"*Forming Families, Forming Saints*  family. Written in a style to either that are of most pressing interest with illustrative anecdotes and deep wisdom. Fr. Griffin's years of faithfully shepherding future priests gives him ample insight to offer faith-focused parents who seek to elevate their child-rearing goals above secular standards and raise future saints. As founders of a Catholic apostolate that helps heal men and women wounded by broken families of origin, we applaud Fr. Griffin for providing such meaningful support to striving parents today and re-proclaiming the beautiful and lofty vocation of Catholic families. This book will heal many souls and prevent family wounds by giving a trustworthy, practical, and reliable blueprint for marriage and parenting that is so desperately needed today. We wholeheartedly recommend it!"

—Daniel and Bethany Meola
Co-authors of *Life-Giving Wounds: A Catholic Guide to Healing for Adult Children of Divorce or Separation* and Founders of Life-Giving Wounds Ministry

"Father Griffin has created a lovely collection of reflections on family life that will bring inspiration to many Catholic families."

—Jennifer Fulwiler
Author of *Something Other Than God* and host of the *Jen Fulwiler Show*

"*Forming Families, Forming Saints* is a beautiful book. This is immediately evident in its design, but even more so through the wisdom that Fr. Griffin reveals in every page. Fr. Griffin draws from his many years of experience forming seminarians and from St. John Paul II's teaching on whole-person formation (human, spiritual, intellectual, and apostolic). As a father, a grandfather, and a family therapist for many years, I have personally witnessed the power of living out these realities in raising healthy and holy children. I have also witnessed the damage when these principles and practices are neglected. I recommend this book to all families, especially those Catholic families who desire to raise well-balanced and wholesome children to become saints and apostles in this current age."

—Bob Schuchts
Founder of the John Paul II Healing Center

"As a now-long-experienced parent and consumer of a great deal of Catholic and family literature, I cannot recommend this book enough. It will assist Catholic parents in guiding their children toward a love of the faith even in the world as it is, not the world as we wish it to be. Its proposal to instill a sense of 'humble exceptionalism' about the faith is spot-on. And it provides tremendous spiritual formation for parents as well."

—HELEN ALVARE
Robert A. Levy Endowed Chair in Law and Liberty,
Antonin Scalia Law School, George Mason University

"*Forming Families, Forming Saints* offers a compelling look at the virtues necessary for Catholic parents to shape their children as human beings and Christians. Drawing on his years of experience of forming young men for the priesthood, the Church's tradition of spiritual formation, and the testimony of Catholic parents, Fr. Griffin has given us a gem of a book that is at once inspiring and deeply practical. A treasure for Catholic parents!"

—JOHN AND CLAIRE GRABOWSKI
Co-Authors of *Raising Catholic Kids for Their Vocations*

"Fr. Carter Griffin has added an insightful and genuinely new perspective to a discussion near to my heart—the hard work of raising a Catholic family. Drawing on the Church's centuries of wisdom on formation of the whole person, Fr. Griffin offers a guidebook that is both deep and practical. For any Catholic parent concerned about raising children in the faith in the modern world, this book provides a guide and a boost of confidence. The Church really is our Mother; and she does know what is best for her children. If we follow her wisdom, good things will happen for us, and our children."

—PATRICK KELLY
Supreme Knight, Knights of Columbus

"Fr. Griffin's brilliant application of the four pillars of seminary formation to raising children is accessible and practical. His extensive knowledge of the Church's wisdom about whole-person formation makes this gem of a book a uniquely powerful resource for parents."

—JOHN CUDDEBACK

Author of *True Friendship: Where Virtue Becomes Happiness* and Professor of Philosophy, Christendom College

"As parents of fourteen and grandparents of thirteen, we are always looking for advice and suggestions on how to better form our family. Fr. Carter Griffin shares reasonable and practical guidance in his book, *Forming Families, Forming Saints*. The ideas for families on human, spiritual, intellectual, and apostolic formation are spot-on and doable for parents looking for balanced approaches to parenting."

—Sam and Rob Fatzinger
Co-Authors of *A Catholic Guide to Spending Less and Living More: Advice From a Debt-Free Family of 16*

"Parents must read this book. We often point out to parents in our podcast that in our vocation we don't have a seminary, we just have kids! But although marriage and family life is naturally designed for self-sacrifice, we all need formation. Parenting today is more difficult than ever, and although, as Father says, there is no manual for parenting, this book may be close! Drawing on the wisdom of the Church's priestly formation, Fr. Griffin offers insightful and practical tools for the modern family that will encourage and inspire!"

—Mike and Alicia Hernon
Founders of *The Messy Family Project*

Forming Families
Forming Saints

Forming Families
Forming Saints

Fr. Carter Griffin

Steubenville, Ohio
www.emmausroad.org

Emmaus Road Publishing
1380 University Blvd.
Steubenville, Ohio 43952

©2024 Carter Griffin
All rights reserved. Published 2024
Printed in the United States of America

First printing 2024

Library of Congress Control Number: 2024944318

ISBN: 978-1-64585-411-1 Paperback | 978-1-64585-412-8 Ebook

Nihil Obstat:
Dr. John S. Grabowski, Ph.D.
Ordinary Professor of Moral Theology/Ethics
School of Theology and Religious Studies
The Catholic University of America
Censor Deputatus

Imprimatur:
His Eminence Wilton Cardinal Gregory
Archbishop of Washington
The Roman Catholic Archdiocese of Washington
July 12, 2024

The nihil obstat and imprimatur are official declarations that a book or pamphlet is free of doctrinal or moral error. There is no implication that those who have granted the nihil obstat and the imprimatur agree with the content, opinions or statements expressed therein.

Unless otherwise noted, Scripture quotations are taken from The Revised Standard Version Second Catholic Edition (Ignatius Edition) Copyright © 2006 by the Division of Christian Education of the National Council of the Churches of Christ in the United States of America. Used by permission. All rights reserved.

Photograph of the painting of St. Martin de Porres at the Basilica of San Domenico, Bologna, Italy (p. 97) courtesy of Fr. Lawrence Lew, O.P.

Cover design and layout by Emily Muse Morelli

Cover image: *First Catholics of Sydney, Circa 1818*, Copyright © Paul Newton 2011

DEDICATION

To the many exemplary Catholic couples I have had the privilege to serve as a priest. You grew into your own vocations as mothers and fathers while I grew into mine as a priest. I am forever grateful for your friendship, your encouragement, your example, and the parental wisdom that you have shared with me. Thank you for allowing me into your family circle.

CONTENTS

Introduction 1

PILLAR I: Human Formation

Introduction to Human Formation 11
Order 15
  Physical Order 16
  Ordering Our Time 19
   St. Benedict 20
Sincerity 23
  Fruits of Sincerity 24
  Sincerity with God 27
   St. Athanasius 29
Chastity 31
  Growing in Chastity 32
  A Personal Reflection from Parents: Richard and Leah Moss 35
   St. Cecilia 38
Fortitude 41
  Teddy Roosevelt: The Man in the Arena 42
  The Need for Fortitude Today 45
   St. Thomas More 47
Magnanimity 49
  Magnanimity in the Life of Jesus 53
  The Urgent Need for Magnanimity 55
   St. Ignatius of Loyola 56

PILLAR II: Spiritual Formation

Introduction to Spiritual Formation 61
Sons and Daughters of God 65
  Forming Children to Be Children of God 66
  Be Child*like*, Not Child*ish* 69
   St. Thérèse of Lisieux 71

Supernatural Outlook 73
Fruits of a Supernatural Outlook 74
How to Acquire a Supernatural Outlook 77
St. Rita of Cascia 80

The Eucharist 83
Fruits of the Mass 84
A Personal Reflection from Parents:
Michael and Maureen Ferguson 88
Bl. Carlo Acutis 89

Sacrifice 91
Principles for Choosing Mortifications 92
Examples of Mortifications 95
St. Martin de Porres 97

Angels and Saints 99
"Saints and Angels Rallying Us On" 102
Spiritual Battle 105
St. Frances of Rome 106

PILLAR III: Intellectual Formation

Introduction to Intellectual Formation 111
Humility 117
How to Foster Humility 118
Effects of Humility 121
St. André Bessette 124

Faith 127
How Do We Grow in Faith? 128
Obstacles to Faith 130
St. Josephine Bahkita 133

Prudence 135
Too Many Rules? 137
How to Form Prudence 139
St. Frances Xavier Cabrini 142

Spiritual Reading 145
Reading Suggestions for Parents 147
Reading Suggestions for Children 151
St. Teresa Benedicta of the Cross (Edith Stein) 153

Beauty 155
- Beauty in the Liturgy 158
- A Personal Reflection from Parents: Daniel and Kari Flynn 161
  - *Bl. John of Fiesole (Fra Angelico)* 162

PILLAR IV: Apostolic Formation

Introduction to Apostolic Formation 167

Interpersonal Skills 171
- St. John Henry Newman's Definition of a Gentleman 172
- The Dinner Table 176
  - *Bl. Pier Giorgio Frassati* 178

Love for Souls 181
- Where to Exercise Apostolate 182
- Love for the Church 186
  - *St. Teresa of Calcutta* 188

Apologetics 191
- Ten Topics to Jump-Start Your Study of Apologetics 192
- Ten Scripture Verses to Memorize 194
  - *St. Miguel Pro* 198

Vocations 201
- Vocation to Single Life? 202
- A Personal Reflection from Parents:
  - Eric and Grace Morrison 204
  - *Sts. Louis and Zélie Martin* 207

Hope 209
- Nurturing Hope 212
- Desire for Heaven 214
  - *St. Mark Ji Tianxiang* 216

Conclusion 219
Acknowledgements 223

INTRODUCTION

Raising a Family on the Four Pillars of Formation

I know what you might be thinking. What is a celibate priest doing giving advice to parents?

It's a fair question.

Let me try to answer with another question: What resources are available to parents who wish to raise their children well?

The first resource is *above* us. God wants us to succeed and thrive even more than we do. It is important, then, for spouses and parents to prayerfully ask for his help and to develop the interior life, which is the substance out of which children are formed. Catholic parenting is above all a work of grace.

The second resource is *inside* us. It is the collection of virtues, abilities, and intuitions that parents have. Mothers and fathers have been endowed with gifts that are meant to be spent on themselves and their children, and those gifts can always be developed and honed further. Personal growth of parents is never just personal; it will have a decisive effect on their children too.

The third resource is *outside* us. It is the counsel, assistance, and encouragement of other people. Young couples can learn so much from people who love them and can accompany them along the path of parenting. Older couples, for instance, who have already raised a family can provide invaluable mentoring. Their own family and friends are often a source of strength and inspiration for parents, especially in difficult moments.

There is someone else, however, who can also be of immense help to Catholic parents. Someone who is an expert on human nature, someone who has successfully raised countless holy children, someone who has learned difficult lessons from children who went astray, and someone who has been doing this for centuries.

I'm speaking, of course, of the Church.

It is by handing on the wisdom of the Church that priests have much to offer mothers and fathers who wish to raise their family well—who wish, that is, to form a family of saints.

A Unique Approach for Parents

It is sometimes said that there is no textbook for raising children. That is true as far as it goes, but what if there were at least a sketchbook grounded on a profound knowledge of human nature? What if the millennia-old insights of the Church in forming human beings could be condensed and recast in a twenty-first-century context? That is the aim of this book.

There are already many excellent resources to help raise a family: books, videos, and podcasts that give detailed advice on understanding the temperaments of children, on communicating as spouses and in front of children, on establishing family rituals and traditions, on taking children to Mass, on sustaining marriage, even on decorating the home.

This is not intended to replace resources like those. What this book offers instead is a recapitulation of the deliberate, insightful, comprehensive formation in which the Church has been engaged for centuries. Young Catholic couples are often looking for deeper moorings for their families. I hope that these pages can help provide some of those solid foundations.

In its most concentrated form, the Church's experience of formation is in the formation of future priests, with which I am most familiar, as well as consecrated men and women. There is no reason why such formation need be hidden or limited to priests and religious. In fact, there are many lessons from such formation that could benefit every Catholic mother and father.

Let's return to our opening question. Celibate priests have something to say to parents because they have inherited a deep understanding of human nature, in part from their own experience of priestly formation. That inheritance can assist parents in several ways.

First, the Second Vatican Council described the family as the "domestic church." The family is where Christ's disciples are ordinarily generated, formed, and sent out on apostolate. Seminary formation has the same aims, only oriented to the priesthood. The Catechism teaches that Matrimony and Holy Orders are the two sacraments directed to the salvation of others; as such, they reinforce each other. St. John Paul II famously said that the family is the "first seminary" for those called to the priesthood. There is a great deal of overlap, in other words, between their missions. Much of what applies to family formation therefore applies to the seminary, and vice versa.

Second, the family, like the seminary, has a broad approach to formation. As parents you are interested in the body, mind, heart, and soul of your child—in every aspect of his or her existence. The seminary, like the family, exists to form the whole person. To ensure that no part of formation is omitted, in fact, formation is divided into four pillars: human, spiritual, intellectual, and pastoral. (We will use that same basic structure in this book.)

Third, our increasingly secularized environment calls for more intentional family formation, the kind of formation that goes on in seminaries. Ask yourself who is actually forming children today. I once saw a report stating that children stare at a screen for an average of eight hours each day (TV, videos, social media, and games) and listen to their parents for an average of ninety seconds a day. I'm not sure how precise that is, but it makes the point. Children are already being formed, very deliberately, by the "influencers" in the media, entertainment, and technology sectors. Families need resources to even out the odds. Some of those resources can be gleaned from seminary formation.

Fourth, the seminary environment provides a fairly clear benchmark by which to gauge what does and does not work in formation, as well as what has and has not worked in seminarians' families of origin. In forming young men across a range of backgrounds, abilities, and temperaments, seminaries have on-the-ground experience that can be beneficial to those in the early stages of parenting.

Seminary formation, admittedly, is far from foolproof. There have been spectacular failures in living memory, as we know only too well in the wake of the sex abuse crisis. For centuries, however, there have also been countless generous, faithful, virtuous priests formed in seminaries, including truly holy priests and a growing army of canonized saints. Though these good priests usually receive less attention, they make up the vast majority and bear witness to the quality of seminary formation, on the whole, that the Church has honed through the centuries.

INTRODUCTION

The Importance of Family Formation

Raising a family has never been easy. It takes generous, sacrificial, sometimes herculean efforts on the part of the parents to cultivate the physical, intellectual, emotional, and spiritual lives of their children, forming them into men and women of character and maturity and nurturing the next generation of responsible citizens who are ready to find their place and profession in the world. Even more importantly, parents are called to raise up future disciples of Christ who are prepared to embrace their vocation, raise a family of their own, and hopefully finish their earthly lives as friends of God ready for the joys of heaven.

That's a lot to ask for in any age, let alone an age like ours which is undergoing such turbulent change. Many believe that culture and technology are changing so quickly that it is practically impossible to handle them with wisdom and in the light of faith. Such pessimism is probably overstated, but the skeptics are right to warn that it has become more difficult.

Social and technological change has given us so many options that we can easily forget the endgame, our goal in life, and how to get there. We spend more time trying to live well-calibrated, optimized lives without actually living good and meaningful lives.

Young people are relentlessly pressured to discover themselves—literally discover who they are, from their deepest beliefs about reality to their sexual proclivities, their gender, and often their very species. Parents need every support we can provide to help children navigate such complicated waters.

Raising a Christian family today is, quite simply, harder than it was—even just a generation ago. As an insightful analysis of our cultural situation put it, parents

> know they will have to think through every aspect of their family's life if they are to maintain its Christian vitality. They understand that they will not be able to depend on the wider culture as a pattern for how they should raise or educate their children, or how they should spend their money, or use technology, or choose among entertainment options. . . . They will need to raise their children differently from how they themselves were raised, not

necessarily because their parents did a bad job, but because the surrounding environment has so radically changed.[1]

As St. John Paul II said, "the future of humanity passes by way of the family."[2] Neither throwing our hands in the air nor simply circling the wagons and shutting off the outside world are viable options. Seminary formation can, I believe, offer a structure and vision to help parents cope with the massive changes that are influencing their families. That is precisely what I propose to do in this book.

How to Use This Book

As already noted, seminary formation is divided into four pillars of formation: human, spiritual, intellectual, and pastoral. This book is divided into those same four pillars, only replacing "pastoral" with "apostolic" as more suitable in a family context.

The idea is not simply to give a summary of seminary life in each area of formation—which would not be as helpful to families—but to select some aspects of seminary formation, under each of the four principal headings, and to adapt them for the context of contemporary family life.

You might consider reading a chapter a week with your spouse and committing to a time when you can discuss how the content might be useful in your unique situation. The goal is to find practical ways that it can be implemented to best serve your family's needs. Perhaps you could take a few notes and renew or adapt those resolutions as the children grow up.

Yearly in the seminary, each seminarian commits to two or three goals in each of the four areas of formation, together with some ways to achieve them. Those goals are then reviewed in monthly meetings with a faculty advisor and formally evaluated once a year. In my experience, young people want to feel that they are growing. Young men in seminary often compare themselves to how they were a year ago, two years ago, three years ago. They love feeling like they are being stretched and formed into better men.

---

[1] University of Mary and Monsignor James P. Shea, *From Christendom to Apostolic Mission: Pastoral Strategies for an Apostolic Age* (Bismarck, ND: University of Mary Press, 2020), 45.

[2] Pope John Paul II, Encyclical Letter on the Role of the Christian Family in the Modern World *Familiaris Consortio* (November 22, 1981), § 86.

That hunger to improve, when properly cultivated with positive reinforcement and lots of encouragement, is not exclusive to seminarians. Something similar might be achieved in a family by encouraging children who are old enough to have a goal or two in different areas of life, together with some practical ways to achieve them. Perhaps those goals might be reviewed every month or two, and evaluated more formally each year, together with the parents.

Formation inevitably means that there will need to be correction and suggestions for growth. An important part of forging a healthy family culture is figuring out the best way, adapted to each child, to convey these opportunities for positive change. I tell every seminarian when he arrives, for instance, that *everyone* receives suggestions to improve. It helps take the sting out of a correction from a faculty member or even from a brother seminarian.

Advice given with tact, respect, and perhaps even a touch of humor can be a reminder that the individual before you is known and loved and that his growth and well-being are more important than a bit of embarrassment or momentary awkwardness. In ways that you think best, this environment conducive to personal growth can be instilled in your family too.

For most of my priesthood I have been involved in the formation of young men for the priesthood. It has been a challenge and a privilege for which I am profoundly grateful. The accumulated wisdom of the Church in forming souls has been a blessing to me personally, to the seminarians I have served, and to the people whom *they* serve now as priests.

With the Lord's help, I pray that these pages may allow those blessings to overflow into your family as well.

PILLAR I

Human Formation

"A true education aims at the formation of the human person in the pursuit of his ultimate end and of the good of the societies of which, as man, he is a member, and in whose obligations, as an adult, he will share. Therefore children and young people must be helped . . . to develop harmoniously their physical, moral and intellectual endowments so that they may gradually acquire a mature sense of responsibility in striving endlessly to form their own lives properly and in pursuing true freedom as they surmount the vicissitudes of life with courage and constancy. Let them be given also, as they advance in years, a positive and prudent sexual education. Moreover they should be so trained to take their part in social life that properly instructed in the necessary and opportune skills they can become actively involved in various community organizations, open to discourse with others and willing to do their best to promote the common good."

POPE ST. PAUL VI
Declaration on Christian Education *Gravissimum Educationis*

INTRODUCTION TO HUMAN FORMATION

ITALY IS KNOWN FOR MANY cultural achievements. It has beautiful churches and the ancient ruins of a great empire, centuries of artistic masterpieces and sublime sacred music, the latest fashions and luxury automobiles.

For many, however, Italy is most famous for its cuisine. Ask any Italian chef for the secret of his cooking, however, and the answer will likely be simple and straightforward: use fresh ingredients!

Formation is a bit like fine cuisine. You might know how to make the most elegant, complex, and expensive dishes, but it won't work if you don't use fresh ingredients. Human formation seeks to bring the best ingredients into the lives of our children so that they can be free, upright, confident, and generous human beings. It provides the raw material, so to speak, for the other areas of formation.

Each pillar of formation boasts its unique importance. Human formation stands out as the precondition for the other three pillars of formation, but that is not all. It also stands out as the one best formed early in life—that is, in the family. Certainly, a solid spiritual, intellectual, and apostolic foundation should also be laid in childhood, but when that does not happen, much of it can be regained later.

In the case of human formation, however, such remediation in later life is often only partly successful. Since many elements of our personality are so deeply rooted in our childhood, parents can have a decisive impact in their children's futures by paying close attention to their human development.

Given the complexity of human nature, the aims of human formation are a bit sprawling. Of first importance, it is about building character, especially moral character, by cultivating a well-formed conscience, the capacity to discern right from wrong, and the self-discipline to choose the good.

Human formation also includes developing balanced habits of life, physical fitness, the capacity for personal organization, and an ordered use of time. It strives to cultivate temperance, sincerity, and self-confidence. It helps us to harness the power of technology without being enslaved by social media, the internet, and the allure of digital devices.

Interior freedom is cultivated in human formation, especially the freedom of "affective maturity"—that is, the capacity to understand and be enriched by our feelings without being driven and dominated by them. Affectively mature people are pure of heart, possessing both interior and exterior chastity and healthy boundaries in their friendships. They are open to correction and are able to both exercise and respond to authority well. They are able to acknowledge and channel their frustrations and angry feelings in wholesome ways—a quality so needed (and rare) today.

Human formation also has a communal character, fostering a capacity to give oneself to others, to fight against selfishness and individualism, and to be generous in serving. It includes affability and discretion, humility, courtesy, hospitality, compassion, and loyalty. Well-formed individuals listen and communicate well, are quick to understand and forgive, and are able to create and sustain deep, virtuous, life-giving friendships.

All four pillars of formation tend to rise or fall together. Without the human qualities of moral uprightness and affective maturity, for example, it is difficult to see how the interior life fostered in spiritual formation can thrive. Without a balanced life, personal order, and a good use of time, intellectual formation will falter.

The importance of human maturity is especially evident in the apostolic dimension of formation. If we lack humility or compassion, how can someone encounter Christ through us? If we cannot listen or communicate well? If we lack generosity or discretion? As St. John Paul II wrote in *Pastores Dabo Vobis*, the human personality of the priest is to be "a bridge and not an obstacle for others in their meeting with Jesus Christ."[1] This is true not only of priests but of all Christians.

---

[1] Pope John Paul II, Post-Synodal Apostolic Exhortation on the Formation of Priests in the Circumstances of the Present Day *Pastores Dabo Vobis* (March 15, 1992), § 43.

The following chapters on order, sincerity, chastity, fortitude, and magnanimity cover some of the key themes in human formation. Though not comprehensive, these five are all core ideas, mainsprings for other aspects of human development. Reflecting on them will help incorporate these "fresh ingredients" into our families so that our children are given the opportunity to grow into mature human beings, to live full and flourishing lives, and to prepare for steady growth in the other pillars of formation as well.

ORDER

As a boy on summer vacation, I was fascinated by ocean tides. I marveled at the vast expanse of water, slowly creeping up, rising to high tide, then receding again. As the ocean began its long march up the beach, one of my favorite pastimes was to gather some friends and build an enormous wall of sand to see how long we could keep out the encroaching sea. We knew that our fort would eventually give way before the rising tide of water; the fun was seeing how long it would last.

Many families feel much the same way when it comes to putting order into a tumultuous home. Parents establish ground rules for family life, figure out the morning schedule for school and afternoon schedule for sports and other activities, periodically clean the house, and try to keep everyone's extracurriculars straight—while trying to keep their own personal and professional lives on track too.

But such efforts often feel like ramparts of sand that eventually come crumbling down in the face of the rising tide of watery turmoil. It's not a matter of *if* but *when* the walls will collapse and they have to start over with a new approach. Even when it does seem to work for a while, holding back the tide leaves everyone feeling exhausted and distressed.

Some have given up and, with a shrug of the shoulders, make little attempt to put order into family life. They simply "go with the flow" and react to new pressures as they arise. Others double down and erect higher and thicker walls, contributing to a mounting anxiety as more and more complicated lives, of both parents and children, erode the walls of sand.

There is another way to handle the rising demands of modern life. We must set realistic expectations. We must establish clear priorities for our lives. Above all, though, we must learn to practice *flexible firmness* in maintaining our standards of order.

That last term points to a constructive tension in how we approach order. A healthy approach is *flexible* enough so that family life does not become rigid and, ultimately, brittle and breakable. It is also *firm* enough

15

to resist the clamor of present demands. Flexible enough to change when needed and yet firm enough to stand fast otherwise. Flexible enough to avoid panic and anxiety when demands mount and yet, in the face of those same demands, firm enough to avoid sloth and defeatism.

Order, I am convinced, leads to human flourishing on so many fronts.

In his autobiography, Ben Franklin identified thirteen necessary virtues. The third highest was "Order." He wrote, "Let all your things have their places; let each part of your business have its time." He ranked this virtue so highly because, he said, it gave him time to attend to other matters.

In effect, order multiplies our time. When we order our time well, not rushing from one thing to another but having a vision for our use of time, we get more things done, with less time, and with greater focus, and usually with greater success.

Spiritually, our souls thrive best in an ordered environment. When our external environment is ordered, it gives interior peace. When

PHYSICAL ORDER

It's been said that if you want to see the state of someone's soul, look in his closet. A bit simplistic, but it conveys an important point: our external order has a real impact on our interior order.

Every morning at St. John Paul II Seminary, the Vice-Rector checks to make sure that the bed in each room is made, clothes are put away, and the space is tidy. The seminarians also shave in the morning, dress in a shirt and tie for Mass and class, and use good manners at the table. These are small details of external order that might seem inconsequential to the formation of future priests. I am convinced that they have everything to do with that formation, in part because they have a noticeable impact on their interior lives.

One challenge, however, is approaching these expectations with that *flexible firmness* that is so important.

On the one hand, we must be flexible in our expectations of these seminarians. The standards are reasonable; we're not bouncing quarters off the beds like Marine Corps Drill Instructors.

our day is ordered, it gives time needed for contemplation. Protecting some time each day for prayer, spiritual reading, and (if possible) daily Mass will yield immeasurable benefits in our own lives and in the lives of our families.

Our moral lives, too, benefit from order since every virtue—such as justice, courage, temperance, prudence, charity, and humility—requires order to live it well. Put differently, there is no such thing as *disordered* justice, courage, or charity. In fact, one definition of sin is "moral disorder." It is no wonder that great saints like St. Augustine speak often about order. "Safeguard order," he said, "and order will safeguard you."

Finally, order is the surest way to live a humanly creative and thriving life. It is like a protective wall that opens a space for freedom. Order is not opposed to spontaneity or fun but rather serves them. Venerable Fulton Sheen said that the order imposed by the Church's teachings "might be a rock in the sea, surrounded by great walls; inside of those walls the children may dance and sing and play as they please." But take

Their clothes should be presentable and clean; they needn't (and shouldn't) look like they emerged from the pages of a fashion catalog. For some people, physical order is difficult and we have to be patient and look for incremental improvements.

On the other hand, there has to be enough firmness to bring about the external order that has such a positive impact on interior wellbeing.

What does that flexible firmness look like in a family? In a home, a playroom will have a different standard of order than a living room but *every* room will have an expectation that is clearly conveyed. Each child (and parent for that matter) should meet standards of attire, hygiene, and manners, which are also spelled out in advance. Evaluating those details of physical order is done routinely, with due flexibility, and there are reasonable and effective consequences for falling short. What would that look like in your family?

17

down those walls because they appear to be a restraint, he said—and this is true of order across realms—and "you would find all the children huddled in the center of the island, afraid to play, afraid to sing, afraid to dance, afraid of falling into the sea."[1]

Fostering order does not mean trying to hold back the encroaching ocean of responsibilities, commitments, family crises, soccer games, band practices, and personal goals. It means approaching each day with a sense of calm and purpose. It means setting realistic expectations, establishing an ordered environment and schedule, and navigating new circumstances with a healthy dose of both flexibility and firmness. It means structuring your family's life so that the priorities—the *real* priorities, the priorities that lead to everyone's flourishing and peace—enjoy the lion's share of your time and attention. The fruits of such order in a family are priceless.

> How can you work toward greater order in your family?
>
> Pick one area (such as bedrooms or the kitchen) that needs special attention in your home this week. What can each member of the family do to foster order?
>
> Spend some time reflecting on aspects of order that are the strong suit of each family member. Your spouse loads and unloads the dishwasher efficiently. Your teenager starts using a task list and calendar. Your preteen is developing the habit of folding his or her own laundry. Be sure to praise each of them for the good order you see them cultivating.
>
> What is one spiritual commitment that you personally feel God is calling you to make at this time?

---

[1] Fulton Sheen, *Peace of Soul* (New York: Whittlesey House, 1949), 285.

ORDERING OUR TIME

Not long ago I spoke to a mother of seven children who found herself oscillating between excessive flexibility and excessive firmness in her approach to time. After a particularly hectic stretch she would give up and just see how the days played out. Finding this even more stressful, she eventually tried again to impose a strict, uncompromising plan on her family's schedule. Not surprisingly, this didn't work either.

Frustrated by the failures of both, she eventually spoke to a priest mentor who encouraged her to "embrace the chaos," by which he meant not giving in to the chaos but "embracing" it—that is, give it some realistic parameters without trying to control too much. That one simple piece of advice, she said, changed her life as a wife and mother.

She discovered that proper order gave the flexibility to accommodate the unexpected without compromising the firm adherence to a plan.

A calendar and a to-do list are basic elements of any good system. A third element is a weekly plan with recurring events. In order to prepare this weekly plan for yourself and your family, map out the times for prayer, school or work, study, exercise, and recreation for each day of the week.

Now it's time to apply these three elements—a calendar, a to-do list, and a weekly plan—to an actual week in your family's life.

- Choose a day, perhaps Sunday evening, to plan for the coming week.
- On a physical or digital calendar, note the recurring events from your weekly plan for each of the coming days.
- Add the events from your calendar as well as those tasks you plan to tackle each day.
- Make sure that you focus first on items that are both *important* and *urgent*—like tests and doctors' appointments.
- Then add the items that are *important* but not necessarily *urgent*—like prayer, family time, and parents' date nights.
- Only then are other less important items added to the week's schedule.

By planning your week in advance, the family is better able to keep focus and balance, including an appropriate space for creativity and relaxation, while remaining flexible enough to accommodate changes to the routine.

Forming Families, Forming Saints

ST. BENEDICT

Abbot
Born in Italy
D. 543
Feast day: July 11

Whatever your task, work heartily, as serving the Lord and not men, knowing that from the Lord you will receive the inheritance as your reward; you are serving the Lord Christ.

Colossians 3:23–24

St. Benedict was born to a noble family in central Italy around AD 480. During his studies in Rome, he realized that worldly allurements were endangering his soul, so he left the city to become a hermit in Subiaco, about fifty miles to the east. Benedict took shelter in a cave, and his only contact with the outside world was through a monk named Romanus, whose monastery was nearby. Romanus vested him with a monk's habit and provided for his spiritual and material needs. Benedict spent the next three years in prayer and solitude.

Over time, monks began to gather around Benedict as he encouraged them to live in a monastic community of "prayer and work": *ora et labora*. He founded twelve monasteries with twelve monks each, as well as a thirteenth monastery for novices and those who needed education to adopt the life of a monk. Later he founded the huge monastery of Montecassino, where his reputation for holiness and miracles continued to spread. One of Benedict's priorities was evangelizing the local population, who were still immersed in pagan practices.

Benedict's twin sister, St. Scholastica, founded an order for nuns based on the same plan of life. The Rule of St. Benedict, as it came to be known, is a masterpiece of order with prescribed times of prayer, study, manual labor, and tempered asceticism. It includes times for liturgical prayer, the Divine Office, silence, and recreation.

St. Benedict died on March 21, 547. He had foreseen and told his disciples of his approaching death. Six days before dying, he ordered the monks to open the grave that he was to share with his sister. Then, exhausted from a life of working for the glory of God, he asked to be carried to his oratory, where, after receiving Viaticum, he died in the company of his fellow monks.

The monastic tradition established by St. Benedict has thrived for almost fifteen hundred years. He is rightly called the Father of Western Monasticism. Regulating the life of a monastery with an explicit rule seems rather obvious to us, but it was an important innovation that changed the direction of the Church. Because of the well-ordered monasteries that spread quickly in the centuries that followed, much of Western culture and intellectual life survived the difficult centuries sometimes called the "Dark Ages."

The measured life that he offered countless monks and the villages and even cities that grew up around their monasteries are a powerful reminder of the importance of order in the life of every Christian. Because of the influence of Benedictine monasteries, St. Benedict is considered one of the patron saints of Europe. Even more importantly, the Benedictine Order has given the Church tens of thousands of known saints and thirty-five popes, seventeen of whom are saints or blesseds.

> Heavenly Father, as you inspired St. Benedict to gather disciples in prayer and work with an ordered way of life, guide our family as we strive to bring order into our lives, our work, our recreation, and our worship. May St. Benedict intercede for us so that, following his holy example, our home may be a place of peace and order for all who live here and for those who receive our hospitality. May the consecrated men and women who follow the Rule of St. Benedict continue to be an inspiration for those of us who serve you in the world, and may our prayers join theirs in worshipping you ceaselessly, through our Lord Jesus Christ, your Son, who lives and reigns with you and the Holy Spirit, God forever and ever. Amen.

SINCERITY

It had been a long day for Jesus. Since arriving in Capernaum that morning, Jesus had healed a paralyzed man on his bed, called Matthew the tax collector to follow him, cured a hemorrhaging woman, raised a girl to life, and restored sight to two blind men. At that point, as if to culminate the Lord's miraculous healing, a "mute demoniac" (Matt 9:32–33) was brought to Jesus for healing.

It was an unnerving scene. Like other demoniacs, the man thrashed and jerked about, writhing in pain, but unlike other demoniacs, no sound came from his tormented face. The man was in agony but unable to express it and powerless to seek healing on his own.

St. Josemaría Escrivá, reflecting on this scene, saw in that "dumb devil" the temptation that we all face to keep things hidden. "If that dumb devil mentioned in the Gospel gets into your soul," St. Josemaría wrote, "he will spoil everything. On the other hand, if you get rid of him immediately, everything will turn out well; you will carry on merrily, and all will be well."[1]

The greatest weapon we have against the dumb devil is sincerity, represented in the Gospels by the apostle Nathaniel. Philip convinces him to meet Jesus despite Nathaniel's skepticism that "anything good" could come out of Nazareth. As Nathaniel approaches the Lord, before he gets a word out, Jesus greets him (I'm sure with a broad smile) and declares to everyone in earshot, "Behold, an Israelite indeed, in whom is no guile!" (John 1:47).

Jesus did not bestow compliments lightly. Why was he so taken by Nathaniel's openness, his sincerity, his transparency?

In part, because openness to the truth would enable Nathaniel to receive the Good News of salvation. Equally important, though, his guilelessness was the raw material from which Jesus could forge a holy man, a faithful disciple, and a great apostle.

---

[1] St. Josemaría Escrivá, *The Way, The Furrow, The Forge* (New York: Scepter Publishers, 2011), 597 (*The Forge*, § 127).

That remains true in any formation environment, whether it is Jesus forming his group of disciples, a seminary forming priests, or parents forming young saints. The foundational virtue is sincerity.

Someone going to the doctor who refuses to open up about his ailments cannot be healed. As one spiritual writer observed, such a person should not go to the doctor but to the veterinarian, since the medical professional will need to figure out what is wrong without the patient's help.

Similarly, those in formation—such as children in a family—cannot be healed, advised, corrected, praised, or affirmed if they are not sincere with those whose responsibility it is to promote their growth.

Sincerity means having the courage to say what is really happening in our hearts to the person who is able to help us. The word "sincerity" literally means "without wax," from the ancient practice of covering up

FRUITS OF SINCERITY

Being a person of sincerity is not only a condition for receiving formation; it is also an ingredient for a joyful life. It is exhausting to keep wounds hidden and a profound relief to bring them into the light. As seminarians have learned to trust formation and open up to formators and brother seminarians, I have frequently witnessed a dramatic growth of joy in their hearts.

There is something deeply satisfying about a single-hearted life, a life without pretense, a life that is an open book. By having in our lives people like parents, spouses, friends, priests, and mentors to whom we can open up, we can make daily progress towards that interior unity. Giving children the opportunity to have such people around—starting with their parents—is a gift that will continue to yield fruit throughout their lives.

The Evil One thrives in darkness, fear, and confusion. Unwittingly, our lack of sincerity plays into his strategy. When, on the other hand, we embrace sincerity and transparency, we grow in spiritual power over the "dumb devil" and foster a heart open to grace.

blemishes on sculptures with wax. Sincerity allows our blemishes (and our virtues, for that matter) to be known. It means opening up about our faults, our temptations, and our hidden grievances, as well as our joys, our hopes, and our dreams. It means being transparent, allowing light to shine into a soul.

In a family, a culture can emerge that subtly discourages sincerity. Children are naturally open, even to the point of bluntness, but quickly learn from their parents whether such openness is welcome. When it is not, children must try to cope with problems on their own, without the benefit of their elders' wisdom and experience.

Much of the fractured, disintegrated lives that our young people are living today, their anxiety, resentments, and emotional wounds, can be attributed to family environments in which they did not feel they could be honest and open.

How can parents create a culture of sincerity in their families?

Above all, sincerity is nurtured by fostering an environment of trust. We instinctively open up to those whom we know have our best interests at heart. Trust, even for parents, must be earned, especially as children mature towards adolescence and beyond.

Parents who wish to build such a culture will help children learn the art of speaking about difficult matters with clarity, disclosing their struggles rather than keeping them hidden. They should be encouraged to keep things simple when speaking about problems, without getting twisted into knots, starting with the most difficult things, learning to "just say it" without worrying about how the parents will react. They will hopefully be pleasantly surprised when parents receive them and their concerns—whatever they may be—with calmness, compassion, and a readiness to help.

When seminarians have courageously opened up about their struggles, I have witnessed again and again a new and profound sense of freedom and often dramatic growth. It is no different in families when children are honest and straightforward about their difficulties.

An old spiritual director often reminded us that "the truth is never a problem." Not a bad motto for parents. When children are bold in revealing their struggles, praise them warmly. Your promotion of a trusting environment will pay huge dividends in your family and throughout the lives of your children.

Sincerity can also be fostered by engaging your children in decision-making whenever possible. When children are young and cannot contribute much to the discussion, parents will explain how decisions are made in the best interests of the family. As children grow up, parents will include them in decisions about family life, whether it's something as minor as selecting a movie to watch or something as important as deciding whether to move to a new home. Even though the final decision rests with the parents, they give children a degree of agency and show the benefits of open and sincere discussion.

Limiting the use of social media is another way to promote sincerity. Although social media boasts a veneer of radical authenticity with people posting about their every thought and life experience, in reality it often leads to a carefully curated depiction of what we wish our life were really like. What we see in social media is often what people wish us to see, not the reality itself. Given these pretenses, social media is no friend of sincerity. Parents who wish to create an environment that prizes honesty will be very cautious in allowing their children access to such technologies. Teenagers in particular are vulnerable to the highly artificial culture of social media and most susceptible to its deceptions.

Also essential to building a culture of sincerity is openness to children's individual temperaments, preferences, and goals. Children will instinctively know when you secretly (or overtly) desire them to conform to an image, a set of preconceived expectations for them. It is hard to divest ourselves of such expectations, and some soul-searching by parents may be needed.

If children are to become healthy and autonomous human beings, they cannot live to meet the expectations of their parents. They will feel hollow and frustrated since their own personalities have not been allowed to develop. Much of the distrust of authority so prevalent today is rooted, I believe, in these parental expectations which children intuitively feel are unhealthy and, however unintentionally, manipulative.

Perhaps the most important way that parents can promote sincerity in their children is by living it themselves. When parents are honest with their children—for instance, by answering difficult questions forthrightly—they give an example of sincerity, even when they cannot fully disclose matters that are confidential or inappropriate for children to hear. In those cases,

SINCERITY WITH GOD

While on retreat, a priest friend of mine enjoyed taking long walks around the retreat center. A friendly dog would accompany him on these walks, capering around him. They both enjoyed the company.

However, the dog never let himself be touched. As soon as the dog was approached, he tucked his tail between his legs and ran away. Through that dog, my friend realized that God was teaching him a lesson.

We, too, want to be with God, near him, capering around him, but we are often afraid to really let ourselves be touched by him. We keep a healthy distance from God, fearful of getting too close, afraid of what he might demand of us.

Just as sincerity is the necessary condition for growth in a formation environment like the family, so too is sincerity the necessary condition for growth in our relationship with God.

Learning to be truly open with God, pouring out our hearts to him, being truly ourselves with him, asking for wisdom and illumination from God to know ourselves, allowing ourselves to be healed by the Holy Spirit—in short, allowing ourselves to be touched by the Lord—is the foundation of a deep interior life.

God's love for us is radically unconditional and he desires nothing more than to pour his love into our hearts. If we are hiding ourselves from him, we cannot receive that love as fully as he desires. If, on the other hand, we are boldly sincere with God, we will find it easier to receive that love and to be more sincere with ourselves and with others.

being honest about the limitations of the discussion and the reasons for it can be just as instructive.

Even ordinary, everyday quarrels between parents can teach children that good people can disagree without losing their love for each other, that there is a constructive way to disagree (which is a vanishing art), and that sincerity is more important than a false peacefulness. While children are often exposed to the arguments of adults, it is important that they also witness reconciliation, spouses asking one another for forgiveness and embracing, and the return to calmer communication. In these and other ways, parents model sincerity for their children and promote it in their lives.

Forging a culture of sincerity in a family is not always easy, but it is always worth the effort. Sincerity is the bedrock of formation, the solid foundation on which human growth takes place. It is the rich soil in which children can flourish and grow, like Nathaniel, into mature men and women without guile who are able to unmask the craftiness of the "dumb devil."

Reflect on how your family of origin encouraged or did not encourage sincerity. Are there parents, siblings, or other family members whom you need to forgive? Do you need to repent of having been an obstacle to sincerity for others?

Ask your spouse to give you a candid assessment of whether you are approachable when your children present challenging behaviors or when a difficult situation arises. Take his or her assessment to prayer and perhaps together commit to making one small change in this area.

Is there a child in the family who could directly benefit from you modeling sincerity? If so, find a natural way to have a sincere discussion together about a matter of importance.

Reflect on a time when you experienced the fruits of sincerity.

ST. ATHANASIUS

Bishop and Doctor of the Church
Born in Alexandria
D. 373
Feast day: May 2

He that would love life and see good days, let him keep his tongue from evil and his lips from speaking guile; let him turn away from evil and do right; let him seek peace and pursue it. For the eyes of the Lord are upon the righteous, and his ears are open to their prayer.

1 PETER 3:10–12

St. Athanasius was born to a Christian family in Alexandria, Egypt. One day when Athanasius was a boy, the bishop of Alexandria discovered him playing at administering baptism with some non-Christian friends. Bishop Alexander called the boys over and, after questioning them, he judged that the baptisms were valid! The bishop then decided to train those boys for the priesthood. Athanasius' family had the means to provide him with a solid classical education, and soon he was serving Bishop Alexander as his personal secretary.

Around AD 323, a priest of Alexandria named Arius denied the divinity of Christ and began spreading the false doctrine that Jesus was not truly divine but merely created in time by God the Father. Bishop Alexander deposed Arius and eleven other priests, but Arius left for Caesarea and continue spreading the pernicious heresy. After Alexander's death, Athanasius became the new bishop of Alexandria and continued the fight against the heresy that came to be known as Arianism.

Though Athanasius is now sometimes called the Father of Orthodoxy and Champion of Christ's Divinity, he suffered cruelly for his fidelity, enduring lies, false allegations (even of murder), physical attacks, and several deportations. He was banished from his diocese five times over the course of his life, spending seventeen years in exile. Once while

FORMING FAMILIES, FORMING SAINTS

Athanasius was celebrating the Divine Liturgy, soldiers forced their way into the church and killed several members of the congregation. Athanasius escaped just in time and hid in the desert, where a group of monks kept him safe for six years. The last years of his life, however, were peaceful, and he died in Alexandria on May 2, 373, the day on which we now celebrate his memorial.

St. Athanasius' defense of the doctrine of Christ's divinity, even when it was difficult and dangerous, is a great example to us of adhering to the truth no matter the consequences. At times his commitment to sincerity seemed to court danger. While Athanasius did not shirk that risk, neither was he foolhardy.

There is a story about the Roman emperor, Julian the Apostate, sending imperial officers to pursue Athanasius up the Nile and kill him. Seeing the officers gaining on him, Athanasius approached a bend in the river and swiftly turned his boat around, steering straight for his pursuers. When the boats drew close, the officers called out to him, asking if he had seen Athanasius. The saint called back, "Yes, he is quite near!" The officers continued on, and Athanasius returned to Alexandria, where he hid until Julian's reign ended.

> Father in heaven, your servant Athanasius defended the true divinity of your Son in the face of great opposition. Give us an unshakeable commitment to the truths of our faith and a determination to live in sincerity, honesty, and integrity. May our home be a place where truth reigns, where a culture of sincerity imbues all our relationships with trust, and where each member of our family experiences the blessings of living in freedom and openness with you and with each other. May our adversary, the Father of Lies, be thwarted in his efforts through our sincerity which is sustained by your grace and the intercession of St. Athanasius and all the saints and angels, through our Lord Jesus Christ, your Son, who lives and reigns with you and the Holy Spirit, God forever and ever. Amen.

CHASTITY

Teaching children to read and write is not especially controversial. Parents know that reading and writing, however laborious, are necessary skills for a successful and flourishing life. There are other difficult habits that parents also encourage. Some children learn an instrument, for instance, or a sport or a technical skill. By persevering in these accomplishments, children become more well-rounded and mature.

What if there were a habit that prepared our children not just to read and write well or to perform well, but to love well? We humans are, after all, beings made to love. That is what causes us to flourish most deeply, to have the most satisfying life, and ultimately to be prepared for eternal life in heaven. As a matter of fact, there is such a habit. Chastity is the virtue that enables us to love well.

Forming young people in this virtue has always been important, but perhaps especially today. In the movies they

(continued on p. 34)

GROWING IN CHASTITY

There are many ways to help our children grow in chastity. Here are ten.

In the natural order:

Mental Hygiene Holy purity is fostered above all by monitoring what comes into the imagination. Movies, videos, games, social media, internet access, apps, and books are all on the table for discussion. Dangerous devices such as smartphones, laptops, tablets, and televisions should be protected as diligently as you would a firearm. Unprotected devices lying around the house are like loaded guns without the safety on—only more dangerous because they threaten your children's immortal soul. Accountability software can foster good conversations about the responsible and upright use of the internet and social media. See both CovenantEyes.com and DefendYoungMinds.com for more help in creating a proactive plan for your family.

Sincerity Children must know that they can approach their parents about anything—*anything*—on their minds without it becoming a scene. No matter what you are thinking or feeling when they bring something up, they cannot see shock, annoyance, or fear on your face, but only calm and compassion.

Boundaries As children grow up, their deep friendships should ordinarily become less co-ed. Teenaged girls and boys can, of course, be friends with each other but those relationships need to be guided by wise adults or they may well end in disaster.

Order A clean, orderly environment, in the home and also in the children's bedrooms, as well as order in the schedule, promotes a clean and orderly imagination.

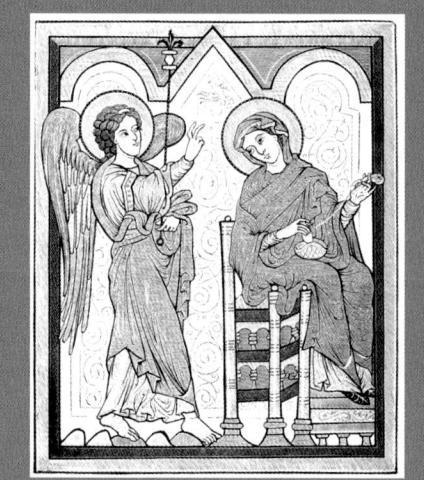

Often souls are most vulnerable in an unbalanced state of mind—for instance, when they are Bored, Lonely, Angry, Sad, or Tired (remember BLAST). Order mitigates the internal swings that can amplify temptations.

BEAUTY Chastity is all about preserving the beauty of love. Having beauty in the house, such as beautiful art and music, reading good literature, and watching good movies, as well as getting outside and enjoying the glories of nature, all contribute to cultured minds that are attracted to genuine beauty and not to its poor substitutes.

In the supernatural order:

PRAYER Regular prayer lifts the mind and the eyes towards God and makes impurity more repellant. Prayer in all its forms is good; a nightly Rosary, for instance, is a cherished tradition in many families. Adoration of the Blessed Sacrament is an especially powerful antidote to a visually lustful culture. If possible, bring young children to adoration for a few minutes every week; give them the gift of the Lord's "radiation therapy." They will grow into the silence as they get older and be able to spend more time in his presence.

SACRAMENTS Regular confession is an incomparable aid to purity, as is the regular reception of Holy Communion.

ASCETICISM The word sounds like "athleticism" because that's what it is on the supernatural plane. Self-denial tempers our bodily cravings and is effective spiritual training for holy purity. Soft living, giving undue priority to our own comfort and convenience, is a breeding ground for temptations of the flesh.

SPIRITUAL READING Reading good books—most especially Sacred Scripture—is like a bath for the mind. It makes us less inclined to pollute it with impure things.

OUR LADY Mary is the most effective ally in the battle, the only human being that God promised victory over the Evil One. There is an old custom of praying three Hail Marys, while kneeling, just before going to bed—especially for holy purity. I cannot recommend it highly enough.

watch, the games they play, their conversations with friends, the clothes they wear, and even in the way sex is discussed in "sex ed" classes, the beauty of holy purity is frequently obscured.

Chastity is particularly undermined by the videos and pictures that are a click away on the portable computers (aka phones) that many children and teens carry around. These images, including the most stomach-churning and violent, do not discriminate by age. The average age of children ingesting the poison of pornography is around eight or nine years old. It does untold damage in young and impressionable minds, leaving them scared, curious, and vulnerable all at the same time. Chastity can help protect their minds and hearts from such injury.

But chastity is more than a protective virtue; it is above all a positive and essential means to flourish as a human being. We are made to love, and to love not as angels but as sexual beings, as male and female.

The mature person, whether married or unmarried, understands his or her sexuality, is unafraid of it, and knows how to channel sexual urges in a wholesome and life-giving way. Chastity helps us become comfortable with our bodies—including the gender with which we were born—as gifts of God and temples of the Holy Spirit.

As children grow up, they need to have clear and calm discussions with their parents about their bodies and their sexual drives. "The talk" cannot be a single conversation, the awkward moment during puberty when Mom or Dad sits down and fumbles through a discussion of the "birds and the bees." There should rather be regular and easy discussions, in age-appropriate ways, while they grow up. The devil thrives on darkness, fear, and confusion. The surest way to frustrate him in his efforts is through open, trusting, sincere dialogue.

If chastity is essential for natural maturity, it is equally essential for supernatural maturity. Quite simply, chastity is necessary to become a saint. It is not the most important virtue—that would be charity—but it is (especially today) the virtue that preserves us from the greatest spiritual dangers.

Chastity unclogs the living waters of grace and allows our hearts to expand freely in love of God and neighbor. Without chastity we cannot make progress in the spiritual life, we cannot grow in holiness, and we cannot be prepared for eternal life.

A Personal Reflection from Parents
— Richard and Leah Moss —

We have attempted to foster chastity in our family by nurturing our children's deep desire to see beauty, and to *be seen* as beautiful. Practically, this has entailed attuning their young "eyes"—and our own—through live music, inspiring art, candlelight meals, leisurely hikes: anything that lifts souls, invites good conversation, and renders cheap counterfeits less appealing.

For us, cultural mediocrity and moral relativism are just as damaging as the explicitly explicit. Without being too reactionary, we fear the effects of a SpongeBob or a Disney princess more than a sensuous Bernini or (when the time is right) a colorfully scripted screwball comedy.

Relatedly, we have encouraged our children to be open to goodness, truth, and beauty in the broader culture beyond the religious context. When we see troubling things, we draw our children's attention to the need for belovedness at the root of every difficult manifestation. This cultural openness only works, however, because we have intentionally fostered an environment of frequent conversation about the good and the bad of everything we encounter.

In that vein, there is no one "talk." Instead, we share the gift of human love naturally over the course of years through *many* conversations. We encourage questions and don't allow ourselves to be shocked, either by questions or mistakes. Such responses cement the bad rather than reframing it as a misdirected good.

Sometimes our children come to us with questions. Other times, if we intuit questions, percolating but unvoiced, we have relied on loving gestures and an invitation to talk to create beautiful encounters. We desire to be our children's go-to resource on matters of human sexuality.

Because modern man listens willingly to witnesses, we have not feared expressing love through physical affection, both with each other as spouses and with our children. Our teens share their desire for a marriage where physical touch—be it a hug or a kiss—manifests a "true" love. Similarly, we have tried to welcome our children's friends into our home, making it a social hub where our teens, especially, enjoy friendship in an environment of freedom. Finally, we have intentionally surrounded our family with the beautiful marriages of relatives and friends who show our children the way.

Sometimes chastity is confused with the demands of chastity. But the demands of chastity aren't chastity; they are simply the necessary means to live in freedom. Someone learning to play the piano does not see the rules about notation and tempo as so many negative impositions, but rather the framework that makes beautiful music possible. So too the rules of chastity are not chastity itself; they are the framework in which beautiful, life-giving, chaste love is made possible. The many noes of chastity are all ordered to one big yes!

Thus, chastity is both a defensive and an offensive virtue. It is a virtue that frees us *from* something and also frees us *for* something. It frees us *from* the shackles of sin that weigh us down. It also frees us *for* the gift of loving well, having authentic friendships and communion with others, interacting naturally and in wholesome ways with both men and women.

In the face of so many temptations today, some doubt our capacity to live truly chaste lives. Chastity, however, is a virtue like any other and it can be both taught and learned. True, lasting, genuine chastity is both possible and, with the assistance of grace, very much within reach.

Still, despite the best efforts of parents, children may fall prey to the many traps set all around them. If that happens, children must know that you are always ready to talk about it, to listen with a sympathetic ear, to offer them practical assistance—in a word, to show them compassion and steady encouragement. In doing that, you will be true representatives of the merciful Lord who is eager to reconcile them to himself, no matter how demanding the struggle.

Chastity is an essential habit to form in our children, more important even than reading, writing, sports, and instruments, because it is the habit of loving well. It is the gateway to a life of freedom, maturity, and joy. Above all, it is the habit that makes the heart capable of loving God himself, both in this life and in the life to come. As the Lord himself said, "Blessed are the pure in heart, for they shall see God" (Matt 5:8).

Make a point to acknowledge to each member of your family at least one way their body reflects the goodness of God's design. Avoid superficial compliments about appearance.

Take time as a couple to assess how you can help each child—in age-appropriate ways—to cultivate chastity. For younger children, your focus might be on virtues like discipline, delayed gratification, and showing basic respect to others. Older children and teens may be ready for more intentional and direct formation.

There are countless canonized saints who are illustrious witnesses of chastity. Together, choose a special patron saint of chastity and encourage all family members to seek help from this saint in times of temptation.

Chastity in marriage has a different character. Spend some time in personal prayer asking the Holy Spirit to offer wisdom and insight into your own growth in chastity for your state of life.

Forming Families, Forming Saints

ST. CECILIA

Virgin and Martyr
Born in Italy
D. circa 230
Feast day: November 22

Do you not know that your body is a temple of the Holy Spirit within you, which you have from God? You are not your own; you were bought with a price. So glorify God in your body.

1 Corinthians 6:19–20

The story of St. Cecilia is somewhat shrouded by time. She was one of the most revered martyrs of ancient Rome, however, with evidence of widespread devotion from an early date. She is one of seven women, apart from the Blessed Virgin, invoked in the first Eucharistic Prayer, also known as the Roman Canon.

Cecilia was born to a wealthy Roman family that instilled in her a devout Christian faith. She wore sackcloth under her clothes, fasted often, and had a great devotion to the saints and angels. Despite the family's Christian faith, her parents arranged for Cecilia to marry a pagan nobleman named Valerian. Cecilia, however, had made a promise to remain a virgin. When she told her husband, he honored her vow and eventually became a Catholic himself, together with his brother Tiberius. These brothers dedicated themselves to burying Christian martyrs, a practice that was forbidden by law, and were subsequently arrested and executed when they refused to renounce their faith.

Cecilia continued to witness to the faith by her life and by speaking boldly to others about Jesus. It is said that she was responsible for the conversion of four hundred people, most of whom were baptized by Pope Urban. When Cecilia herself was arrested, she was condemned to be suffocated in the heat of her own bath, possibly to make it appear that the influential young woman had died of natural causes. She was enclosed for a night and a day, but she still did not die from the excruciating temperatures.

The prefect then lost patience and sent an executioner to decapitate her, but after striking her three times, he was unable to sever the head. Cecilia continued to live for three days. Crowds came to visit Cecilia, collecting her blood while she spoke about the Lord and prayed. Many were converted and sought baptism as she lay dying. She distributed her property to the poor and donated her house to the pope so that it could become a place of Christian worship.

Cecilia was buried by Pope Urban and his deacons in the Catacomb of Saint Callistus. Centuries later, when her body was exhumed in 1599, officials found her to be incorrupt, draped in a silk veil and wearing a gold embroidered dress. They also reported a flower-like scent emanating from the burial chamber.

Since she is said to have heard heavenly music inside her heart during her wedding to Valerian, Cecilia is considered the patroness of musicians. The vow of virginity that Cecilia made, and which Valerian honored, is a reminder that all human love—no matter how noble—is kept pure and intact when we subordinate it to our love for God.

> Heavenly Father, St. Cecilia is a beautiful example of fidelity for our age, which has strayed so far from the ideals of holy purity. May her example of constancy to your divine Son be a reminder to all Christians, both married and unmarried, that chastity in all walks of life is a path to freedom, true love, and peace. With your grace, may we resolve, like Cecilia, to remain faithful in our resolutions of chastity regardless of the obstacles and the suffering that we might face. We ask this through our Lord Jesus Christ, your Son, who lives and reigns with you and the Holy Spirit, God forever and ever. Amen.

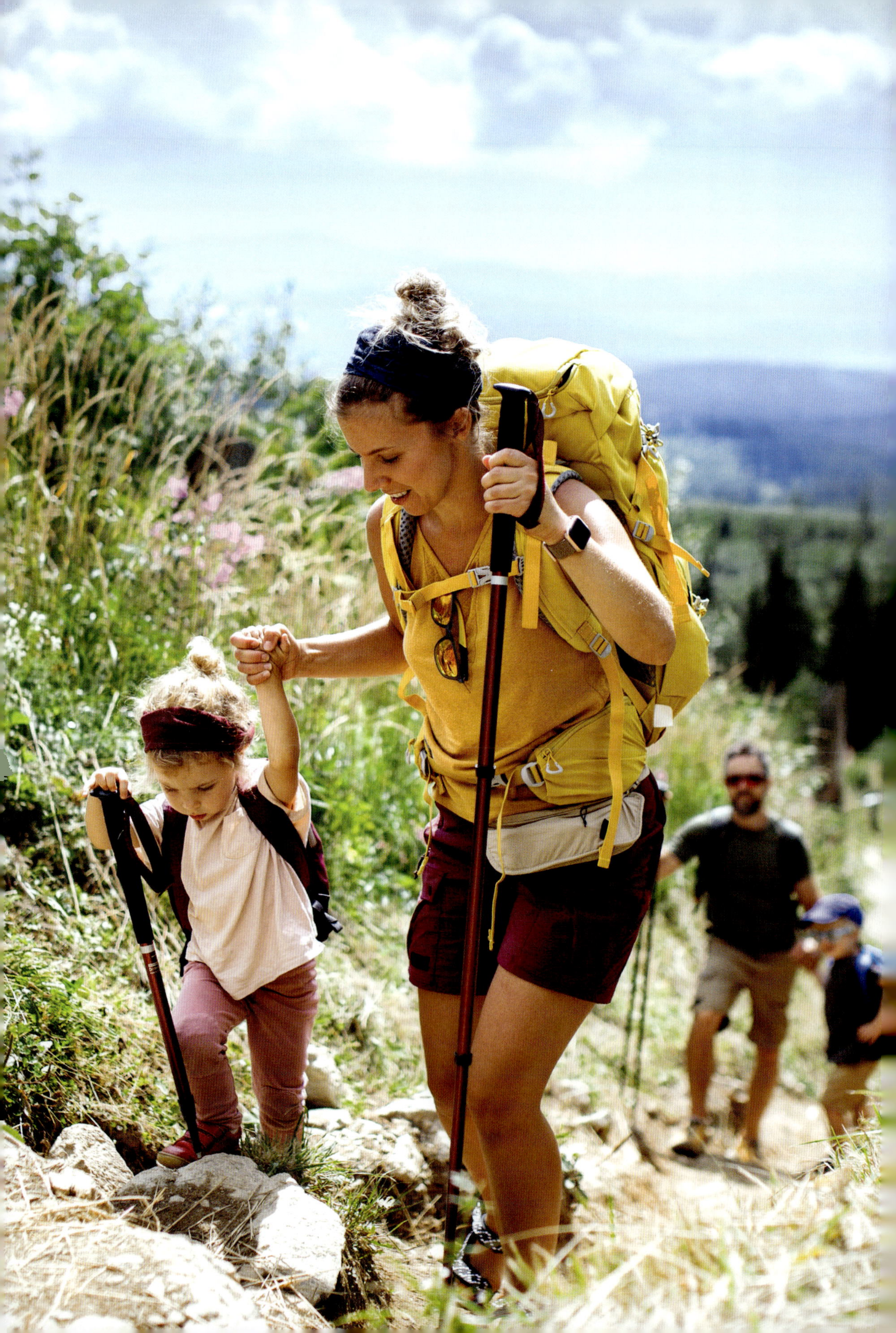

FORTITUDE

Every life is a drama. It is a compelling narrative with a plotline, characters, and—importantly—obstacles to overcome. It is an adventure story. We have to conquer external trials and internal afflictions, our own temptations, weaknesses, and failures. We all have anxieties, illnesses, setbacks, and ordeals to surmount. We all must do battle with an implacable enemy who sets traps along our path. We are the protagonists in this drama and, like all storybook heroes, need the virtue of fortitude to see our way through.

Fortitude is a virtue that invests us with firmness of mind and body both for doing good and enduring evil. All good things in life require fortitude, whether prayer, work, relationships, intellectual growth, skills, athletics, good health—you name it. Every virtue, in fact, requires fortitude to achieve. C. S. Lewis writes that fortitude is "the form of every virtue at the testing point."[1]

Simply, fortitude means discipline, being able to say no to oneself; doing the right thing when it is difficult and without concern for human respect or personal comfort. It means not being overly saddened in the face of difficulties, even when no relief seems to be coming. It is not the absence of fear, but the mastery of fear.

Chesterton says that courage is "almost a contradiction in terms. It means a strong desire to live taking the form of a readiness to die." He continues by saying that a soldier surrounded by enemies

> needs to combine a strong desire for living with a strange carelessness about dying. He must not merely cling to life, for then he will be a coward, and will not escape. He must not merely wait for death, for then he will be a suicide, and will not escape. He must seek his life in a spirit of furious indifference to it; he must desire life like water and yet drink death like wine.[2]

---

[1] C. S. Lewis, *The Screwtape Letters* (London: Fontana Books, 1955), 148–49.
[2] G. K. Chesterton, *Orthodoxy* (Colorado Springs: Waterbrook, 2001 [1908]), 136–37.

How can we help children grow in fortitude—and grow in this virtue ourselves?

Fortitude in its highest form is a Gift of the Holy Spirit. We begin, then, by asking for the grace to give that gift free play in our lives. The natural virtue of fortitude, in which we can freely grow, is the best soil for the Holy Spirit's gift to operate.

Talking to children about the virtue is a good place to start. Take advantage of moments that call for fortitude to have a conversation about it. When a child is tempted to lie, for instance, or witnesses someone being

TEDDY ROOSEVELT: THE MAN IN THE ARENA

In 1910, a year after he left the presidency, Theodore Roosevelt delivered a speech at the Sorbonne in a packed Grand Amphitheater of the University of Paris. The speech was called "Citizenship in a Republic" but it has become more popularly known as his "The Man in the Arena" speech. He powerfully captures the essence, and the grandeur, of fortitude.

> It is not the critic who counts; not the man who points out how the strong man stumbles, or where the doer of deeds could have done them better. The credit belongs to the man who is actually in the arena, whose face is marred by dust and sweat and blood; who strives valiantly; who errs, who comes short again and again, because there is no effort without error and shortcoming; but who does actually strive to do the deeds; who knows the great enthusiasms, the great devotions; who spends himself in a worthy cause; who at the best knows in the end the triumph of high achievement, and who at the worst, if he fails, at least fails while daring greatly, so that his place shall never be with those cold and timid souls who neither know victory nor defeat.[*]

---

[*] Theodore Roosevelt, *In the Words of Theodore Roosevelt: Quotations from the Man in the Arena*, ed. Patricia O'Toole (Ithaca, NY: Cornell University Press, 2012), 27.

bullied, or is ridiculed for his or her beliefs, parents can use the situation to talk about fortitude. Even a child's failure to be courageous in one of these situations—for example, lying in order to get out of trouble—can be a teachable moment about the virtue.

Like all virtues, fortitude grows through repeated actions, and these can take several forms. Life itself offers many opportunities to exercise fortitude. The daily obedience to a schedule, saying yes to the duty of the moment, is a subtle but effective way to grow in the fortitude of perseverance. Being patient when confronted with adversity is another way to grow in it. Coping with illness, a difficult class, frustrations with siblings—all are opportunities to grow in fortitude. Friendships also present us with ways to grow in fortitude when we sort out misunderstandings, handle conflict, forgive, and ask for forgiveness.

In addition to these occasions of growth that come to us, we can create opportunities to cultivate fortitude. One of the best ways is through delayed gratification. A spiritual director of mine used to recommend that I "pick a fight with myself"—choosing small mortifications, tiny, often invisible, ways of delaying a pleasure. These can be physical gratifications like food or other kinds of pleasure like the use of devices, searching the internet, and satisfying our curiosity. Helping children delay gratification is a gift that will reap rewards throughout their lives.

We can also help children grow in fortitude in more direct ways. Encourage them to persevere in difficult things, whether succeeding in school, learning an instrument, becoming a better athlete, remaining loyal to a difficult friend, or even just waking up on time.

Depending on the age of children, families can engage in difficult activities together, such as running in a race to support a cause, hiking a nearby mountain together, or getting up once a month for an early morning adoration time at the parish.

Every child should have chores around the house for which he or she is accountable. Having and maintaining family expectations—standards of dress, room cleanliness, hygiene, etiquette, and conversation—are all ways to help children grow in fortitude.

Finally, children grow in fortitude by becoming accustomed to correction. Many young parents are reluctant to discipline or correct their children, perhaps fearing that it will damage their children's self-esteem. Quite the opposite is the case. Deep down, children know that they need formation. When it is given with love, clarity, consistency, respect, and firmness, they respond well.

We cannot imitate the "bulldozer" parents who, with the best of intentions, try to forcefully remove any obstacles that their children face. Such efforts are often counter-productive. When children grow up without the need to confront challenges, without being allowed to fail at times, without having to stretch and exercise the virtue of fortitude, they are not prepared for the difficulties of life, and they know it. They are not more secure, but insecure, for having their path cleared of all obstacles.

When children grow up learning how to be strong, how to exercise firmness of mind, both for doing good and enduring evil, they will be ready to make a gift of themselves to others and do something great with their lives. St. Teresa of Avila said that "the devil has no dread of irresolute souls."[3] It is the resolute souls whom he dreads!

With God's grace and your help, your children will become men and women of courage able to do anything that needs doing, say anything that needs saying, and overcome any obstacle that needs surmounting. That is not the recipe for a carefree life, but it is the recipe for a virtuous life, for a life of holiness and integrity. It is, in the end, the only recipe for deep joy, both in this life and in the life to come.

---

[3] St. Teresa of Avila, *Way of Perfection*, trans. Alice Alexander (Westminster, MD: Newman Bookshop, 1948), 144. Translated here as "He is terribly afraid of resolute souls."

THE NEED FOR FORTITUDE TODAY

There is a need for fortitude in every age, but there is a particular need for it today, and for several reasons.

First, we live in a highly prosperous time and it is all too easy to fall into the habit of laziness, indulging our desires, and avoiding our responsibilities. It is, quite simply, a soft age. Unless we make conscious efforts to grow in fortitude, the tenor of the age, the advances of technology, and our own fallen nature will conspire to rob us of our strength.

Second, a widespread but flawed notion of self-fulfillment has sometimes warped our understanding of fortitude. When my own fulfillment becomes equated with satisfying my emotional cravings, it is no longer genuine fulfillment but simply selfishness under a different name. Countless marriages have broken up because one or both parties "no longer feel fulfilled." Some spouses actually claim that it is an act of fortitude to break their commitment, abandon their families, in order to courageously "follow their heart." This shallow concept of self-fulfillment is one of the most pernicious lies around. The only true route to personal fulfillment is the one taught by Jesus; the seed must die in order to give life. It is in sacrifice for the sake of love where true joy is found. That will require fortitude.

Third, we live in a time that has an almost clinical fear of commitments. "Keep your options open as long as possible," the wisdom of the age says. "Don't burn any bridges," we are solemnly told. "Nothing lasts forever," the skeptic insists. They are mistaken. Commitments are essential to the good life. Someone who cannot commit to anyone, any mission, anything outside themselves is a person on the road to sadness, loneliness, and anxiety. Only by persevering in commitments, which requires fortitude, will we ever find real peace and joy.

What is your own relationship with fortitude? Do you struggle to persevere and fulfill your duties and obligations?

Fortitude is relevant at virtually every age. Discuss with your spouse areas in which each child could benefit from your guidance with this virtue. Whether it's modeling fortitude, offering advice for a particular challenge, or demonstrating patience as a young child struggles, what can you do this week to help each child overcome his or her unique obstacles?

We all face seasons when our fortitude is tested. Choose a verse or short passage of Scripture to commit to memory for times when you feel overwhelmed, discouraged, or tempted to abandon a commitment.

Choose a reasonable activity in which to engage the entire family in some fortitude building. Provide challenges that stretch but do not break individuals. From service projects to outdoor activities, find something that you and your spouse agree would be suitable for your family.

ST. THOMAS MORE

Martyr
Born in England
D. 1535
Feast day: June 22

Finally, be strong in the Lord and in the strength of his might. Put on the whole armor of God, that you may be able to stand against the wiles of the devil.

Ephesians 6:10–11

St. Thomas More was one of the most highly respected men of his time, not only in England but also throughout Europe. He was a lawyer, a scholar, and a statesman. Under King Henry VIII, he rose to become the first layman to be named Lord Chancellor, the highest office in the land apart from the monarch. More came from a well-to-do family from which he received a strong faith and a good education. As a young man, More thought of becoming a Carthusian, but after two years of discernment with the monks, he determined that it was not his vocation. He married and had four children, though his wife died prematurely. Despite his grief, More remarried soon thereafter in order to provide a mother for his children. He was a beloved father, ensuring that both his boys and—unusually for his time—his girls received the same sterling education that he did.

Beginning his legal practice in London in the year 1502, More soon entered Parliament, where the king noticed his intellect and wisdom. The young man was made a Privy Counselor in 1514 and Lord Chancellor in 1529. When King Henry sought an annulment from a childless marriage, however, and started to break from the Church of Rome, More left the king's service. He did not attend the king's wedding with Anne Boleyn, further angering the monarch. King Henry had him arrested and imprisoned in the Tower of London in 1534. Though More refused to explicitly acknowledge Henry as head of the Church, there was no case against him since he remained silent about his views. The prosecutors were forced to employ false witnesses in order to convict More of treason.

As he climbed the scaffold to be executed on July 6, 1535, More asked the executioners to help him up. "As for my coming down," he said dryly, "let me shift for myself." Addressing the gathered crowd, he then declared himself publicly: "I die in and for the faith of the holy Catholic Church. Pray for me in this world, and I shall pray for you in that world. Pray for the king, that it please God to send him good counselors. I die as the king's true servant, but God's first." He was canonized in 1935 and declared patron of statesmen and lawyers.

St. Thomas More is an exceptional example of fortitude. During his life, he mortified himself with a hairshirt and lived a life of piety, asceticism, and penance. His temperate way of life prepared him well for the more serious trial that came when he had to let go of his position, his reputation, his freedom, his family, his friends, and eventually his life in order to remain true to his faith.

> Dear Father in heaven, St. Thomas More was an outstanding witness of fortitude as he resisted the temptation to acquiesce to the urging of many personal friends and influential individuals to violate his conscience and deny his faith. When we are tempted to take the easy way out, to give up, to get discouraged, or to comply with ideas that we know are wrong, may the prayers and example of St. Thomas More help us to stand fast with fortitude. With your grace, may this virtue help our family to grow in all the virtues and help us to persevere in the faith to the end. Through our Lord Jesus Christ, your Son, who lives and reigns with you and the Holy Spirit, God forever and ever. Amen.

MAGNANIMITY

Fortitude is needed for the protagonist to overcome obstacles. But there is more to a good story than obstacles. The plot needs to have not only adversaries but also a destination, a point toward which everything tends. The battle must be won, the girl swept off her feet, the world saved, the hostages freed, the criminal captured, or the ring destroyed. (Can you tell what kind of movies I like?)

As protagonists in our own drama, the virtue that helps us stretch toward those lofty goals in life is called magnanimity. Magnanimity is a greatness of soul, a largeness of heart, a profound freedom of spirit. The magnanimous person aspires to great things. He or she lives audaciously, deliberately, with purpose and conviction.

Though not as well-known as other virtues, Aquinas and Aristotle taught that magnanimity is "the jewel of all the virtues" since it always decides what is the greater possibility of our human potential.

Magnanimous people do not shrink from ideals and dreams. They recognize the eternal significance of the moment, the "depth" of the present, and are not afraid to let others feel the weight of who God made them to be. In fact, they rejoice in their own existence since they know it can be a positive good for others.

Magnanimity teaches us that our dignity is based not on our capacities or achievements, but on the love that God has for us, his sovereign choice to create us as his beloved children. We are not great because we feel great or do great things, but because God created us to *be* great.

We are sons and daughters of the King and stroll through the palace of creation knowing who we are. We know that God has a plan, that his providence will prevail, that he has counted every hair on our head, that he loves and protects us. Magnanimity is the defining characteristic—the outrageous confidence, the profound hopefulness—of the true lover.

Magnanimity is a virtue with a wide range of qualities. For instance, magnanimous people:

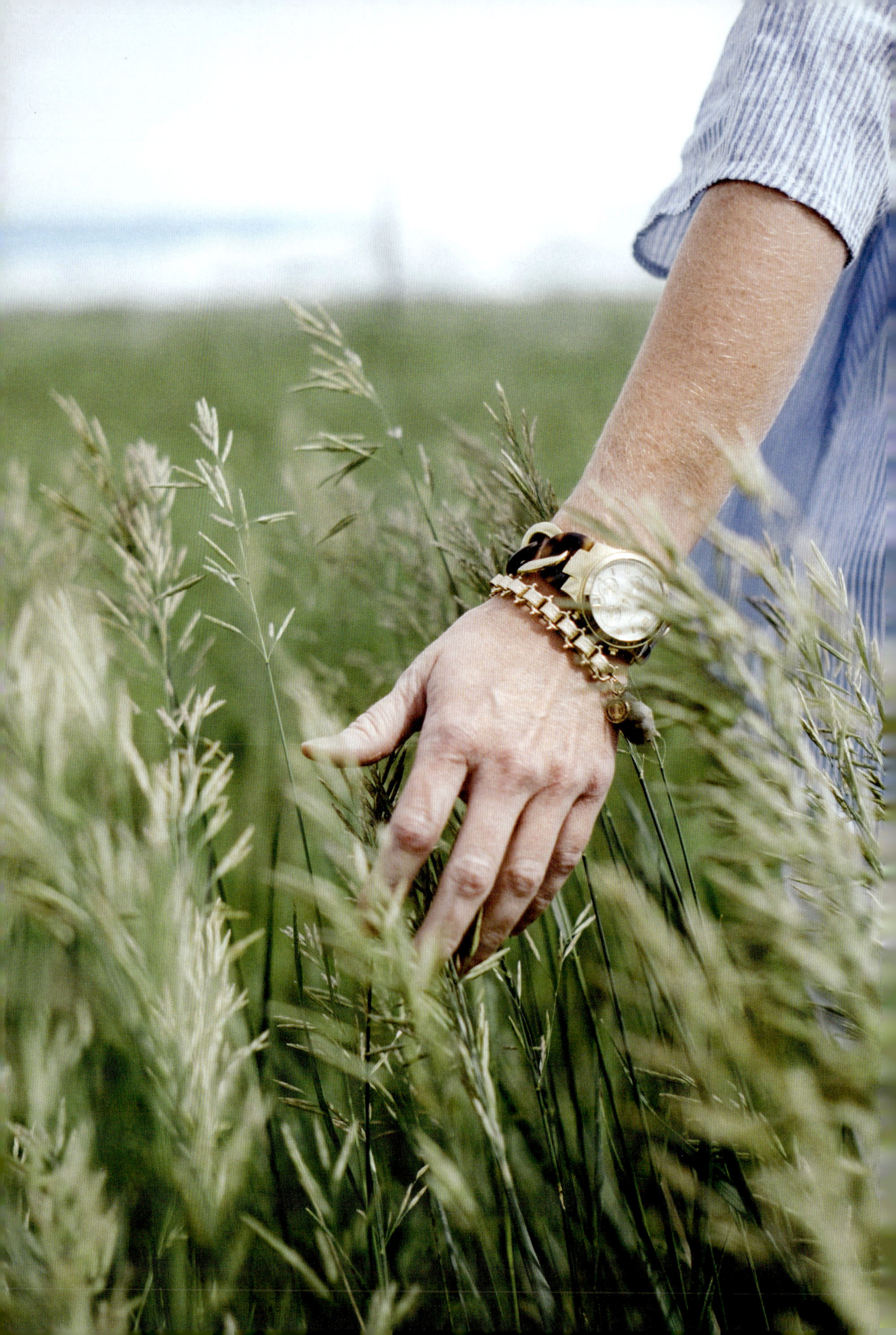

- Do not pay too much attention to what others think. They neither rejoice much in applause, nor become saddened at its absence.

- Are calm and able to focus on one thing at a time, not frenetically multi-tasking. Aristotle makes a point of saying that magnanimous people walk slowly!

- Learn to do without when necessary. They do not complain about things they lack.

- Go beyond the minimum, whether in friendships, doing their work well, or serving others generously. They do not aim for mediocrity, above all in their dealings with God, in giving time to God.

So how do we become great-hearted ourselves, and how do we instill this virtue in our children?

One way to grow in magnanimity is by having a generous spirit towards our neighbors. We rejoice at their gifts and achievements, judge their motives in the most charitable way, and encourage them in their aspirations. The magnanimous person is loyal, never holding onto grudges or giving in to pettiness, and is quick to forgive. He or she is easy and kind, respectful to all regardless of rank, and instinctively sees the best in others. These are all qualities that we can instill in our children.

One of the truly magnanimous souls of our age was St. John Paul II, whose spokesman once said that, in all their many travels together, in over a hundred trips, he never once heard the pope say anything critical of anyone. Even minutes after he had been shot in St. Peter's Square, John Paul was heard murmuring that he forgave his assailant. That is magnanimity!

Another way to grow in magnanimity is by earnestly desiring our neighbor's good: above all, his salvation. If we are convinced of the truth of the Gospel, we will earnestly want every soul on earth to have that same relationship with the Lord. The wider our heart, the more souls we will want to reach, the more attentive we will be to what truly helps them along the path to salvation, whether they are fellow Catholics, fallen away Catholics, separated Christians, those of other faiths, or those of no faith. Magnanimity shines most brightly when we are serving others;

when we imitate the One who "came to serve, not to be served." These, too, are dispositions that we can instill in our children from a young age.

We also grow in magnanimity by fostering our own confidence in God. We might think that magnanimity sounds a bit prideful, but precisely the opposite is true. It is not opposed to humility but presupposes it, since Christian magnanimity rests on the power of grace, confidence in grace, knowledge of the power of God.

The more we grow in childlike trust of our heavenly Father, the more we are certain of God's ultimate victory, the bolder and more magnanimous we become. Even in the face of evil and suffering, the magnanimous person knows in his bones that good will eventually triumph. The ending of almost every great story is roughly the same because every great story is an echo of salvation history. The monster is defeated, the bomb is defused, the poor orphan boy is exalted, the tragedy is averted. Good wins.

Tolkien called this the *eucatastrophe*—the "good catastrophe"—the sudden joyous turn before the happy ending. It does not, as he put it, "deny the existence of *dyscatastrophe*, of sorrow and failure: the possibility of these is necessary to the joy of deliverance; it denies (in the face of much evidence, if you will) universal final defeat."[1] When we know that all will come right in the end, that evil will not have the last say, that in fact we can contribute to the great, final triumph of all that is good and beautiful and true, we have a tremendous motive to act magnanimously.

This virtue is not about emotional euphoria or buoyant feelings. It is compatible with (and in fact presupposes) noble perseverance in the face of the mundane and ordinary. True love is tested not in emotional exhilaration but in commitment, fortitude, and patience—all qualities of the magnanimous soul.

Magnanimity is living with purpose and determination, knowing who we are and what we are about. Magnanimous people know that they have only one life to live and want to live it well. They want their lives to make a difference. They want to do something great with their years on earth. It is irrelevant whether or not their life's work is deemed great in the eyes of the world, because they know its worth from the perspective of eternity.

Good stories, the stories that really stick with us, are about the cosmic struggle between good and evil. They uncover hidden greatness. As in those

---

[1] J. R. R. Tolkien, "On Fairy Stories," in *The Tolkien Reader* (New York: Ballantine Books, 1966), 86, italics in original.

MAGNANIMITY IN THE LIFE OF JESUS

The man who lived magnanimity most perfectly was Our Lord himself. Nobody before or since has lived with such a sense of purpose. Nobody has ever been more sure of who he is and of his mission. Nobody has been more confident of the meaningfulness of his life and work. Jesus knew what he was about and what he was on earth to do.

Even in the quiet Nazareth years, in the ordinary life of a working man, no day was simply routine. He worked for the glory of his Father with a powerful sense of the importance and depth of each moment.

In his Incarnation he lowered himself to assume a human nature, but never thought himself too exalted for humanity. His greatness of soul was shown precisely in his capacity to become small. He was easy, comfortable, respectful, and humble with all—from the high priest to hard-working fishermen to poor, blind beggars. In the Scriptures there is never a hint of the pettiness, grudges, and small-mindedness that we know in ourselves all too well.

Honors, veneration, and compliments did not enthrall him, and indifference, scorn, and even violent persecution did not derail his mission. In the end, as we know, he magnanimously forgave his murderers, even excusing their behavior because they "know not what they do."

The more we come to know our divine Lord the more we will admire and imitate his humanity. He did not work prodigies to exalt himself or, until the Resurrection (and that for our sake), to distinguish himself from our common human nature. He has left us an example to imitate, and that is nowhere clearer than his modeling of the virtue of magnanimity.

stories, our world is larger and deeper, more real and more dramatic, than it might first appear. Our life, no matter how ordinary in appearance, is filled with opportunities to do great deeds. It is the stuff of a magnificent drama. It contains all the splendor of wonder, mystery, and holiness. It is custom designed to nurture magnanimity.

> Make a list of potential obstacles to magnanimity for you and your family. Are there habits, media, or relationships that you need to reconsider?
>
> Who exemplifies magnanimity within or outside of your family? Discuss as a family the qualities in that person or people that are worth emulating.
>
> As a couple, have a conversation about ways you can encourage one another to grow in magnanimity. How do you think this virtue can benefit your marriage and family life?
>
> Do you believe that God created you for greatness? If not, why? Spend some time in prayer this week asking the Holy Spirit to show you the truth of your dignity.

THE URGENT NEED FOR MAGNANIMITY

Today there is a particular need for magnanimity because its opposite vice, that of pusillanimity, or "smallness of soul," is on the rise. This is the tendency to shrink from great aspirations and from the struggle to grow in virtue. Pusillanimity is blind to the greatness of ordinary life. It is satisfied with mediocrity. It leaves us feeling unmoored, bored, isolated, indifferent, and anxious.

Sadly, we see the symptoms of this malaise all around us. There are at least three principal causes of the rise in pusillanimity today.

First, the digital world tends toward an isolation from real relationships in favor of cyber substitutes. Magnanimity grows, in large part, when we are generous in spirit towards other people. The more alienated we are from others, the fewer opportunities to grow in the virtue.

Second, the sexual revolution has contributed to a widespread emotional detachment in which pusillanimity festers. Alan Bloom observed that for those caught in the grip of the sexual revolution "the world is for them what it presents itself to the senses to be; it is unadorned by imagination and devoid of ideals."* Pusillanimity is one of the many toxic byproducts of our permissive age.

Third is pervasive materialism, a practical atheism that diminishes human dignity. The upshot of living as if God doesn't exist is the crushing smallness, the insignificance of humanity, the drive to just try to get what we can out of life. It shrivels the soul and drains it of vitality and fire and energy. It is the toughest ground in which to grow the virtue of magnanimity.

Those afflicted with pusillanimity have two options.

They can try to escape what feels like the suffocating insignificance of life. Whatever it takes to forget the perceived meaninglessness of existence.

The other option is to live a different kind of life, one that is deliberate and intentional. Living with purpose and conviction, finding the depth in the present moment, discovering one's dignity and mission as a child of God. In other words, living magnanimously. It is the very medicine that our world needs!

---

* Alan Bloom, *The Closing of the American Mind* (New York: Simon and Schuster, 2012), 134.

Forming Families, Forming Saints

ST. IGNATIUS OF LOYOLA

**Religious
Born in Spain
D. 1556
Feast day: July 31**

*When I look at your heavens,
the work of your fingers,
   the moon and the stars which
you have established;
what is man that you are mindful of him,
   and the son of man that
you care for him?*

Psalm 8:3–4

St. Ignatius of Loyola was born in 1491, the youngest of thirteen children in a family of minor nobility. When he was seven years old, he was sent to live at an aristocratic home, where he served as a page. This introduced him to the glamor of knighthood and military service. He dreamed of becoming a great military leader.

He was a soldier by the age of eighteen and, having exhibited courage in many battles, he quickly rose in rank and was soon commanding his own troops. In 1521, however, his dream of glory was shattered by a cannonball that exploded near his legs, breaking one and mangling the other. During his convalescence, he read the lives of Christ and of the saints and resolved to turn his life around and become a faithful servant of Christ.

On March 25, 1522, having finally recovered from his wounds, he entered a Benedictine Monastery in Monserrat and laid down his military gear at the feet of the Blessed Virgin. He then walked to a nearby hospital, where he offered his humble services while he begged for food and spent hours each day in prayer. He decided to return to school. He had to start by learning Latin sitting next to schoolchildren, but he eventually earned his master's degree at the University of Paris at the age of thirty-eight.

Ignatius' roommates in Paris were two other future saints, Peter Faber and Francis Xavier. These three friends joined themselves informally into a group called the "Friends of the Lord," but soon others joined them. Their order—the Society of Jesus or "Jesuits"—was approved by the pope in 1540 with a particular focus on education. By the time of Ignatius' death in 1556, the Jesuits ran thirty-five schools and boasted over one thousand members. It is credited with being a significant force behind the Catholic Reformation that finally stopped the growth of Protestantism.

As a young man, Ignatius spent much time daydreaming about romance, chivalry, and human glory. He was ambitious and wanted to be a great commander, leading men into battle and winning fame for himself and his prince. These desires, though they were all too human, fueled his magnanimous heart when he turned his life over to the Lord. His human ambition was transformed into ambition for God. The motto of the Jesuits to this day is *Ad majorem Dei gloriam*, "for the greater glory of God."

After his conversion, Ignatius exemplified the notion of Christian magnanimity since he was utterly dependent upon grace and prayer and yet aspired with a profound freedom of spirit to do great things for God. He lived in trust, with purpose and conviction, and wanted to spend his life well. All for the glory of God!

> Heavenly Father, you raised up St. Ignatius of Loyola to be a faithful son and priest. You inspired his noble heart to seek not the glory of passing fame and fortune but your own glory, which is the true path of peace and joy. May his example and intercession help us and our families to rightly value the things of this world, placing our hope not in them but in you and your kingdom, for which no effort and no sacrifice is too great. We ask this through our Lord Jesus Christ, your Son, who lives and reigns with you and the Holy Spirit, God forever and ever. Amen.

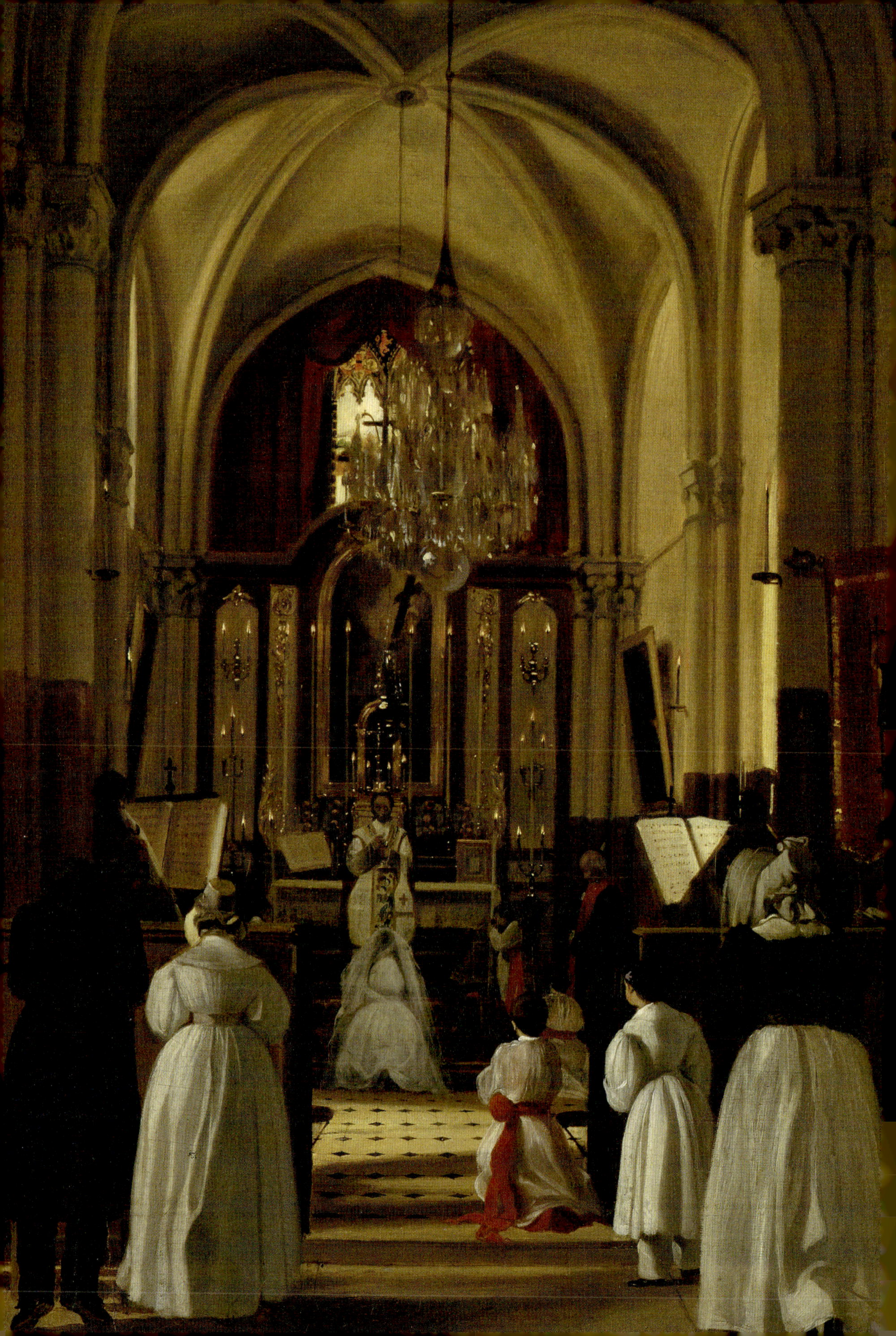

PILLAR II

Spiritual Formation

"By virtue of their ministry of educating, parents are, through the witness of their lives, the first heralds of the Gospel for their children. Furthermore, by praying with their children, by reading the word of God with them and by introducing them deeply through Christian initiation into the Body of Christ—both the Eucharistic and the ecclesial Body—they become fully parents, in that they are begetters not only of bodily life but also of the life that through the Spirit's renewal flows from the Cross and Resurrection of Christ."

POPE ST. JOHN PAUL II
Apostolic Exhortation on the Role of the Christian Family in the Modern World *Familiaris Consortio*

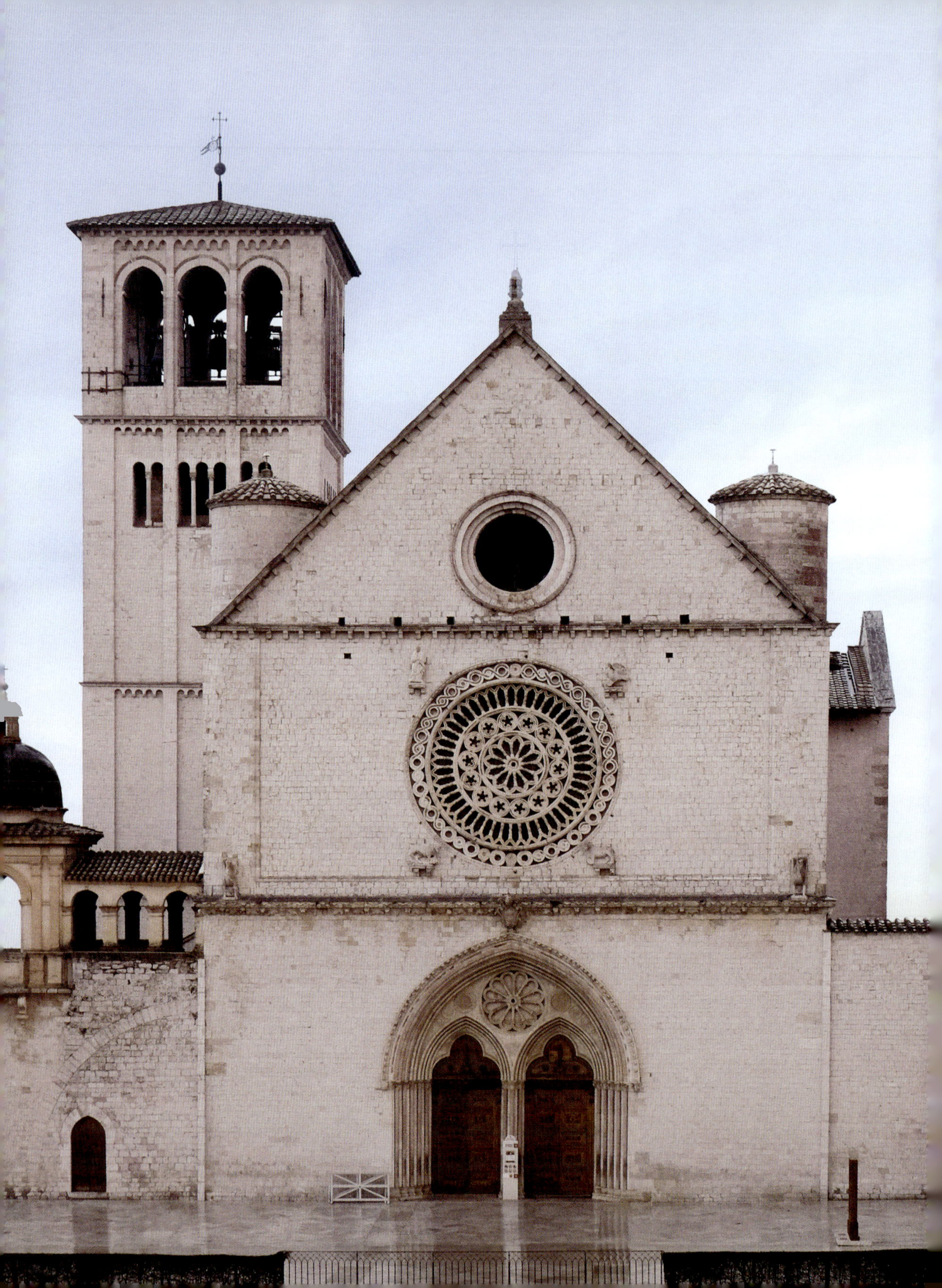

INTRODUCTION TO SPIRITUAL FORMATION

The Basilica of the National Shrine of the Assumption of the Blessed Virgin Mary was the first cathedral built in the United States. When the "Baltimore Basilica" was being renovated some years ago, workers were clearing out the undercroft and, to their surprise, they found it filled with sand. They hauled out all that debris and in the space built a chapel for adoration of the Blessed Sacrament. Removing sand from underneath the building and replacing it with space for divine worship: a fitting image for spiritual formation!

At its heart, spiritual formation is building foundations for growth in holiness. It is molding the soul in love, beginning with our baptism, which forges us into new creatures in Christ. It means being united to Christ, walking in holiness of life, being nourished by the Eucharist, and being healed by repentance and forgiveness.

Spiritual formation is the work of grace, as St. Paul reminds the Ephesians: "For by grace you have been saved through faith; and this is not your own doing, it is the gift of God—not because of works, lest any man should boast. For we are his workmanship, created in Christ Jesus for good works, which God prepared beforehand, that we should walk in them" (Eph 2:8–10).

Many elements of spiritual formation are pertinent to parents who wish to build a solid foundation in their children's interior lives. The most important is helping their children to have a posture of receptivity to God, the humble approach of Our Lady, who teaches us that the most important decisions we make in life are not external but in our hearts. Forming a family culture in which children are encouraged to say yes to God, and made capable of doing so, is, bar none, the most vital task entrusted to parents.

There are many ways to create such a culture, some of which will be explored in the chapters that follow. Instilling in our children a conviction that they are sons and daughters of God, with all the dignity and responsibility of that exalted calling, is an essential way to promote a culture of holiness. Fostering the supernatural outlook which flows from that conviction is a second way, as is a deep and mature Eucharistic piety.

Helping our children grow in love for the Scriptures and to establish habits of prayer are topics woven into each of the chapters that follow. Liturgical prayer, vocal prayer, and quiet mental prayer are all within reach of children. An old professor of mine once cautioned against underestimating the prayer of the young. "Even children can be mystics," he said, and I have witnessed the truth of that statement.

Teaching children the basics of prayer, leading them in prayer, taking them to Mass and Eucharistic exposition, and encouraging daily vocal prayers suited to their age are all ways to promote a prayerful spirit in our children. These can also open them to the gift of simple adoration, which Cardinal Ratzinger observed is "humanity's highest possibility; it alone forms his true and final liberation."[1]

There is a persistent myth that forming children in the faith will somehow lead to a backlash later in life. Nothing could be further from the truth. Certainly harshness has no place in forming children, and that often does lead to a later reaction—sometimes against the religion the parents tried to instill through overly strict methods. But you need not fear a backlash when instilling prayerful habits in your children, forming their minds to think with the Church, and cultivating moral virtue.

Union with God is at the heart of spiritual formation, and flowing from that union is a life of discipleship, conversion, and growth. A saint, the old adage goes, is simply a sinner who keeps getting up. Helping children grasp the importance of the moral life, and an unshakable confidence in God's mercy, are important goals for spiritual formation. Trust in the Father's mercy is taught first in the family setting, by giving and asking for forgiveness when called for, and by frequenting the Sacrament of Confession individually or as a family.

Parents can help their children build habits of self-denial, penance, and a love for the Cross, which are inseparable from Christian discipleship. They can also encourage their little ones to develop sincere friendships with the saints and angels who give us so much inspiration and assistance

---

[1] Joseph Ratzinger, *Introduction to Christianity*, trans. J. R. Foster (San Francisco: Ignatius Press, 1990), 219.

in our spiritual growth. These, too, will be topics explored in the chapters ahead.

After their own holiness, the greatest gift parents can give the Church and the world are children with an interior life. We might be tempted to dwell on everything that seems to be going wrong in the Church and in the world. That is understandable. We need to live in reality and grapple with the many challenges that face us. The most important asset we have, though, is our union with God.

"I'll tell you a secret," St. Josemaría Escrivá wrote, "an open secret: these world crises are crises of saints."[2] The only way to reform the Church is through holiness. The only way to change the culture is through holiness. Most of all, the only way to live lives fit for heaven is holiness. That is the primary subject matter of spiritual formation.

None of the pillars of formation stand alone. Spiritual formation is built on the foundation of human nature. The more mature and well-developed that humanity, the stronger and more robust the potential for interior life. Since love always seeks to know the beloved, intellectual formation will both nourish and be nourished by a deep interior life. And since Christianity only grows when people meet authentic, joyful Christians who truly know Christ, and since apostolate is truly effective only when it is the overflow of an interior life, our apostolic fruitfulness is in direct proportion to our spiritual depth.

Hauling out the sand that lingers beneath our spiritual edifice, and helping our children to do the same, is not an easy task, but it is always worth it. Building a foundation of adoration is the sure path to holiness, and it also happens to be the most beautiful way to live a human life.

"Let us pray God to give us all graces," St. John Henry Newman wrote,

> And while, in the first place, we pray that he would make us holy, really holy, let us also pray him to give us the beauty of holiness, which consists in tender and eager affection towards our Lord and Savior, so that through God's mercy our souls may have not strength and health only but a sort of bloom and comeliness, and that as we grow older in body, we may, year by year, grow more youthful in spirit.[3]

---

[2] Josemaría Escrivá, *The Way* (New York: Scepter Publishers, 1954), no. 301.
[3] John Henry Newman, *The Tears of Christ: Meditations for Lent*, ed. Christopher Blum (Greenwood Village, CO: Augustine Institute, 2019), 190.

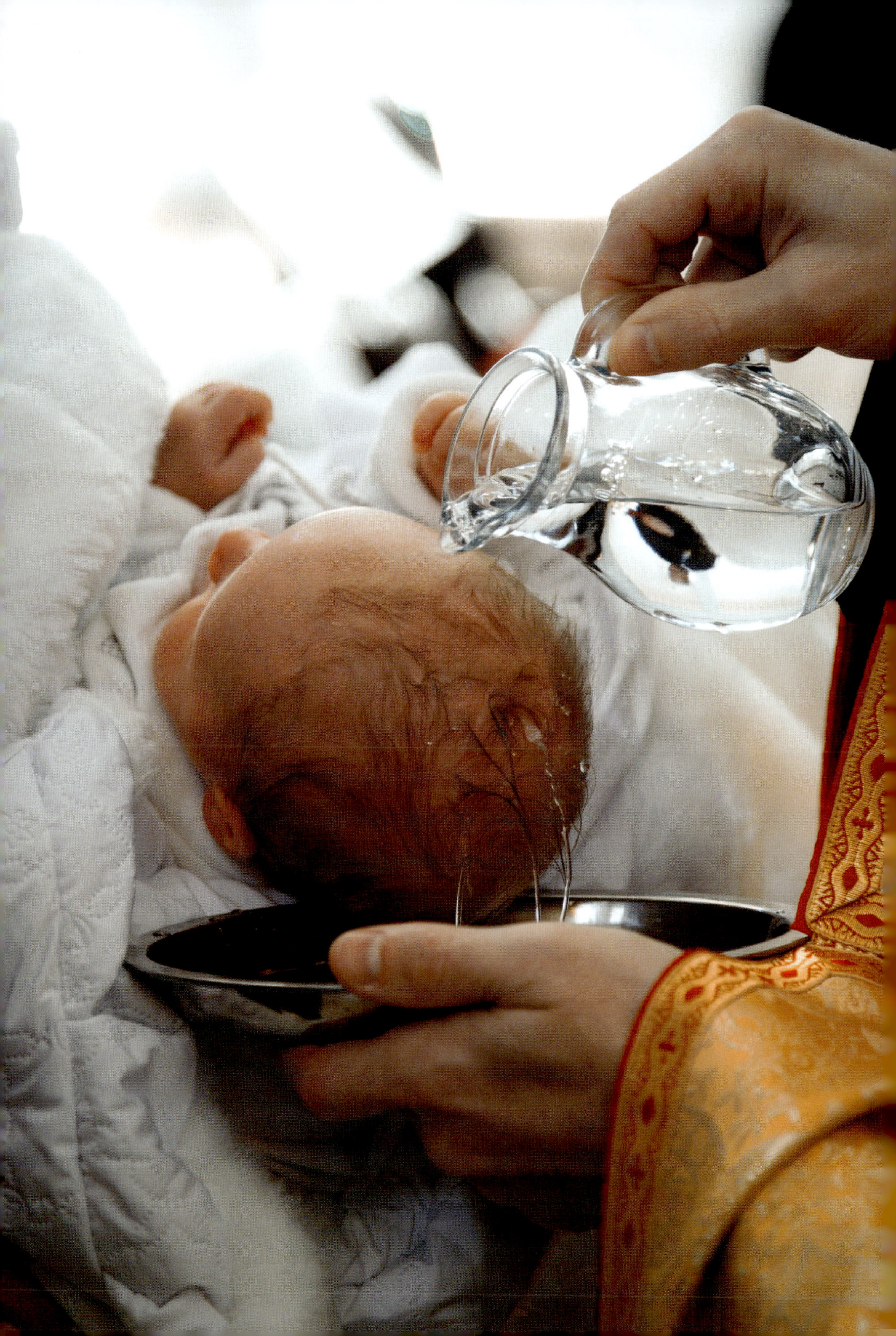

SONS AND DAUGHTERS OF GOD

THERE ONCE WAS A COASTAL village in a distant kingdom, several weeks' journey from the capital. Everyone knew each other. Sometimes they were good to each other, and sometimes they were cruel. It was much like anyplace else.

One day a little orphan boy showed up, and they watched him warily as he made his way to the village square where the other children were playing. Some of the children laughed at him, insulted him, even tried to hurt him, except for one boy who was kind and befriended him.

They became close companions over the weeks and months that followed. Three years later, a magnificent carriage rolled into town, drawn by eight white stallions. Wide-eyed villagers watched as footmen jumped down and opened the door for a man in splendid attire, wearing a golden chain. He looked around at the gathering crowd. As he scanned the villagers, they humbly lowered their heads, until his eyes met those of the young orphan boy who had arrived three years earlier.

As their gaze met, tears welled up in the great man's eyes, and with a broad smile he made a low bow. "Your Highness," he said in a quiet voice, "your father the King says it is time for you to return home."

Upon hearing these words, the amazed townspeople fell to their knees. But the Prince turned to his young friend and lifted him to his feet. "No," he said, "you are not my servant. You are my friend, and I shall never forget it. And what is more, if you wish I shall take you to my home, to live in my palace, and my Father will adopt you so that we can be brothers forever."

This fable tells a deep truth about our Lord's mission. In the Incarnation, Jesus emptied himself of his divine prerogatives. He traveled a great distance to our little village, in the flesh of our poor human nature, so that he might bring us home, so that he might make us sons and daughters of the King. "He came to what was his own," St. John writes, "but his own people did not accept him. But to those who did accept him he gave power to become children of God" (John 1:11–12).

Our adoption as God's sons and daughters is not simply one element of the Christian religion; it is its very heart. It is what Jesus came to do. As St. Athanasius said, "the Son of God became the Son of Man so that sons of men might become sons of God."[1]

In the ancient world, interaction with divine beings was regarded with profound dread. Man cannot look upon the face of God and live (see Exod 33:20). Things changed dramatically with the arrival of Jesus. He did not lack the authority that would inspire awe. He commanded evil spirits, restored sight to the blind and health to the sick, stilled

---

[1] Athanasius, *On the Incarnation*, 54.3, trans. Archibald Robertson (London: D. Nutt, 1891), 93. In this translation, it is rendered, "He was made man that we might be made God."

FORMING CHILDREN TO BE CHILDREN OF GOD

Without a doubt parents play the crucial role in forming children to know that they are cherished sons and daughters of God. The love of parents, like the love of God, is a complete gift, unchosen and unmerited. Wilbur Wright once quipped, "If I were giving a young man advice as to how he might succeed in life, I would say to him, pick out a good father and mother, and begin life in Ohio."*

It is all too apparent when such love is missing. Unworthy parents often leave lasting distrust, fear, and resentment in the hearts of their sons and daughters and impede their ability to know God as a loving Father. On the other hand, just being good, loving, attentive, patient parents does more for the spiritual good of children than we can possibly imagine!

In addition to simple, natural love, there are many supernatural

---

* Quoted in David McCullough, *The Wright Brothers* (New York: Simon and Schuster, 2015), 5.

the wind and waves over the Sea of Galilee, and raised the dead to life. His was unquestionably divine and royal power.

And yet how informally and affectionately the apostles treated him! They spoke to him with ease. They jostled him, pressed him for favors, complained when they couldn't work miracles, goaded him to punish the Samaritans, and brazenly asked what they would receive in return for their loyalty.

Through it all, Jesus delighted in their love, their simple faith, and their unswerving confidence in him. He knew of what they were made and that they were in the first stages of formation. He loved them back and taught them how to relate to God not as slaves but as children.

In ancient times even human royalty shared in the dread of God; people were forbidden, on pain of death, to look into the face of the king. There

---

ways to help children grow in their divine filiation. Here are three:

- Foster in your children a relationship to the Holy Spirit. St. Paul wrote to the Romans, "When we cry, 'Abba! Father!' it is the Spirit himself bearing witness with our spirit that we are children of God" (Rom 8:15–16). By configuring us to Jesus, the Holy Spirit makes possible our adoption through the power of grace. He will teach us how to relate to God as a loving Father.

- Encourage children to pray for their needs with faith and humility. We grow in spiritual childhood when we acknowledge our dependence on God and regard him as worthy of all our trust. The Father loves that confidence in him and will always answer our humble prayers with what we ask for—unless it is not the best thing for us, in which case he will give us something even better!

- Cultivate a reliance on God's mercy. If we find ourselves reluctant to repent, to fling ourselves back into the arms of our loving Father when we stray, perhaps we have grown too big for our own good. Reliance on mercy keeps us small and reminds us that we are, after all, simply children— and we may thank God for that!

was one exception, however. One person could even wake the king up at three in the morning and ask for a glass of water. It was his son, of course. That is the kind of access we have to our Father in heaven. That is the stunning novelty of the Good News.

Jesus promised that he would not leave us orphans (see John 14:18). We are sons and daughters in the Son, and we have an intimacy with the King of Heaven that no one else in history has dared to claim.

A few years ago an Australian priest friend told me a story from the campus chaplaincy where he was serving. One of the young students who lived in that residence brought a Muslim friend around for a visit near Christmastime. They visited the chapel where a Nativity scene had been set up. Curious, the Muslim asked about the custom, the various figures, and what it all means to Christians. He turned to his Catholic friend and said, "I don't know any religion in the world where people feel so good about their God." He eventually became Catholic himself.

When we know and feel that God is truly our Father, our entire perspective on life changes. It changes how we pray, how we trust, how we love God. It changes how we behave, how we suffer, how we love others, how we love ourselves. It changes how we tie our shoes in the morning. If we take seriously that God cares for us with the vigilance of a father, of the best of fathers, what else matters? What can possibly ever disturb us again?

St. John Henry Newman once observed that many look back at their childhood "full of tender, affectionate thoughts towards those first years, but they do not know why." It is not simply nostalgia for the past but a deep intuition that the joy of their lost childhood will one day be regained. "They think it is those very years which they yearn after," he says, "whereas it is the presence of God which, as they now see, was then over them, which attracts them. They think that they regret the past, when they are but longing after the future."[2] It is an intimacy with our Father that begins now when we take seriously the invitation to live as his children.

That is the childhood that Jesus asks us to embrace. The strong and hopeful childhood of grace. It is the reason for our Lord's Incarnation, the condition for our entrance into the kingdom, and the foundation of

---

[2] John Henry Newman, "Christ Manifested in Remembrance," Sermon 17 in *Plain and Parochial Sermons*, vol. 4 (London: Longmans, Green, 1909), 262–63.

BE CHILD*LIKE*, NOT CHILD*ISH*

"Truly," Jesus said, "unless you turn and become like children, you will never enter the kingdom of heaven. Whoever humbles himself like this child, he is the greatest in the kingdom of heaven" (Matt 18:3–4).

To be child*like* is not the same as being child*ish*. We all know that many children are self-absorbed, impetuous, spoiled, and peevish. Once I read an interview with a Catholic mother who had borne ten children. She was asked, "Would you do it all over again?" "Yes," was her instant reply. Then after a pause she continued with a smile, "but perhaps with different children." Childish faults are clearly not what Jesus had in mind when he presented that youngster to the apostles for emulation.

To be child*like*, on the other hand, means to imitate the better qualities of children, to be simple, humble, sincere, docile, and vulnerable. It means to live in freedom and authenticity, without affectation. It means to take pleasure in small things and to live in the moment. Above all, it means to trust in the goodness and love of our Father.

Those are the noble qualities of childhood that Jesus himself lived with his Father. When we imitate them, we imitate him. Our souls expand to receive the Father's love in proportion to our childlike faith. By them we are made capable, as Jesus promised, of entering the kingdom of heaven.

our discipleship. It is the pledge of eternal life, where one day—please God—we will rejoice forever in the Father's house as his beloved sons and daughters.

> Find time to discuss with your children what it means to be a son or daughter of God. Ask them individually how they understand their role as children of God. Do they need more insight from you to feel secure in this identity?
>
> Share with your spouse a memory or experience that has shaped your understanding of what it means to be a child of God.
>
> Strive this week to affirm the goodness in your children by saying yes to them. Rather than saying "maybe" or "later," agree immediately to any reasonable requests for quality time or help.
>
> Read and pray with John 14:1–18. What are the characteristics of the relationship Jesus is describing? Are you growing deeper with the Lord according to his own words?

ST. THÉRÈSE OF LISIEUX

Virgin and Doctor of the Church
Born in France
D. 1897
Feast day: October 1

See what love the Father has given us, that we should be called children of God; and so we are.

1 JOHN 3:1

ST. THÉRÈSE, AFFECTIONATELY KNOWN AS "the Little Flower," was born in 1873 in Alençon, France, to Sts. Marie-Azélie Guérin and Louis Martin. She was the youngest of five living sisters. Theirs was a warm and loving home, filled with faith and a supernatural tone. Her mother died before Thérèse's fifth birthday, but both parents showered their children with affection. All four of Thérèse's sisters entered religious life (three in the same Carmelite convent as St. Thérèse) and St. Thérèse herself entered at the age of fifteen with special permission of the local bishop. She was not to live long, however. At the age of twenty-three, she contracted tuberculosis and spent more than a year suffering intensely before dying in 1897.

St. Thérèse never did great things in the eyes of the world. She had a profound thirst for souls, but she never went on a mission. She had impressive talents, but she never performed great works. At the age of twenty-one, just a few years before she died, she began under obedience to write her autobiography, entitled *The Story of a Soul*, which revealed a simple and pure heart burning with love for the Lord. "The only way I can prove my love," she wrote, "is by scattering flowers and these flowers are every little sacrifice, every glance and word, and the doing of the least actions for love."

Her desire for sanctity in the midst of humble, ordinary tasks became her path to holiness and showed that "little way" of spiritual childhood to countless millions through the years that followed. "Instead of being discouraged, I told myself: God would not make me wish for something impossible and so, in spite of my littleness, I can aim at being a saint," St. Thérèse wrote in her autobiography. "It is impossible for me to grow bigger, so I put up with myself as I am, with all my countless faults. But I will look for some means of going to heaven by a little way which is very short and very straight, a little way that is quite new."

Thérèse learned love of God first through what she experienced in her family. She saw in the intense love of her mother and the irrepressible affection of her father an echo of God the Father's love for her. She knew herself unquestionably to be a beloved daughter of God, and she rejoiced in it. Her unshakeable confidence in his love allowed her even to accept suffering, knowing that he would draw great good out of it. She is a marvelous witness to the truth spoken by Jesus when he put a child before his disciples and said, "Whoever humbles himself like this child, he is the greatest in the kingdom of heaven" (Matt 18:3).

> Loving Father, who first revealed your love for St. Thérèse through the example of her parents, help our family to be a school of charity where our children will come to know deeply your love for them. Through the intercession of St. Thérèse, may we receive the grace to overcome whatever defects we have that obscure your love, and so together as a family advance in holiness as your beloved sons and daughters. We ask this through our Lord Jesus Christ, your Son, who lives and reigns with you and the Holy Spirit, God forever and ever. Amen.

SUPERNATURAL OUTLOOK

A CHILD'S WORLD REVOLVES AROUND THE home. It is where he or she *belongs*. As children, sleepovers were fun but it was not the same as being at home, where you did not have to ask permission to play a game or raid the refrigerator. At home a child thinks, sees, and behaves differently.

There is a similar dynamic in the life of faith. Knowing that we are sons and daughters of God means that we are at home in the house of the Father. We belong there. And that, in turn, means that we should think, see, and behave differently. This "supernatural outlook" imparts a new way of seeing reality, a new approach to life, a new mindset and attitude. It is a way of seeing the world that is not limited to the natural but is infused with faith; that is, it is above or "super" natural.

Strange as it may sound, even devout Christians can struggle to really see the world from a supernatural point of view. The great theologian Fr. Romano Guardini, whose clarity and wisdom were so vital in the tumultuous twentieth century, admitted that "God certainly does not dominate my life. Any tree in my path seems to have more power than he, if only because it forces me to walk around it! What would life be like if God did rule in me?"[1] Learning to see the world through the lens of faith takes some practice, both for us and for the children we are forming.

The struggle to have a supernatural outlook is partly due to what Max Weber called the "disenchanted" modern condition. In our herculean efforts to understand, dissect, and control material creation, contemporary man has gained much knowledge but has also lost some wisdom, especially an appreciation for the unseen world.

---

[1] Romano Guardini, *The Lord*, trans. Elinor Castendyk Briefs (Washington, DC: Regnery Publishing, 1954), 44.

FRUITS OF A SUPERNATURAL OUTLOOK

THE FIRST FRUIT OF A supernatural outlook is peace of soul. Seeing through the lens of faith ensures that we remain focused on the present moment, since it is in the present where God encounters us through grace, through his inspirations and his help. As every spiritual master—and modern psychologist for that matter—will tell you, being rooted in the present is essential for peace of mind.

Living in the present helps us avoid those tendencies we all have to dwell on the past with its memories and hurts and grudges, as well as the future with its flimsy promises and often needless worries. In the present we stay in touch with reality, with ourselves, and most of all with God. One writer describes it this way:

> The infinity of God comes to us through a funnel. It becomes so little and so narrow that it is difficult for us to recognize it. It comes only drop by drop through the small opening. The funnel is the present moment. When I put my mouth to the funnel, I am nourished by infinity. . . . Those who live in the present

Supernatural Outlook

Sir Arthur Conan Doyle remarked that people in the Middle Ages perceived "a great wonder and mystery in life. Man walked in fear and solemnity, with Heaven very close above his head, and Hell below his very feet. God's visible hand was everywhere."[2] Our ancestors knew, as we so often forget, that it is a thin membrane which divides the supernatural from the natural.

When we have a supernatural outlook, we recover this appreciation for invisible realities. The world is re-enchanted.

A couple of years ago I grew tired of blurry vision. I went to the eye doctor and she told me in no uncertain terms that I needed glasses. Right

---

[2] Arthur Conan Doyle, *Sir Nigel Page* (New York: McClure, Phillips, 1906), 7.

---

moment drink unceasingly of eternity.[*]

A second fruit of supernatural outlook is courage. No life is without its sufferings, but a believer can approach those sufferings from a different point of view. We can use them to renew our trust in the providence of God, we can grasp their redemptive value, and we can see beyond them to a future life where "death shall be no more, neither shall there be mourning nor crying nor pain any more, for the former things have passed away" (Rev 21:4). That point of view is a wonderful font of courage.

A third fruit of supernatural outlook is joy. Life is not always easy. It is often a school of hard knocks, as the saying goes. Truth be told, sometimes we Catholics are not always the beacons of joy that we should be as the result of our faith in Jesus. "His disciples," Nietzsche wryly observed, should "look more redeemed."[†]

Having a supernatural outlook will keep our hearts free from discouragement and our eyes fixed on the goodness of God. It will allow us to remain joyful, even in the midst of life's challenges.

---

[*] Wilfrid Stinissen, *Into Your Hands, Father: Abandoning Ourselves to the God Who Loves Us*, trans. Sister Clare Marie (San Francisco: Ignatius Press, 2011), 61.

[†] Friedrich Nietzsche, *The Portable Nietzsche*, ed. and trans. Walter Kaufmann (London: Penguin, 1954), 204.

away. "You're barely legal to drive," was her precise phrase. I asked whether I was nearsighted or farsighted; she said "yes." Then came a crash course on what it means to have an astigmatism. We lucky winners, it seems, have trouble seeing things *both* close at hand and far away. When I first put on my new glasses, the world was so clear that it gave me headaches.

The upshot is that my new specs gave me the perfect metaphor for a supernatural outlook.

To begin with, seeing with the lens of faith is *not* like putting on sunglasses. If you think about it, sunglasses are the opposite of corrective lenses. They *change* our perception of reality to make it more comfortable, whereas prescription lenses *correct* our vision to see reality more accurately. Supernatural outlook is not about putting on "rose colored sunglasses" to make reality more pleasant. Instead, it corrects our vision, both nearsighted and farsighted, to make reality more clear.

Spiritual nearsightedness occurs when we can see things right in front of us but have a hard time perceiving the larger picture. That traffic jam, that complaining child, that minor illness, or that humiliation overwhelms us by its present force. Seen through the lens of eternity, though, such events take on more modest proportions. What seems so big with uncorrected vision is often in reality quite small. Pausing to reflect on supernatural realities can protect us from giving the present "urgent" matters a significance that they don't always deserve.

On the other hand, spiritual farsightedness sees right through those moments which, though not clamoring for attention, are actually much more important from a supernatural point of view. Consoling a crying child, smiling at the grocery store clerk, calling a friend who lost a loved one, or offering up a small mortification at a meal might seem insignificant compared to the great things of life. But from a supernatural point of view, those can be the most enduring things we do, the most pleasing in the sight of God.

With corrected supernatural vision, we can see the greatness that reverberates in the smallest detail of our lives. We can find God in the moment, however routine or monotonous the activity might seem. It is a deeply contemplative way to live.

Maintaining a supernatural outlook on life will help us recover the sense of wonder that we have lost in a disenchanted world. Cardinal Robert

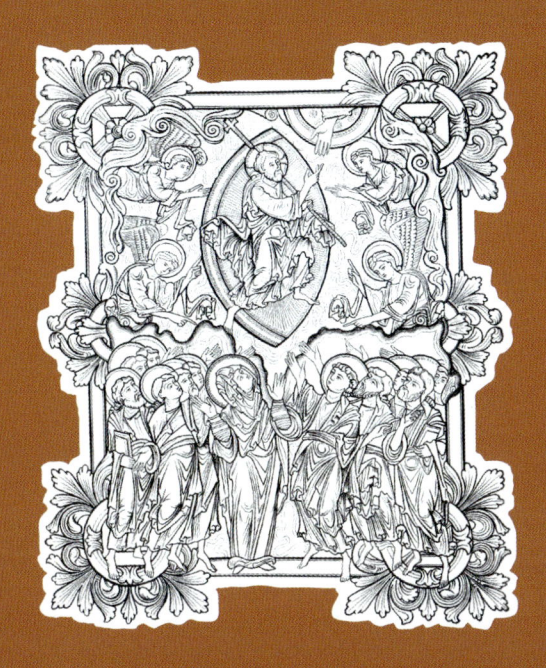

HOW TO ACQUIRE A SUPERNATURAL OUTLOOK

A SUPERNATURAL OUTLOOK CAN BE DIFFICULT to sustain and teach to our children because our physical senses clamor for attention and can overwhelm the more subtle senses of faith. The visible world has an immediacy and a power that seem so permanent, so vibrant, so real.

Today, especially, there are ever more powerful amplifiers for our sense-knowledge through technology and the means of media and entertainment. Having a supernatural outlook is at once more important, and more difficult, than ever. We have to take a step back and make it a deliberate choice through daily habits.

Daily devotions, both individual and in the family, are one way to forge the habit. Mental prayer, spiritual reading, Marian devotions, and weekly or even daily Mass are opportunities to encounter God repeatedly and breathe the air of eternity. They become spiritual heat sources that warm the rest of our day and make a supernatural outlook possible. Spending a few moments in the morning going through our day and inviting the Holy Spirit into each upcoming event can also help.

Another way to grow in supernatural outlook is to pray about our own death. We humans suffer a 100% mortality rate, but we also have a 100% immortality rate! revise to: Meditating with your children on the last things and, as they grow up, helping them realize the shortness of life gives some needed clarity and perspective. The *Imitation of Christ* says it well: "Every action of yours, every thought, should be those of a man who expects to die before the day is out. . . . If you aren't fit to face death today, it's very unlikely you will be by tomorrow."*

Finally, like an archer who pauses for a moment before releasing his arrow, we can find ways to pause throughout our day in order to take better aim and identify the presence of God in each moment. Here are some ways to do this and instill good habits in our children.

- Repeat aspirations during the day. These can simply be the names of Jesus and Mary, or a short text from Scripture, or an act of faith or gratitude. Children can be taught how to make a spiritual communion at a young age, even before they can receive Our Lord in the Blessed Sacrament.

- Take three to five seconds before starting a new task to place yourself in God's presence and offer him your work. Parents can model this habit when helping children with homework, for instance, by offering it for a certain intention.

- Place an image of Jesus, Mary, or another saint, or a small crucifix, on bedroom walls, next to the desk, in the car, near the sink and ironing board, by the television—anywhere you spend time. Your home needn't look like a monastery, however; these can be discreet, natural, and tasteful.

- Show children how to use the bookends of the day to revive a supernatural outlook. Teach them to make a short morning offering when they get up by kissing a small crucifix, greeting their guardian angels, and offering up the day's activities. In the evening, they can make a short examination of conscience, say a prayer, kiss the crucifix again, and give their last thought of the day to God.

---

* Thomas á Kempis, *The Imitation of Christ*, trans. Ronald Knox and Michael Oakley (San Francisco: Ignatius Press, 2005), 63.

Sarah compares the West to an old man who is "no longer astonished by anything, no longer enchanted by anything." He writes,

> Spiritually, the continents that came to know the Good News more recently are still astonished and enchanted by the beauties of God, the marvels of his action in us. The West is perhaps too accustomed to it. It no longer shivers with joy before the manger scene; it no longer weeps with gratitude before the Cross; it no longer trembles in amazement before the Blessed Sacrament. I think that men need to be astonished in order to adore, to praise, to thank this God who is so good and so great. Wisdom begins with wonder, Socrates said. The inability to wonder is the sign of a civilization that is dying.[3]

Supernatural outlook recovers the sense of astonishment that many have lost. It helps us and our children to see that everything, from the most mundane reality to the most sublime truth of faith, is charged with spiritual force and meaning. Every believer can have this corrected vision so that reality—all of reality, visible and invisible—never has to be blurry again.

Together with your spouse, evaluate what you are doing to help cultivate a supernatural outlook within your family. Is there room for improvement? Use the list on pages 77–78 to consider new ways to form your children's view of their life experiences.

Do you recognize any fruits of a supernatural outlook in yourself? In your spouse? In your children?

Candidly discuss with your spouse one area of your life where you are struggling to see things supernaturally.

What "invisible realities" do you treasure most? Spend some time in prayer this week meditating on God's wondrous works and thanking him for them.

---

[3] Robert Sarah, *The Day Is Now Far Spent* (San Francisco: Ignatius Press, 2019), 127.

ST. RITA OF CASCIA

Widow and Religious
Born in Italy
D. 1457
Feast day: May 22

For those who live according to the flesh set their minds on the things of the flesh, but those who live according to the Spirit set their minds on the things of the Spirit.

ROMANS 8:5

Margherita (Rita) Lotti was born near Cascia, Italy, to older parents who saw in the birth of their daughter an answer to years of prayer. She was raised in a Christian home and displayed signs of extraordinary devotion at a young age, even asking her parents to set up a small chapel in their home in which she could pray. She begged her parents to allow her to enter a convent, but instead, in a practice common at the time, they gave her away in marriage at the age of twelve.

Her marriage to a man named Paolo Mancini was not happy. He was an angry man who mistreated her mentally, emotionally, and physically. After eighteen years of marriage, her witness of faith, patience, and forgiveness eventually won him over, and he finally turned to Christ. Shortly after that, he tried to restore peace with a rival family, but rather than accept his offer, they betrayed and murdered him. Though Rita forgave his assailants publicly at her husband's funeral, her two sons were out for revenge. Rita begged them to reconsider and prayed to God that he would preserve them from the great sin of murder, even if it meant taking their lives before they could commit such a crime. They both died of an illness without having taken their revenge.

Rita again asked for admission to enter the convent, and after many trials, she was eventually admitted. She lived forty years as a religious sister, adopting severe penances, eating very little (the daily Eucharist was her primary nourishment), and praying long hours in the chapel. When she was sixty years old, she received a stigmata on her head, inflicted by one of the thorns that crowned the head of Jesus. Her wound was so painful and unsightly that she remained in seclusion in her convent for the last decade of her life. She died of tuberculosis at the age of seventy.

St. Rita is sometimes invoked as an intercessor for impossible causes, in part because of the extreme sufferings she endured from her husband and the other trials she experienced in life. Through it all, she maintained an attitude of faith and hope, sustaining a supernatural outlook even when, from a purely natural standpoint, there seemed little cause for a positive point of view. She knew that God continued to love and cherish her even when life seemed bleak, and she found many opportunities in her daily occupations to encounter him. Despite her trials, she never lost her early devotion, and for that she is an exceptional witness for seeing through the lens of faith.

> Dear Heavenly Father, your servant St. Rita retained her capacity to see life as a journey of faith. Even in her great sufferings, which you permitted for her sanctification and that of many around her, she always had recourse to you. Give us the faith to see with correct vision through the trials of our life to the warmth of your love and to the end of our journey, when in your mercy, and if we are faithful, you call us home to live in your presence forever. We ask this through our Lord Jesus Christ, your Son, who lives and reigns with you and the Holy Spirit, God forever and ever. Amen.

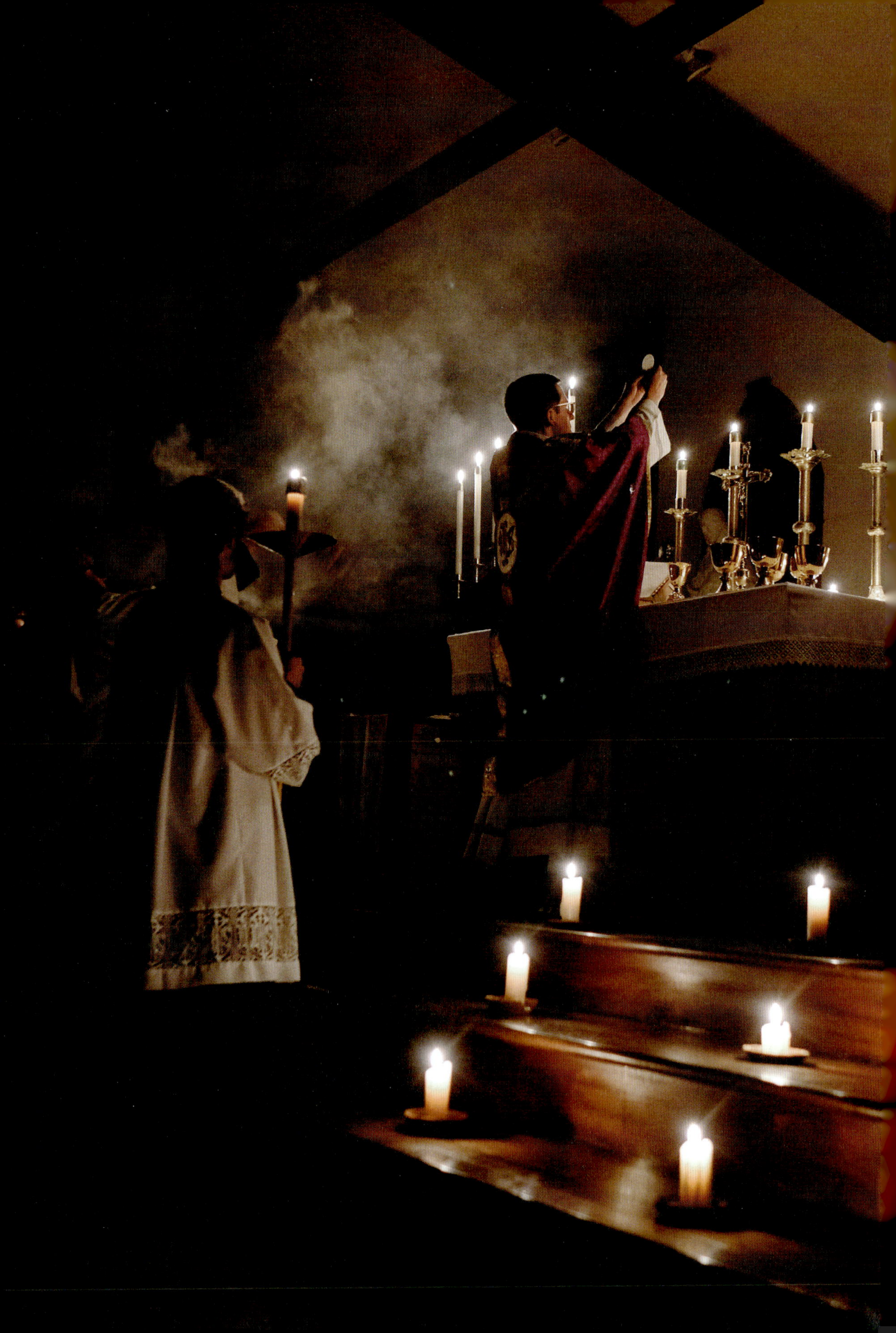

THE EUCHARIST

ELIZABETH HAD BEEN MARRIED TO William Seton for eight years when his tuberculosis began to worsen. Doctors advised them to move to a warmer climate, and they decided to spend time with friends in Italy. Upon arrival they were held in quarantine, but this proved a fatal blow to William's precarious health.

After her husband's death, Elizabeth was in profound mourning and she felt keenly the separation from her family in the United States. Though an Episcopalian, she was moved by the Catholic faith of her hosts, the Filicchi family. She wrote to her sister:

> My sister dear, how happy would we be if we believed what these dear souls believe, that they possess God in the Sacrament and that he remains in their churches and is carried to them when they are sick; oh my—when they carry the Blessed Sacrament under my window while I face the full loneliness and sadness of my case, I cannot stop the tears at the thought. My God, how happy would I be even so far away from all so dear, if I could find you in the Church as they do (for there is a chapel in the very house of Mr. Filicchi); how many things I would say to you of the sorrows of my heart and the sins of my life.[1]

When Elizabeth Ann Seton returned home, she began instruction to become a Catholic. In the meantime, still attending her Episcopalian church, the future saint found herself yearning for the Real Presence on Sunday mornings. She sat as close to the nearest Catholic Church as she could manage. "I got in a side pew which turned my face toward the Catholic Church in the next street, and found myself twenty times speaking to the Blessed Sacrament there," she later wrote.[2]

Words cannot capture the wonder that is the Holy Eucharist. The fact that God invented this way of being present means only one thing: he

---

[1] Elizabeth Ann Seton, quoted in Joseph I. Dirvin, *The Soul of Elizabeth Seton* (San Francisco: Ignatius Press, 1990), 68.
[2] Seton, quoted in Dirvin, *The Soul of Elizabeth Seton*, 70.

wants to be with us. Jesus wants to be united to us. He loves us and likes our company.

In a way, the Eucharist is not even surprising. After all, people who love each other leave mementos when they separate. Family members swap pictures and lovers used to give small lockets of hair. New ways to communicate today allow us to see and hear the ones we love. In the end, though, these are all imperfect substitutes for really being present to each other.

Jesus, however, suffers no such limitations. He could remain with us physically even after he had ascended to heaven. That is why we can say, without any irreverence intended, that the Eucharist is not even surprising. It simply follows the logic of love. Some might ask, "Why would Jesus institute the Eucharist?" They do not yet grasp the power of God and the eagerness of his love. We Catholics ask, "Why wouldn't he? Wouldn't you?"

FRUITS OF THE MASS

The most important fruit of the Mass is the glory that Jesus offers to his Father through his loving obedience in the Passion, made present at every Eucharistic celebration.

In our adoration and praise, in uniting ourselves to Christ, we also offer glory to God. Worshipping God is the highest and greatest human act, and the Mass is the supreme way it is exercised since it is the very prayer and offering of Jesus to his Father.

At Mass, too, we have the opportunity to intercede for the whole world and all our personal and family needs. We bring our loved ones, all those we have promised to pray for, together with all of our own sacrifices, and we unite them to the sacrifice of Christ on the Cross. There is no more powerful prayer on earth, and not only for the visible Church. The souls in purgatory hang on the words of the priest at Mass and are refreshed and renewed by the power of the Holy Sacrifice.

Finally, at Mass we humbly beg pardon for our sins and those of every human being. Once I had

THE EUCHARIST

The most elemental duty and desire of all parents, in every time and place, is to feed their children well. Jesus' desire to remain with us is so intense that he wanted to (quite literally) become a part of us, to feed us with himself, to give us the only food that can nourish our souls.

You, too, desire to feed your children, and that desire is not limited to their mortal bodies. Their immortal souls, too, need nourishment. That is why forming your children to attend Mass reverently and, when they are old enough, to receive Holy Communion well is so important. What are some ways to do that?

Preparing for Mass does not begin when we drive into the church parking lot. The remote preparation for Mass is the way we live our lives. It is living according to God's commandments and having a regular life of prayer. Going to Confession regularly is an indispensable part of preparing our hearts to receive Jesus. Teaching your children about the various steps of the Mass can help them follow along. Reading and discussing the

the opportunity to offer Mass in a former abortion clinic, in the very room where the gruesome procedure took place. It is a place that epitomizes evil, where the lives of tiny, innocent human beings were snuffed out by the thousand.

As I prepared for Mass, I began to wonder if it was unseemly for me to offer something so holy and beautiful in such a wretched place—and then I realized how wrong I was.

That dark place was precisely where Jesus wanted to be. He wants to bring his light and his grace to wherever he is most needed.

Every Mass calls down his healing love into the dark places of the earth, and especially the dark corners of our hearts that still need conversion. It is a furnace of love where everything evil is burned away and purified, leaving our hearts cleansed, healed, and free to love God with renewed devotion.

weekly readings in advance can prepare their minds and imaginations for the Sunday liturgy.

If you can visit an adoration chapel once or twice during the week, with the children if possible—even for a few minutes—you will find it remarkably effective in fostering a Eucharistic hunger in their hearts. Many families have even begun to attend daily Mass after building a habit of weekly adoration.

Proximate preparation means preparing ourselves inside and out before going to Mass. Dressing in special Sunday clothes, giving enough time so that you do not have to rush to church, and arriving a bit early so that you can spend some moments in prayer are beautiful ways to show love to our Eucharistic Lord.

During Mass, sitting up close and letting the children see what is happening can help reduce distractions. When they (or you) are distracted, do not worry or lose your peace. Gently turn your attention back to the Lord and know that he sees the love that is in your heart for him. Remember that the saints and angels, a "great cloud of witnesses," accompany you and your family at every Mass. They look with delight at your efforts to be present to the Lord and they accompany you with their prayers.

Holy Communion is the most intimate moment between a soul and God. In every sacristy of Mother Teresa's Missionaries of Charity a sign reads, "Priest of God, celebrate this Holy Mass as if it were your first Mass, your last Mass, and your only Mass." You can modify the text: "*Receive Holy Communion* today as if it were your first time, your last time, and your only time." There is no surer path to sanctity than humble, attentive, devout reception of the Holy Eucharist.

Lastly, spend a few minutes after Mass kneeling down and thanking God for his indescribable love of us. Throughout the day—in fact, throughout the week—try to make short spiritual communions. By habitually asking him to come into our hearts, we will be better prepared to receive him sacramentally.

Our Lady is called the Mother of the Eucharist for many reasons, not least because the blood that poured out of Jesus' veins on Golgotha came from her; it was *her* body and blood that she gave to Jesus in her womb and that he in turn gives to us. Mary is the human source of the Precious Blood that Jesus, who is both human and divine, offered for the salvation of the world. Her prayers will never be lacking as we strive to prepare our families for the most important moment of our lives, when we kneel before the altar as Jesus is made present and are fed, as beloved children of the Father, with his own Body and Blood.

> Choose one Eucharistic devotion to do with your family this week. Keep expectations low and don't add unnecessary pressure on your children. We want to encourage a loving relationship with the Blessed Sacrament, and the best way to do so is with patience, joy, and reverence.
>
> Many saints throughout the ages have promoted Eucharistic piety. Share the story of one such saint with your children.
>
> Discuss with your spouse whether the Eucharist is the focal point of your family life. What can you do to ensure that it is?
>
> Find time this week for both you and your spouse to pray before the Blessed Sacrament.

A Personal Reflection from Parents
— Michael and Maureen Ferguson —

Kids do what you do. They learn what's important by seeing what's important to you. For the Eucharist to matter for them, it has to matter for you. You have to believe in your own heart that it is the Body, Blood, Soul, and Divinity of Jesus. (And if you doubt, pray with the father in Mark's Gospel, "I do believe, help my unbelief.") If your kids love and trust you, they'll value what you love and value.

Strive to set a visible example. Strive to make Mass part of your daily routine. We want our children to see that we prioritize receiving the Eucharist daily. This is especially important for fathers. For whatever reason, kids especially notice if their dad arranges his busy work day around Mass, perhaps getting up early before work or finding a noon Mass during lunch.

On Sundays when we go as a family, we try (though we often fail) to arrive on time and well prepared for Mass. Dressing well to show respect, encouraging reverence during Mass, and praying after receiving Communion helps to drive home the importance of the Eucharist. Your kids' belief will be nurtured if you behave like it's the real thing, because it is.

Bring your kids to adoration. Sit still before the exposed Eucharist with them on an evening or weekend afternoon. You can also make visits with them—your parish church or school chapel are often empty and silent during the day. It takes just a few minutes to pop in, genuflect, and say a prayer or two, but helps form habitual reverence for what's present there.

And in all of this, it is an incredible blessing if you can find a school (or homeschool) community to reinforce all you are trying to teach your children. A good Catholic school is a treasure and worth every penny and sacrifice required to send your children there.

An important word on technology: Practicing reverence for the Eucharist requires contemplation and the ability to sit in silence. You do your kids a favor if you protect their sense of wonder and awe by keeping them off screens and social media. A teenager with a smartphone habitually in his or her pocket (and it's actually a supercomputer, not a phone) has a crippled ability to sit still in prayer.

Being physically present at adoration is one thing, but actively contemplating the mystery of the Eucharist is another. It takes practice. It's hard to do if one's mind and attention span has been short-circuited and manipulated by Silicon Valley algorithms.

BL. CARLO ACUTIS

Layman
Born in England (Raised in Italy)
D. 2006
Feast day: October 12

"For my flesh is food indeed, and my blood is drink indeed. He who eats my flesh and drinks my blood abides in me, and I in him."

JOHN 6:55–56

Blessed Carlo Acutis was born on May 3, 1991, in London. His well-to-do Italian parents eventually settled down in Milan when Carlo was still an infant. They were not especially religious, but Carlo demonstrated a great interest in the faith from a young age and often urged his parents to take him to church on Sunday. There he was frequently observed praying in front of the Blessed Sacrament before and after Mass. When he was a little older, he went to confession weekly. His devotion eventually led to the conversion of his mother. As she later said on EWTN Nightly News, "He used to say, 'There are queues in front of a concert, in front of a football match, but I don't see these queues in front of the Blessed Sacrament' . . . So, for him the Eucharist was the center of his life."

Rajesh Mohur, who worked for the Acutis family as an *au pair* when Carlo was young, converted from Hinduism to Catholicism because of Carlo's witness. Carlo taught Mohur how to pray the Rosary and told him about the Real Presence of Jesus in the Eucharist. Mohur said that one of the things that impressed him most was the witness of Carlo's love and concern for the poor, especially his interaction with homeless people, to whom Carlo would bring dishes of food.

Carlo had a heart for others and especially those who were suffering. He comforted friends whose parents were going through a divorce by inviting them over to his own home. He stepped in to defend special-needs students from bullies. He regularly gave away his pocket money to the destitute. He was not afraid to defend Church teaching; high school classmates remember him passionately defending the Church's stand on the sanctity of life in class even when most of the other students disagreed with him.

Above all, however, Carlo loved the Eucharist. From the age of three, he showed an unusual interest in the Blessed Sacrament. After he taught himself to code and build websites, he used his knowledge to recount Eucharistic miracles from around the world based upon a catalog he had compiled since he was eleven. He completed the website shortly before his death. The exhibit on Eucharistic miracles that emerged from that research has been displayed at thousands of parishes on five continents.

Carlo developed leukemia as a teenager and offered up his sufferings for Pope Benedict XVI and the Church, saying, "I offer all of my suffering to the Lord for the pope and for the Church in order not to go to purgatory but to go straight to heaven." He died on October 12, 2006, at the age of fifteen and was beatified in 2020.

> Loving Father, you instilled in the heart of your son Carlo a profound devotion to Jesus in the Blessed Sacrament. May his witness and intercession rekindle in the members of our family a steady and deep love for our Eucharistic Lord. May the miracles that continue to adorn the Catholic religion inspire us to trust in you more fully and to surrender to your love so that, even apart from miraculous signs, our faith may be steadfast, especially in the midst of trials. We ask this through our Lord Jesus Christ, your Son, who lives and reigns with you and the Holy Spirit, God forever and ever. Amen.

SACRIFICE

SEVERAL YEARS AGO I TOOK our seminarians to visit the Tomb of the Unknown Soldier at Arlington National Cemetery. After the visit we chatted with one of the guards about his ceremonial duties. He recalled standing his post by the Tomb in perfect spring days as well as in blistering heat, ice storms, and even a hurricane. "What weather do you like best when guarding the tomb?" one of the seminarians asked him. The soldier thought for a moment and said, "I think every guard here prefers bad weather. That's when it's a greater sacrifice."

As far as I could tell, the young man was not particularly religious. He was committed to honoring the Unknown Soldier, though, and he intuitively and deeply understood the notion of sacrifice. He knew that it is more than self-discipline. It is more than hard work. It is a way to give oneself in love.

Unless we are willing to sacrifice, to endure suffering for the sake of others, we cannot become proficient in love. As Pope Benedict XVI said,

> The one who desires to avoid suffering, to keep it at bay, keeps life itself and its greatness at bay.... There is no love without suffering—without the suffering of renouncing oneself, of the transformation and purification of self for true freedom. Where there is nothing worth suffering for, even life loses its value.[1]

---

[1] Pope Benedict XVI, "Celebration of First Vespers of the Solemnity of the Holy Apostles Peter and Paul for the Opening of the Pauline Year," June 28, 2008.

Deep down everybody knows this. Imagine a young man, kneeling in front of his beloved with a diamond ring, asking her to marry him. Misty-eyed, he says, "I love you, my dear, and I will love you forever." Then, after a pause, he continues, "Or at least as long as things are easy." You can imagine how that would go over.

It is vital, then, to cultivate in ourselves and in our children the capacity for sacrifice. Being able to give of oneself is a defining mark of maturity. It is also a condition for Christian discipleship. "If any man would come after me," Jesus said, "let him deny himself and take up his cross and follow me" (Matt 16:24).

So how do we grow in our capacity for sacrifice, and hence for love? How do we encounter the Cross?

Often we do not need to go in search of sacrifices; they come to us. As Jesus said, we are to take up the crosses sent (or at least allowed) by

PRINCIPLES FOR CHOOSING MORTIFICATIONS

In choosing some small sacrifices to make, here are a few principles to keep in mind:

They should never hinder us from fulfilling our vocation, doing our duty, or completing our work well.

> **Examples:** fasting that leaves us too tired to work well, devotions that crowd out ordinary mental prayer, or almsgiving that prevent us from giving to those who have a right to our help.

The best sacrifices, in fact, are those which *help* us to fulfill our vocation, do our duty, or complete our work well.

> **Examples:** getting to bed on time in order to be better rested for work, mortifying the use of our phone so that we can be more attentive to our children, spouses getting up earlier so that they have some quiet time to pray together before the children wake, or getting over our moodiness by smiling and being cheerful, even when we don't feel like it.

God. These can be the small annoyances and contradictions of everyday life or bigger trials like severe illness, financial setbacks, or the death of a loved one. Sometimes these are the hooks by which God pulls us out of our self-absorption or frees us from disordered attachments. They act like surgical operations on the soul—painful, but also healing. When we bear our crosses well, they can open our eyes to the needs of others, expand our capacity to love, and cause us to cling more tightly to the Lord.

Forming a habit of sacrifice also includes small self-denials that we consciously choose in order to grow in love and freedom. The man who turns off the television when his wife asks him to (or even better, when she doesn't) shows that she is more important to him than entertainment. The mother who puts the phone down in order to focus on her children is growing in freedom from those addictive devices. Mortifications like

Usually, the more hidden the mortification the better, since self-denials can become a source of spiritual pride. There is one important exception. Children ought to know that their parents are practicing self-denial, even when they are too young to really understand or practice it themselves. It is a crucial witness in forming a habit later in life.

If you wish to practice more intensive mortifications, such as longer fasts or other corporal self-denials, first clear it with a prudent spiritual guide to make sure that it will not impede your health or your other duties—or your humility.

A few sacrifices done well are always better than many sacrifices done half-heartedly or grudgingly.

Mortifications should contribute to a life of greater temperance. It makes no sense to deny ourselves in one or two areas while otherwise indulging ourselves.

It is a good practice to change our list of small mortifications periodically. Even sacrifices that seem hard at first can soon become routine, sometimes even pleasant. Many have given up cream in coffee during Lent and eventually started preferring black coffee! Adjusting our list of mortifications will ensure that this part of our spiritual life remains fresh.

this educate and form the will. When we put God and others first in our lives through practical choices, our will is strengthened to love better.

One way to look at mortifications is embedded in the very word—mortification means "putting to death." They are ways of dying a little to ourselves in order to avoid a greater spiritual death, like a vaccination against a virus. We take something in a small dose which in larger doses would kill us. Paradoxically, the "putting to death" of mortifications is an essential ingredient in spiritual life and fruitfulness. "Truly, truly, I say to you," Jesus said, "unless a grain of wheat falls into the earth and dies, it remains alone; but if it dies, it bears much fruit" (John 12:24).

A friend of mine once spent a summer working at a vineyard in California where he learned an important lesson about vines. It turns out that the branches of a vine must be stretched in order to bear fruit. They must be pulled and strained against the trellis. Soft, loose branches produce few grapes. When Jesus told his disciples that they are like branches on a vine that will be fruitful as long as they abide in him (see John 15:4), they knew what he had in mind. They were to be stretched on the trellis of his vineyard.

The Catholic view of suffering and sacrifice is, in my opinion, a more counter-cultural doctrine than any of the hot-button issues of the day. In a world frantically trying to pursue comfort and avoid suffering at all costs, the most shocking teaching of the Church is that suffering is not the worst thing that can happen to us. Separation from God—sin—is far worse.

In fact, when suffering does come, it can sometimes be the *best* thing to happen to us when we unite it to the sufferings of Jesus. Redemptive suffering releases untold graces for us, our loved ones, and the whole world. As Venerable Fulton Sheen wrote, "there is nothing more tragic in all the world than wasted pain."[2]

Children are not born with a natural instinct for sacrifice. Helping your children to accept suffering out of love is a habit that must be sown early and tended patiently. Teach them, through your own example, to grasp the spiritual fruitfulness of embracing the small crosses of everyday life. As they grow, encourage their generosity by suggesting small mortifications they can offer—or you could both offer—for their various intentions. It is not easy to see our children suffer in the moment, of course, but it is far worse to see them suffer in the future, when an inability to sacrifice leaves them crippled in heart and spirit, unable to really love and be loved.

---

[2] Fulton Sheen, *Calvary and the Mass* (Garden City, NY: Garden City Books, 1936), 61.

EXAMPLES OF MORTIFICATIONS

These are five general areas of self-denial with some sample mortifications.

Spiritual Being more intentional about avoiding distractions during Mass or prayer by leaving the phone in the car, pausing for a moment during the work-day to offer up work for specific intentions, praying the Rosary with greater focus on the mysteries, doing spiritual reading more attentively.

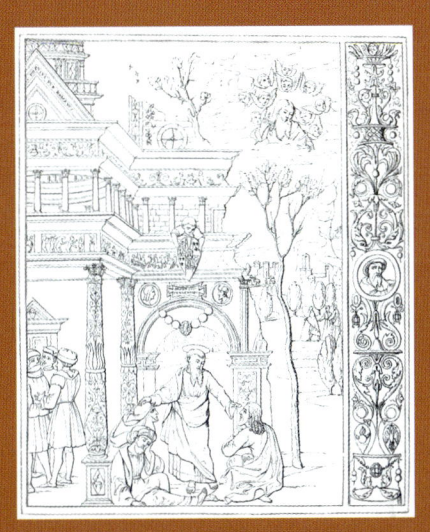

Physical Getting up and going to bed on time, being faithful to regular exercise, keeping a good posture, closing doors with less noise, taking the stairs instead of an elevator, putting a small pebble in our shoe.

Intellectual: Fasting from social media, not talking about or drawing attention to ourselves, refraining from consulting our phone especially in conversations, being temperate in our phone use when at home or at work, starting and stopping tasks on time, avoiding music or podcasts while working or studying, keeping custody of our sight, imagination, or memory.

Meals Avoiding second helpings, taking less of food we like and more of food we don't care for, skipping breakfast or lunch on Fridays, foregoing some condiments, eating more slowly and with better manners.

Simplicity of Life Waiting a day before making non-urgent purchases, not getting the latest gadgets, avoiding restaurants when possible, ordering something on the menu that is less expensive than the item you prefer.

How about the children? Young children will ordinarily live a spirit of sacrifice not through active mortifications but by being taught how to accept the small pinpricks of daily life well. Nevertheless, it is important that your children see you actively denying yourself in small ways. It will be an important witness when they are old enough to practice self-denial on their own.

One of the recurring lies of the Evil One is that we and our children will be miserable if we do penance. In fact, the opposite is the case. Generous sacrifice will be a surprising source of joy in our lives. We will be at peace, even about the inevitability of death, since our mortifications are little deaths that we embrace each day—little deaths that open our hearts to true life.

Done with generosity and love, mortification will help us become saints. There can be no holiness without sacrifice, and suffering increases our capacity to love. So "pick a fight" with yourself. You might be surprised at the result!

> Reflect on your attitude toward sacrifice. Do you struggle to embrace sufferings and inconveniences? What are some ways you can sacrifice more generously?
>
> Discuss with your children some age-appropriate mortifications. Help them choose one practice to take up for a period of time. Then re-evaluate whether they'd like to continue or choose a new sacrifice.
>
> With your spouse, take an inventory of your family's customs and habits. How are you modeling simplicity of life for your children? Are there certain purchases or practices you need to consider foregoing?
>
> Choose one mortification to offer for your spouse and children.

ST. MARTIN DE PORRES

Religious
Born in Peru
D. 1639
Feast day: November 3

I consider that the sufferings of this present time are not worth comparing with the glory that is to be revealed to us.

Romans 8:18

Martin de Porres was born in Lima in what was then the Viceroyalty of Peru. His father was a Spanish nobleman, and his mother was a freed slave, probably of African descent. According to the custom of the time, this made Martin a "mulatto," an illegitimate child of mixed race. After Martin's sister was born, the father abandoned the family, and Martin's mother, Ana, supported her children as a washerwoman. When Martin was twelve, he was able to attend school for a couple of years before being apprenticed to a barber-surgeon, where he learned basic medical treatments and procedures.

Even as a child, Martin had a deep faith, spending hours in prayer and giving alms when he could. He had a particular attraction to the Dominican friars in Lima, and while he could not become a fully professed Dominican because of a Spanish law that marginalized people of mixed race, he asked to become a lay brother to serve the community and the poor. He lived and dressed as a Dominican, doing menial work around the convent, working in the kitchen, the laundry, and the infirmary, where he served for the next twenty-five years. Because of his evident integrity and good sense, he was put in charge of the community's alms to distribute to the poor. After eight years, convinced by the young man's virtue, the prior ignored the Spanish law and allowed Martin to take formal vows of priesthood at the age of twenty-four.

Though he labored under the racial prejudices of the time, his reputation for holiness continued to grow. He spent long hours in prayer and subjected himself to severe penances. He received many extraordinary gifts, including bi-locating (some claimed to have encountered him in Europe and Africa), levitation, and the ability to read souls. The most learned of men sought his counsel. Many fellow Dominicans took him for their spiritual director. His medical treatments, which he offered willingly to anyone from Spanish nobles to African slaves, often had miraculous effects. He opened a home for orphans, supporting it by begging for alms throughout the city. He even had a special relationship to animals, with whom he seemed to communicate preternaturally.

By the time of his death at the age of sixty-one, Martin had a widespread reputation for sanctity, helping to break down the walls of prejudice that infected Spanish society at the time. Sufferings, rejections, and humiliations never led to bitterness but only to an increase of holiness. As someone who took on penances for his own sins and gave himself generously for the good of others, Martin is a formidable example of the sanctifying power of sacrifice.

> Heavenly Father, St. Martin de Porres followed your Son closely in pouring himself out for his neighbors even when he was met with rejection and humiliation. Through his intercession, may we learn to become souls capable of sacrifice for our own sanctification and for the good of others, and so become the saints that you wish us to be. Through our Lord Jesus Christ, your Son, who lives and reigns with you and the Holy Spirit, God forever and ever. Amen.

ANGELS AND SAINTS

PEOPLE, IT SEEMS, ARE LONELIER by the day. Every year—practically every month—another study emerges that demonstrates how isolated people feel from one another. As Christians, we feel deeply the sadness of those who have no real friends, often no close family. In reaching out to them we perform a great work of mercy. With God's help, however, such loneliness will not ever be ours; it certainly never needs to be.

The Letter to the Hebrews teaches that we are surrounded by a great "cloud of witnesses" who help us "run with perseverance the race that is set before us" (Heb 12:1). Every Christian child is born into a family of faith that extends far beyond the home. The Church into which we are incorporated at baptism is more than a mere institution; more even than a communion of persons on earth. The far larger portion of our family, in fact, is assuredly in heaven or being prepared for heaven in purgatory. Absorbing that reality and making it come alive in our families is an essential element of Christian formation.

Children are fascinated by new siblings. A baby sibling is the first experience of a human being who is suddenly, intimately, mysteriously united to them. Sometimes children are not sure what to make of their tiny new family member. "Dear God," one little girl wrote, "thank you for my baby brother. But what I prayed for was a puppy!" Our family members are not the result of our choices or preferences, but the result of a fact: the fact of our birth. So too our communion with each other in the Church on earth and the Church in heaven is the result of a fact: the fact of our baptism.

Learning about our spiritual family members is one of the great joys of growing up in a Christian home. Many people are fascinated by their family history, their ancestors, often using DNA testing to gain greater insights into their family tree.

How much more important, though, is learning about our spiritual family members who continue to be deeply involved in our lives through their example and prayerful assistance?

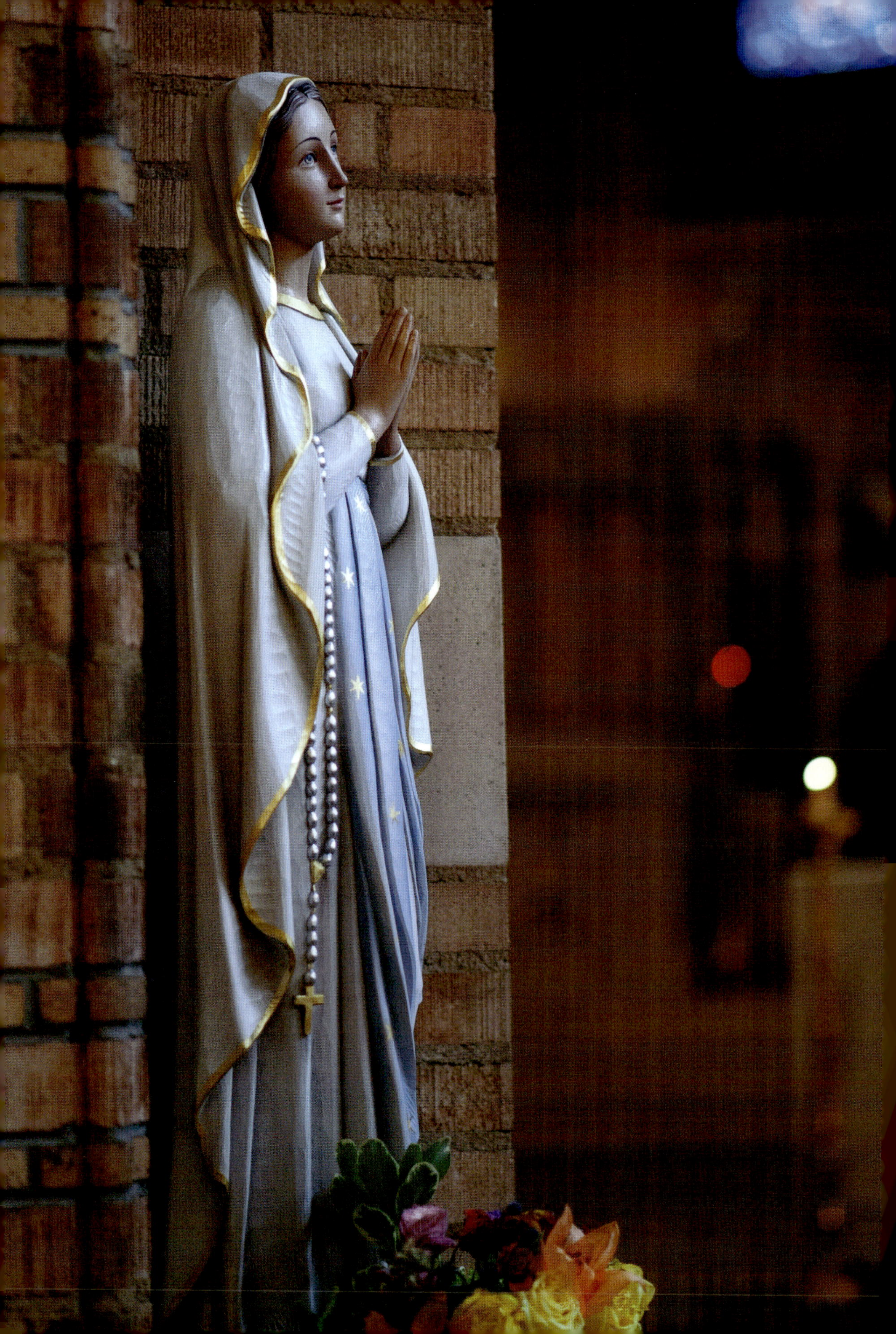

The first members of the Church were the angels. Mysterious and powerful, these friends of God, especially our guardian angels, are not as distant from our everyday lives as we might think.

Jacob dreamed of a ladder reaching up to heaven on which "the angels of God were ascending and descending" (Gen 28:12)—an image restated by Jesus to Nathaniel. Notice the order: angels are *ascending* and *descending*, not the reverse. They are with us, abiding with us, in a priestly role, carrying our needs to heaven and bringing down the blessings of God. Their place is at our side.

The Catechism of the Council of Trent teaches us about these heavenly allies:

> Just as parents, whose children are about to travel a dangerous and infested road, appoint guardians and helpers for them, so also in the journey we are making toward our heavenly country our heavenly Father has placed over each of us an Angel under whose protection and vigilance we may be enabled to escape the snares secretly prepared by our enemy, repel the dreadful attacks he makes on us, and under his guiding hand keep the right road.[1]

Another portion of the Church is populated by those who are undergoing purification after death. The devotion of a young priest friend of mine to the holy souls in purgatory began when he was imprisoned in a Communist jail for his outspoken Catholic faith. In that jail cell he reflected on the many who were praying for him, supporting him, trying to release him. It was a moment of insight into the plight of the souls in purgatory who have only us to help them. In return they pray earnestly for us—who often have prisons of our own, perhaps even more confining than a jail cell of concrete and steel.

The Church Triumphant is made up of our brothers and sisters who are already enjoying the *lumen gloriae*, the light of glory, the special grace that allows a created mind to experience the immediate vision of God. Saints, especially those explicitly recognized through a process of canonization, demonstrate that the teachings and means of sanctification provided

---

[1] *Catechism of the Council of Trent,* trans. John A. McHugh and Charles Callan (Fort Collins, CO: Roman Catholic Books, 2002), 502.

"SAINTS AND ANGELS RALLYING US ON"
From The Christian in Complete Armour *(1655)*

You march in the midst of gallant spirits, your fellow soldiers, every one the child of a King. Some are in the midst of battle, like you enduring affliction and temptation on every side, taking heaven by storm and force. Others, after many assaults, repulses, and rallyings of their faith, are already upon the wall of heaven as conquerors. From there they look down and encourage you, their fellow brethren on earth, to march up the hill after them. This is their cry: "Fight on and the city is yours, as now it is ours!"

For a few days' conflict, you will be crowned with heaven's glory. One moment of that joy will dry up all your tears, heal all your wounds, and make you forget the sharpness of the fight, through the joy of your victory.

In a word: God, angels, and the saints are spectators, observing how you quit yourselves as children of the Most High. Every victory of your faith against sin and Satan causes a shout to go up from heaven, every time you valiantly defeat a temptation, scale a difficulty, or regain ground lost to your enemies.

Your dear Saviour stands by with reserves for your relief at a moment's notice. His very heart leaps for joy to see the proof of your love and zeal for Him in all your combats. He will not forget your faithfulness in His wars on earth. And when you come off the field, He will receive you as joyfully as the Father received Him upon His return to heaven.[*]

---

[*] William Gurnall, *The Christian in Complete Armour* (London: Richard Baynes, 1821), 11. Some of the original text was rendered by the author into more contemporary English.

by the Church are effective. They give us hope and encouragement and examples of holiness to follow.

Saints also assist us through their prayers before the throne of God, and they do so as former sinners like us. "I believe the Blessed in Heaven have great compassion for our miseries," St. Thérèse of Lisieux wrote to a young seminarian near the end of her life. "They remember that when they were weak and mortal like us, they committed the same faults themselves and went through the same struggles, and their fraternal tenderness becomes still greater than it ever was on earth. It's on account of this that they never stop watching over us and praying for us."[2]

There are many reasons to teach our children about the saints and to encourage deep and lasting friendships with heavenly friends. It instills in our little ones an eager anticipation for heaven, a resolve to imitate the virtues of the saints, and even prepares them, at a young age, to confront the reality of death with realism, hope, and peace. It nurtures a supernatural view of the world that will help them navigate the challenges of life from the perspective of faith.

Saints are, if anything, more real than you and I since they are no longer afflicted by the temptation to sin that saps us of life. Once I met someone painting the crypt church in the Basilica of the National Shrine of the Immaculate Conception in Washington, DC. On the walls of the crypt are mosaics of many saints from the ancient Church. This painter had rendered them alive and walking around, conversing with each other. That is the kind of vivid awareness of the saints that we wish for our children throughout their lives.

Parents can foster a love for the saints in their children by, first of all, having a love in their own hearts for Our Lady and St. Joseph, for their patron saints and guardian angels, and for other saints whose patronage is especially applicable. The parents of St. Thérèse, Sts. Louis and Zélie Martin, and other married saints can be called upon for wisdom and strength. Patron saints of professions and other activities, even hobbies and interests, can become lifelong companions. The children will learn what devotion looks like by seeing it in their parents.

The liturgy is a natural setting for speaking about the saints. Learning about the saint of the day—even obscure saints who might not be on the

---

[2] Patrick Ahern, *Maurice and Thérèse: The Story of a Love* (New York: Image Books, 1998), 209–10.

universal calendar of the Church—is a way to incorporate these devotions in small doses over time.

You might help children to learn about their favorite saints and to ask for their intercession with the little problems that crop up in their lives. Encourage them to dress up as their favorite saint for Halloween or costume parties. On long car rides the whole family can play the "Name that Saint" game as a way to have fun while learning more about the saints. There are so many ways to make these heavenly allies come alive in the hearts of our children!

> Do your children have favorite saints? Ask them to share which saints they are most drawn to and why.
>
> How are you promoting devotion to guardian angels in your family?
>
> What is your relationship with the Blessed Mother like? What devotions to her are particularly meaningful to you?
>
> Discuss with your spouse what you could do to make better use of the Church's liturgical calendar to celebrate our rich treasure of saints.

SPIRITUAL BATTLE

The reality of our heavenly friends reveals, as well, the existence of spiritual enemies. We do no service to our children if, together with an encouragement to make celestial friends, we do not also (in ways appropriate to their age) caution them about our infernal enemies.

As St. Peter taught, the devil "prowls around like a roaring lion." Lions are famous for their "mock charges"—roaring, making noise, stamping their feet, shaking the ground, and moving around in zigzags, but as long as we stand our ground, they will not attack. The Evil One only has the power of a mock charge: he cannot actually touch our person, our inmost self. Sin, the only real danger to us, is always a self-inflicted wound.

One way to teach children about spiritual combat is through fairy tales, which teach not only the reality of personified evil but also that it can be defeated. Every child, Chesterton wrote, "has known the dragon intimately ever since he had an imagination. What the fairy tale provides for him is a St. George to kill the dragon."* The truth in fairy tales, in other words, is not only that they tell us dragons exist but that they tell us dragons can be beaten.

How are they beaten? Above all by availing ourselves of grace to live an upright life, by repentance and forgiveness, especially in the Sacrament of Confession, and by an interior life. The devil loses track of someone the moment he or she surrenders in adoration to God.

We must teach our children to respect the power of demons but also to have utter confidence in the Lord, especially the power of the Cross that marks our souls through baptism.

As St. Gregory Nazianzen said,

> Strong in the sign of the Cross with which thou hast been marked, say to him (the devil): I also have been made in the image of God and I have not been like thee cast down from heaven on account of my pride. I have put on Christ; by baptism, Christ has become mine own. It is for thee to bend the knee before me![†]

---

* G. K. Chesterton, "Red Angel," in *Tremendous Trifles* (New York: Dodd, Mead, 1920), 130.

† Gregory Nazianzen, "Select Orations of Saint Gregory Nazianzen," in *S. Cyril of Jerusalem, S. Gregory Nazianzen*, ed. Philip Schaff and Henry Wace, trans. Charles Gordon Browne and James Edward Swallow, vol. 7, A Select Library of the Nicene and Post-Nicene Fathers of the Christian Church, 2nd ser. (New York: Christian Literature, 1894), 363.

Forming Families, Forming Saints

ST. FRANCES OF ROME

Religious
Born in Italy
D. 1440
Feast day: March 9

For he will give his
angels charge of you
   to guard you in all your ways.
On their hands they will bear you up,
   Lest you dash your foot
against a stone.

Psalm 91:11–12

Frances was born to a noble family in Rome. At the age of eleven, she asked to become a nun, but her father had promised her in marriage to a wealthy man named Lorenzo, who was commander of the papal army. She reluctantly consented and was married at the age of twelve. The demands of society life took their toll on the pious girl, and she soon fell ill with a life-threatening condition. She recovered only after she received a vision from a fourth century saint named Alexis, who urged her to follow God's will. After that, she surrendered herself entirely to the Lord. Following the illness, she embraced her vocation wholeheartedly. She was a loving wife (and soon a mother) for the next forty years. Lorenzo was a worthy man who loved her in return and was even a little awed by her spiritual depth.

She spent much time in prayer, though she always put her family duties first. "A married woman must," she said, "when called upon, leave her devotions to God at the altar to find Him in her household affairs." It is said that once while praying the psalms, Frances was called away four times to attend to her family, and when she came back the fifth time to finish her prayers, the words of the psalm were etched in gold as a sign of God's pleasure with her fidelity to duty.

St. Frances of Rome

Together with her pious sister-in-law, Frances spent much time serving the poor of Rome. She herself embraced a life of simplicity, penance, fasting, and prayer. She wore simple garments and often a hairshirt next to her skin. She endured many sufferings, including the death of one son to the plague, the kidnapping of another as a hostage, the exile of her husband, and the destruction of her home. It was a time of tumultuous civil war. Through it all, she continued to fulfill her duties as wife and mother while sustaining a deep relationship to the Lord and an extensive outreach to the poor and the sick.

When Frances was tending to her husband after his return from exile, she received the grace of seeing her guardian angel for the rest of her life. He was her constant companion and spiritual advisor. We all live surrounded by a cloud of saintly and angelic witnesses; St. Frances was simply able to see them and interact with them as easily as we do each other.

After her husband's death, Frances joined the Benedictine Oblates of Mary, which she had helped found, and was made superior. Three years later, when her guardian angel informed her that her mission was complete, she died peacefully. Her last words were, "The angel has finished his task—he beckons me to follow him." Pope Pius XI declared St. Frances the patron saint of automobile drivers because her angel always went before her, lighting the way as headlights illuminate the way for a car.

> Gracious Father, St. Frances remained ever attentive to the guidance of the saints and her guardian angel. May we, too, always trust in the powerful aid your heavenly servants give us. When we feel alone, help us through the power of faith to know of your paternal care through these friends and allies, who accompany us along the path of salvation. Through our Lord Jesus Christ, your Son, who lives and reigns with you and the Holy Spirit, God forever and ever. Amen.

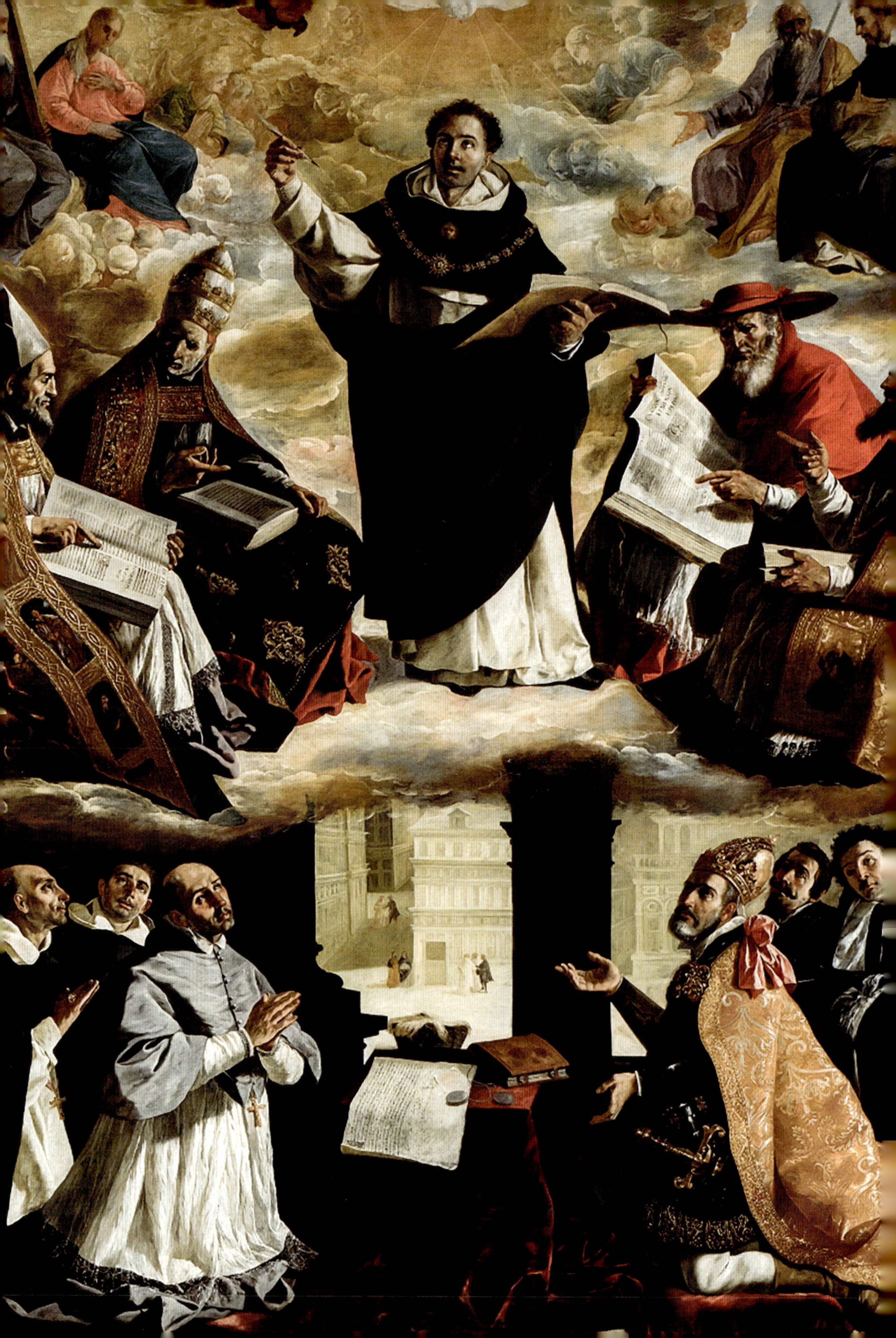

PILLAR III

Intellectual Formation

"The profound responsibility to lead the young to truth is nothing less than an act of love. Indeed, the dignity of education lies in fostering the true perfection and happiness of those to be educated. . . . It strives to articulate the relationship between faith and all aspects of family and civic life. Once their passion for the fullness and unity of truth has been awakened, young people will surely relish the discovery that the question of what they can know opens up the vast adventure of what they ought to do."

Pope Benedict XVI
Address to Catholic Educators
Washington, DC
April 17, 2008

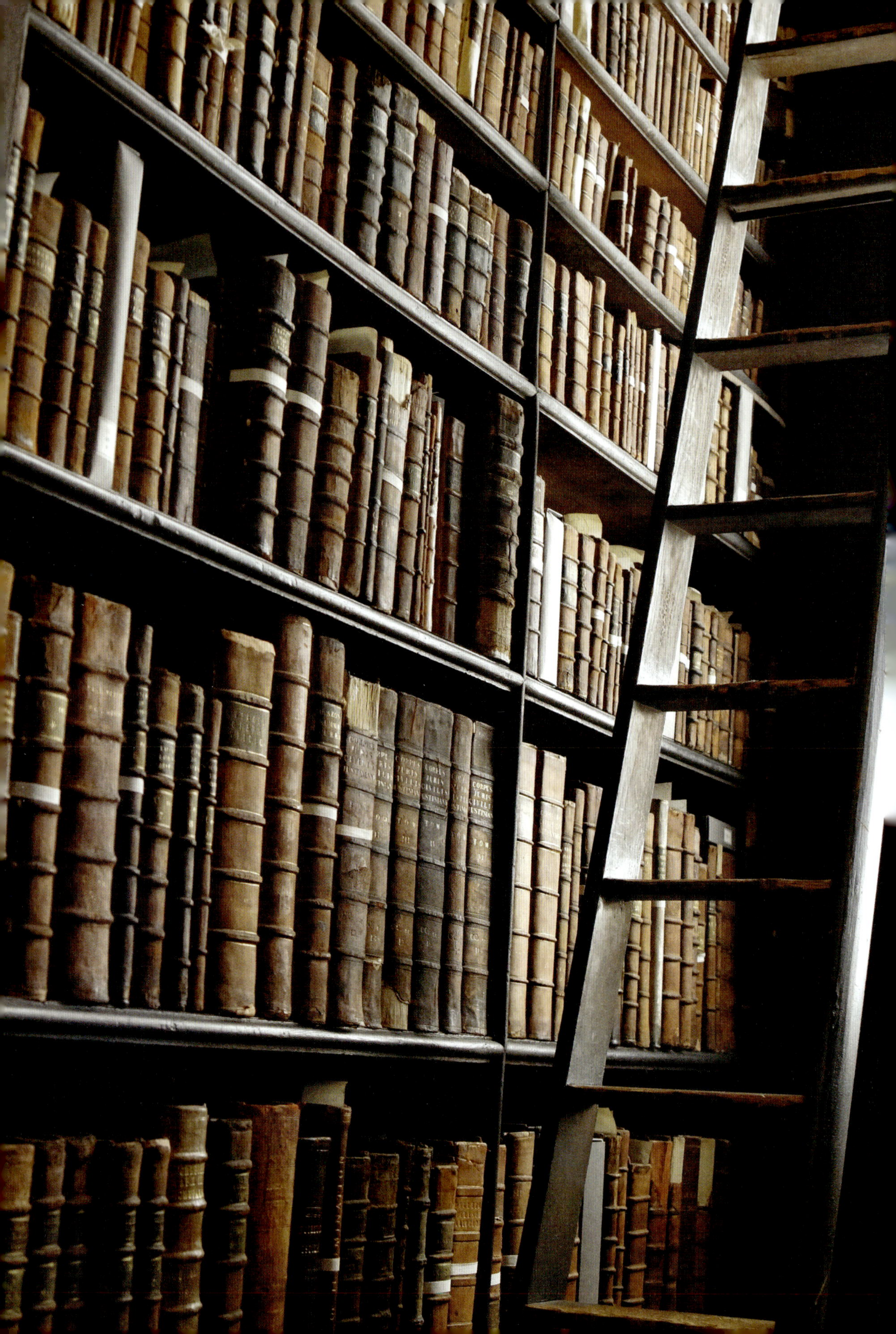

INTRODUCTION TO INTELLECTUAL FORMATION

A FRIEND OF MINE VISITED EAST Berlin in 1983, while it was still under Communist rule, and noticed some graffiti scrawled on the Berlin Wall. It was neither lewd, nor angry, nor even political in nature. It simply read, "1+1=2." In the face of a relentless effort on the part of the government to disseminate lies and half-truths, that simple statement of reality was an act of rebellion. It is also an apt image of what parents are called to do when they give their children tools to grasp reality in a digital age steeped in lies and half-truths.

We are rational beings, and it is through our minds that we come to know the truth about God, about ourselves, and about creation. It is through our minds that we ask the most important questions in life: Who am I? Where have I come from? Where am I going? What is there after this life? It is through our minds that we know Jesus as "the way, the truth, and the life" (John 14:6).

Just as the Church has been entrusted with the truths of revelation to ensure that each generation receives the deposit of faith intact, so the domestic church of the family has been entrusted with preparing children to receive the Gospel and, in a broader sense, to grasp the nature of reality itself.

Intellectual formation of children is ever more challenging. We have inherited the many achievements of scientific advances, but those gains are often accompanied by a flawed approach to reason.

St. John Paul II observed that the search for knowledge, when divorced from transcendent truths, is reduced to an unsatisfying pragmatism and a "belief that technology must dominate all." Reason, he continued, "has wilted under the weight of so much knowledge and little by little has lost the capacity to lift its gaze to the heights, not daring to rise to the truth of being."[1]

In our day this reduction of reason has reached the stage of nihilism, a "philosophy of nothingness" in which there is no hope or possibility of attaining truth. Life becomes a closed loop of sensation and experience without meaning, objective truth, or transcendence. Nihilism is the ultimate denial of our dignity, our immortality, and our eternal destiny. It leads "little by little either to a destructive will to power or to a solitude without hope. Once the truth is denied to human beings, it is pure illusion to try to set them free. Truth and freedom either go together hand in hand or together they perish in misery."[2]

A recent cultural analysis argues that evangelization today is inseparable from a renewal of the mind since a "daily onslaught of false gospels" has led, through a barrage of distractions, "away from invisible realities to concerns solely of this world." As a result, it suggests

> a counter-narrative to the overwhelming non-Christian narrative currently on offer. . . . Such conversion of mind is especially needed in those who lead: in bishops and priests, parents and teachers, writers and scholars and artists. The great apostolic task of our time is to gain a genuine conversion of mind and vision.[3]

Today the task of intellectual formation is made even more daunting by the digital world that engulfs our lives. Children growing up in a world of screens and online avatars are increasingly detached from the reality that makes our existence truly human. Many young people today express a preference for the easy pleasures of virtual reality over the more arduous but genuine experience of authentic reality.

For years we have been taught that visible realities are more important than invisible realities by the simple fact that they happen to be visible. This effort to uproot knowledge from its intellectual and spiritual sources has already robbed our intellectual life of much of its richness. It is useful knowledge, not wisdom, that is held in highest honor. Young people today, however, go even further. In their habits, if not in conscious belief, they

---

[1] Pope John Paul II, Encyclical Letter on the Relationship between Faith and Reason *Fides et Ratio* (September 14, 1998), § 5.
[2] Pope John Paul II, *Fides et Ratio*, § 90.
[3] University of Mary and Monsignor James P. Shea, *From Christendom to Apostolic Mission: Pastoral Strategies for an Apostolic Age* (Bismarck, ND: University of Mary Press, 2020), 66 and 69.

often reject not only invisible realities but even the visible. Their refuge is not hard science but humanly created, digital worlds. It's more comfortable, more controllable, and more comprehensible.

In the film *The Matrix* there is a scene in which Cypher (a Judas-type character) has betrayed his friends and is rewarded by his digital overlords with artificial happiness. "I know this steak doesn't exist," he says. "I know that when I put it in my mouth, the Matrix is telling my brain that it is juicy and delicious. After nine years, you know what I realize? Ignorance is bliss." Living in a lie is unworthy of a child of God, though, and a strong intellectual formation for your children will help inoculate them from Cypher's tantalizing escapism.

How can we form children intellectually in an age of nihilism and virtual reality? To be sure, protecting children from excessive exposure to screens is a top priority.

When parents refrain from giving younger children smartphones and access to social media, however demanding and inconvenient that may be, they are giving a gift that will reap enormous rewards in their children's lives. As countless studies show, children free of screen addictions study better, learn better, and fare better in school. Even more importantly, they are less anxious, less distracted, and less depressed, which is to say they are calmer, more focused, and happier.

Parents of my acquaintance who have successfully delayed their children's introduction to digital devices almost all have one thing in common: they did not do it alone. The pressure to conform to other families, the fear that children "won't have any friends" if they do not have a smartphone, and the convenience of every family member being a click away are almost irresistible.

Good resolutions to preserve children from the dangers of smartphones and the unhealthy effects of social media are more likely to succeed in union with other like-minded parents. I encourage you to arrange a meeting of couples with young children to discuss the effects of devices and social media on children and to make some common resolutions.

In addition to that healthy protectiveness of children's minds, nothing substitutes for simple experiences of real things. Exposing children early and often to three-dimensional reality through family hikes, outdoor play, physical labor, and works of service may not seem like intellectual formation, but these activities help children connect with reality in powerful, visceral ways.

Catholic speaker and apologist Jason Evert makes the point that the explosive surge in gender dysphoria among children is partly due to a lack of such contact with nature. The notion that our gender is a personal choice is largely a product of children's online experience of digital characters with limitless options. This confusion can be remedied by experiences with three-dimensional reality. When children spend time outdoors

> they are better able to connect with their bodies than if they spend endless hours immobile on a screen, taking on the roles of various avatars . . . they are surrounded with the inherent goodness of nature and the solidity of reality, where all things are created good (including them). Even when they engage in fantasy play outdoors, they're immediately confronted with the reality of natural laws that cannot be denied. They cannot fly, and thus they learn to reconcile fantasy from reality regarding the limits of the human body. However, no such limits exist when one's face is aglow with the endless possibilities offered online.[4]

In recent years we have learned a great deal—often the hard way—about how our new intellectual and digital environment is affecting the hearts and minds of children. That knowledge can help parents prepare for what lies ahead. With support from like-minded friends and families, as well as a proactive, intentional approach to fostering their children's well-being, parents have more resources than they realize. And of course, we can never underestimate God's grace!

Intellectual formation begins by teaching children to read and to grow in ordinary knowledge as well as knowledge of our faith. There are innumerable and excellent resources to help parents with these twin aspects of natural and catechetical intellectual formation.

The following five chapters do not seek to replicate those resources but rather to provide guidance on more foundational elements of intellectual formation. They explore ways to put children in touch with reality.

The first chapter treats humility, the root of it all, since without humility we cannot embrace the truth of things. Faith, the subject of the second

---

[4] Jason Evert, *Male, Female, Other?* (Scottsdale, AZ: Totus Tuus, 2022), 202.

chapter, enables us to absorb realities that surpass the capacity of reason alone. In the third chapter, we will consider the virtue of prudence, which gives us tools for moral reasoning. The fourth chapter is about intelligent reading, especially spiritual reading, which is a lifelong means to grow in our understanding of the greatest realities—namely, God and the things of God. Finally we will explore the importance of beauty, which makes it easier for us to receive the truth and to aim for the good.

These foundation stones of intellectual formation will keep us grounded in the midst of an uncertain time and help our children, even in an age beguiled by lies and half-truths, navigate reality and live in freedom.

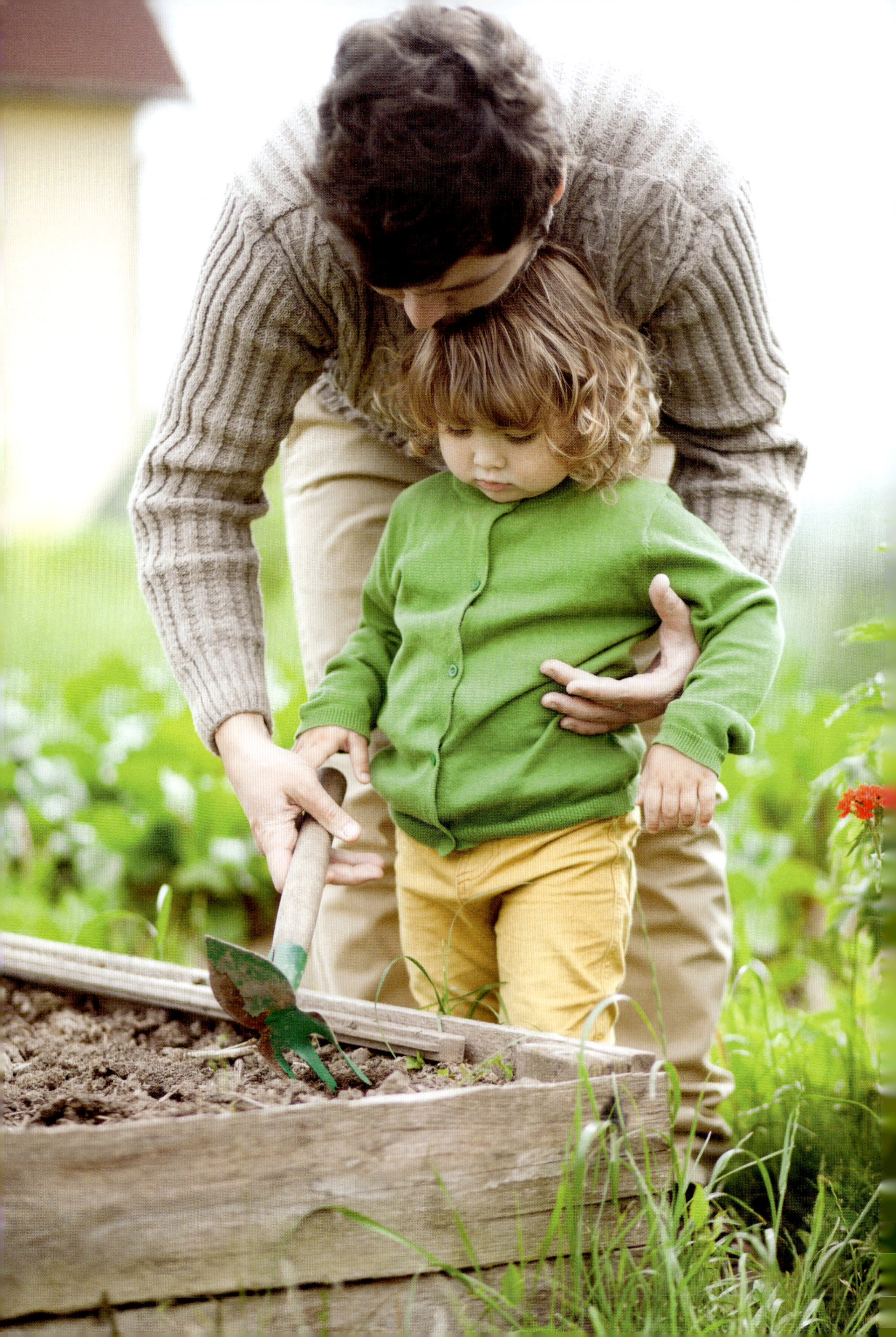

HUMILITY

THE FIRST CONDITION FOR PUTTING our children in touch with reality is nurturing in them an attitude of openness to real things. That might sound obvious. Have you noticed, though, how often disagreements, whether in families or the Church or the political arena, seem to produce a lot of heat but little light? How often people seem to speak past each other and throw up their hands in frustration when the other side just doesn't get it?

Much of that gridlock, I believe, is due to different worldviews that make it difficult for people to have fruitful conversations. These different perspectives on reality can be called the classical (or realistic) approach and the post-modern (or liquid) approach. In the first, the key to grasping reality is humility. In the second, the key to grasping reality is control or power. Which worldview we embrace will dramatically affect our lives and those of our children.

The classical or realistic worldview sees reality primarily as "out there," beyond ourselves. As rational creatures, we can study that reality and, over time, come to a greater awareness of the truth of things.

We can do so together since there is an objective *something* to study. In fact, as the history of ideas demonstrates, we grasp reality far more effectively when we do it together.

The first virtue needed in this worldview is humility, since we do not create reality but discover it. Humility is an openness to the truth of things.

The other worldview, so widespread today in the West, is a post-modern or "liquid" approach that perceives reality primarily as the fruit of our subjective thoughts and choices.

Truth, according to this outlook, is not discovered outside ourselves but inside. This is no longer a fringe idea of radicals and activists. The United States Supreme Court itself, in *Planned Parenthood v. Casey*, stated that "[a]t the heart of liberty is the right to define one's own concept of existence, of meaning, of the universe, and of the mystery of human life."[1]

(continued on p. 120)

---

[1] Planned Parenthood of Southeastern Pa. v. Casey, 505 U.S. 833 (1992).

HOW TO FOSTER HUMILITY

Humility about Ourselves

- Take advantage of humiliations: nobody enjoys being embarrassed or humbled! Moments like that, though, can be precious opportunities to grow in humility. Certainly we should resist being treated unfairly and should tell the truth when the cause of our humiliation is unfounded—that too is an act of humility. But many small humiliations, for instance when our imperfections are seen by others, can be occasions to grow in humility.

- Create an atmosphere of affectionate correction: humility is fostered when children know that they are loved despite their imperfections. Giving correction in a way that is encouraging and supportive, reflecting a positive opportunity to grow as human beings, clears the way for a humble approach to themselves. Children should know that everyone has faults, even their parents! Acknowledging our limitations, while working to overcome them, is an important element of humility.

Humility toward God

- Demonstrate a simple, childlike piety as adults: Mom and Dad kneeling in church before God does more to form the religious imagination of a young child than hours of intellectual instruction. Praying a family Rosary, simple devotions, and your own daily spiritual practices all reveal and foster humility.

- Give honor to God: living in gratitude to God, thanking him for blessings, for successes, and even for failures and sufferings show how to live as beloved children of God, safe in the arms of a loving Father.

Humility toward Others

- Focus on the other: anything that gets our eyes off ourselves and onto the needs of others is a way to grow in humility. "Do nothing from selfishness or conceit," St. Paul wrote the Philippians, "but in humility count others better than yourselves. Let each of you look not only to his own interests, but also to the interests of others" (Phil 2:3–4). Praise children when they show concern for others, engage others in conversation, or ask interested questions—these are all solid ways to grow in humility.

- Rejoice in the good of others: when children see that others have an ability they don't have or are praised for an achievement, they may naturally experience some jealousy. Try to redirect that towards a humble gratitude for the gifts of others, as well as their own gifts. It will be easier if they have witnessed that selfless gratitude in their parents.

- Be understanding towards others: when children witness others' faults, help them to take a measured, humble approach by making excuses for weaknesses whenever possible, highlighting their good qualities, and avoiding gossip. They will, once again, take their cue from how their parents talk (or don't talk) about others' faults.

A great deal of the anxiety, depression, and despair that young people experience today can be traced to the enormous pressure, even at a young age, to invent themselves, to "define [their] own concept of existence, of meaning, of the universe, and of the mystery of human life" as the Supreme Court advocated. How terrifying must it be for ten year olds to be pressured by responsible adults, including parents, teachers, and social media influencers, to decide what is true, what is real, who they are, what their sexual proclivities are, what gender they are, and even what species they are!

If humility is necessary to discover truth in the realistic worldview, the liquid worldview demands power and control. The only way to secure a measure of security, and perhaps even sanity, when I must decide my own "concept of existence" is to have power over myself and my surroundings. The liquid worldview sees reality as a constructor set, bits and pieces—including our very bodies as, to use a crude phrase in circulation, "meat lego"—that can, if we have enough power, be molded into anything.

Through technological advances, some feel like we have achieved a degree of dominion over existence. There are many advocating a "transhumanism" who see technology as a way to enhance humanity, expanding our physical abilities and mental capacities and even, ultimately, overcoming the limitation of death itself.

That desperate grasp for more and more control, though, comes at a dreadful cost. You do not have to look far to see the misery, loneliness, and hopelessness that it has spawned, especially in young people.

The coexistence of these two worldviews is precarious because they differ in fundamental ways. If reality is grounded in subjective choice, there is little common ground from which even to have a conversation. The liquid worldview, by definition, does not accept the notion of objective truth, much less a reality that we discover together. In a liquid worldview, without a reference point outside of ourselves, the definitions of truth and goodness are defined by those who have the power to enforce them. In the judgment of many sober thinkers, this perilous slide to tyranny is already well underway.

When we form children in humility, we are preparing them to embrace a worldview that is not only correct—from our Catholic perspective and that of the vast majority of human beings who have ever lived—but also gives them a fighting chance for happiness. Humility allows our children

EFFECTS OF HUMILITY

Joy The privilege of a humble soul is to rejoice in the small and common things that others fail to notice. A proud life is a boring, unhappy existence. How much better is the childlike simplicity and wonder of humility!

Wisdom Since humility is a necessary condition to grasp reality, it is the starting point of true wisdom. Only those who humbly seek the truth about themselves, creation, and God can make good judgments about the things of God and apply them to human affairs.

Freedom When we cease craving constant attention and approval, when we live and work for God alone—that is, when....ourselves—we live in freedom. Someone pridefully focused on themselves and on sustaining their status in the eyes of others lives a life of self-imposed slavery.

Holiness An expert on the canonization causes of saints once said that saints had very different qualities, temperaments, and missions, but one thing united them without exception. They were all known for genuine humility. That is not surprising, since all holy people are conformed to Christ, whose Incarnation, life, teaching, and Passion were all steeped in humility.

to resist the tantalizing offer of a liquid worldview that promises, like the serpent in the Garden, nothing more than a lie: the chance to create their own reality, the chance to be like God—indeed, the chance to be their own god.

Truly to be like God, though, does not mean dominating or fashioning reality after our own tastes. It means conforming ourselves to the One

> who, though he was in the form of God, did not count equality with God a thing to be grasped, but emptied himself, taking the form of a servant, being born in the likeness of men. And being found in human form he humbled himself and became obedient unto death, even death on a cross. (Phil 2:6–8)

Humility is important, then, not only in fostering our perception of reality, but in conforming ourselves to the Source of that reality. It is the lynchpin of our lives as Christians. "Humility is to the various virtues what the chain is in a Rosary," the Curé of Ars said. "Take away the chain and the beads are scattered; remove humility, and all virtues vanish."[2]

We grow in humility by embracing the truth about ourselves, about God, and about others. Some practical ways to foster humility, and the beautiful fruits of humility, can be found in the sidebars throughout this chapter. First, though, let's consider some concrete ways we might lack humility in each of these areas.

We lack humility about ourselves when we have an excessively high opinion of our dignity or achievements. Vanity, for instance, is a focus on our physical appearance and intellectual attainments. Using ourselves as examples in conversation, giving our opinions too stridently, considering small tasks beneath us, and being overly sensitive when others criticize us are all ways we can lack humility. Social media has a particular talent in fostering narcissistic self-absorption!

We lack humility before God when we neglect our dependence upon grace and consider ourselves the cause of our own spiritual excellence. Taking pride in our spiritual practices is a particularly dangerous lack of humility since it robs God of the glory that is due to him. Rejecting the sufferings that God permits is another way we can lack humility towards God.

Finally, we lack humility with others when we place ourselves above them, strive to dominate, or consider ourselves superior. Craving approval from others and fishing for accolades and compliments are subtle forms of pride, a desire to be exalted above others. Dwelling on the faults of others, envying their gifts, talents, and successes, and gossiping about others betray not just a lack of charity but also a lack of humility.

Humility is a beautiful virtue that strikes at the very heart of Original Sin, which was fundamentally a sin of pride. Growing in authentic humility puts us in touch with reality. It is a lifelong struggle that leads us ever deeper into lives of holiness. Starting our children on their own path to humility, both by fostering the virtue and by giving an example of humility ourselves, is one of the most precious gifts we can give.

---

[2] John Vianney, quoted in Abbé Francis Trochu, *The Curé D'Ars*, trans. Dom Ernest Graf (Charlotte, NC: TAN Books, 1977), 490.

Are you aware of any struggles your children might have with feeling they have to define their own identity? How can you help them to remain oriented to the truth about who they are?

Consider reflecting on and praying the Litany of Humility on a weekly basis.

Make a critical assessment of areas where you need to grow in humility. Are certain relationships or situations spiritual pitfalls for you?

Discuss with your spouse whether "affectionate correction" is an apt description for your method of discipline. Do you need to revisit your approach to correcting faults in your children?

FORMING FAMILIES, FORMING SAINTS

ST. ANDRÉ BESSETTE

Religious
Born in Canada
D. 1937
Feast day: January 6

If there is any encouragement in Christ, any incentive of love, any participation in the Spirit, any affection and sympathy, complete my joy by being of the same mind, having the same love, being in full accord and of one mind. Do nothing from selfishness or conceit, but in humility count others better than yourselves. Let each of you look not only to his own interests, but also to the interests of others.

PHILIPPIANS 2:1–4

Brother André was born Alfred Bessette in Quebec, Canada, the eighth of twelve children. His parents died before he was seven, and Alfred, a sickly child, became an orphan. Adopted at twelve, he tried various trades, including working in a factory in the United States during the Civil War. None worked out for him. When Alfred was twenty-five, his pastor encouraged him to apply for acceptance into the Congregation of the Holy Cross in Montreal. The pastor wrote to the religious superior, "I am sending you a saint." There was only one problem: the Congregation is a teaching order, and Alfred could not even read or write.

Still, Alfred was allowed to join as a lay brother, taking the name Brother André. He helped around the community in various humble tasks: cleaning, hauling wood, and carrying messages. Above all, he was the doorkeeper, a post he held for the rest of his long life. As he later quipped, "When I joined this community, the superiors showed me the door, and there I remained for forty years."

Brother André had an exceptionally warm personality. He was welcoming, calming, and approachable. In his role as doorkeeper, Brother André engaged with innumerable people over four decades. His humility and gentleness won the hearts of all, rich and poor, saints and sinners. He was a man of deep prayer and trust who inspired confidence in the mercy of God, especially through the intercession of St. Joseph. Whispers of miracles through Brother André's prayers began to surface. Soon his name was known throughout Canada and beyond. Near the end of his life, he needed four secretaries to handle the eighty thousand letters he received each year. Every time his conversation inspired a soul to turn to God, every time a miracle happened through his prayers, he would attribute it to the intercession of St. Joseph. "Go to St. Joseph. He will help you," he repeated throughout his life.

"It is with the smallest brushes that the artist paints the best paintings," Brother André said of himself. When he died at the age of ninety-two, it is estimated that a million people paid their respects during the week that his body lay in state. During his life he built a small chapel to St. Joseph, which over time was expanded to accommodate the thousands of visitors each year. Finally being completed only after Brother André's death, it is now the impressive St. Joseph Oratory on Mount Royal near the Collège Notre-Dame. Brother André's final act of humility was bequeathing to future generations this impressive basilica in honor of St. Joseph, to whom he attributed all his apostolic fruitfulness.

> Heavenly Father, the humility of St. André Bessette, like that of his patron St. Joseph, allowed him to be fashioned by grace into a great saint and intercessor for others. So often we allow pride to obstruct the workings of grace in our lives and in our family. Give us the courage and insight, through the prayers of St. André, to know how we can grow today in humility and so become more like your divine Son, who lives and reigns with you and the Holy Spirit, God forever and ever. Amen.

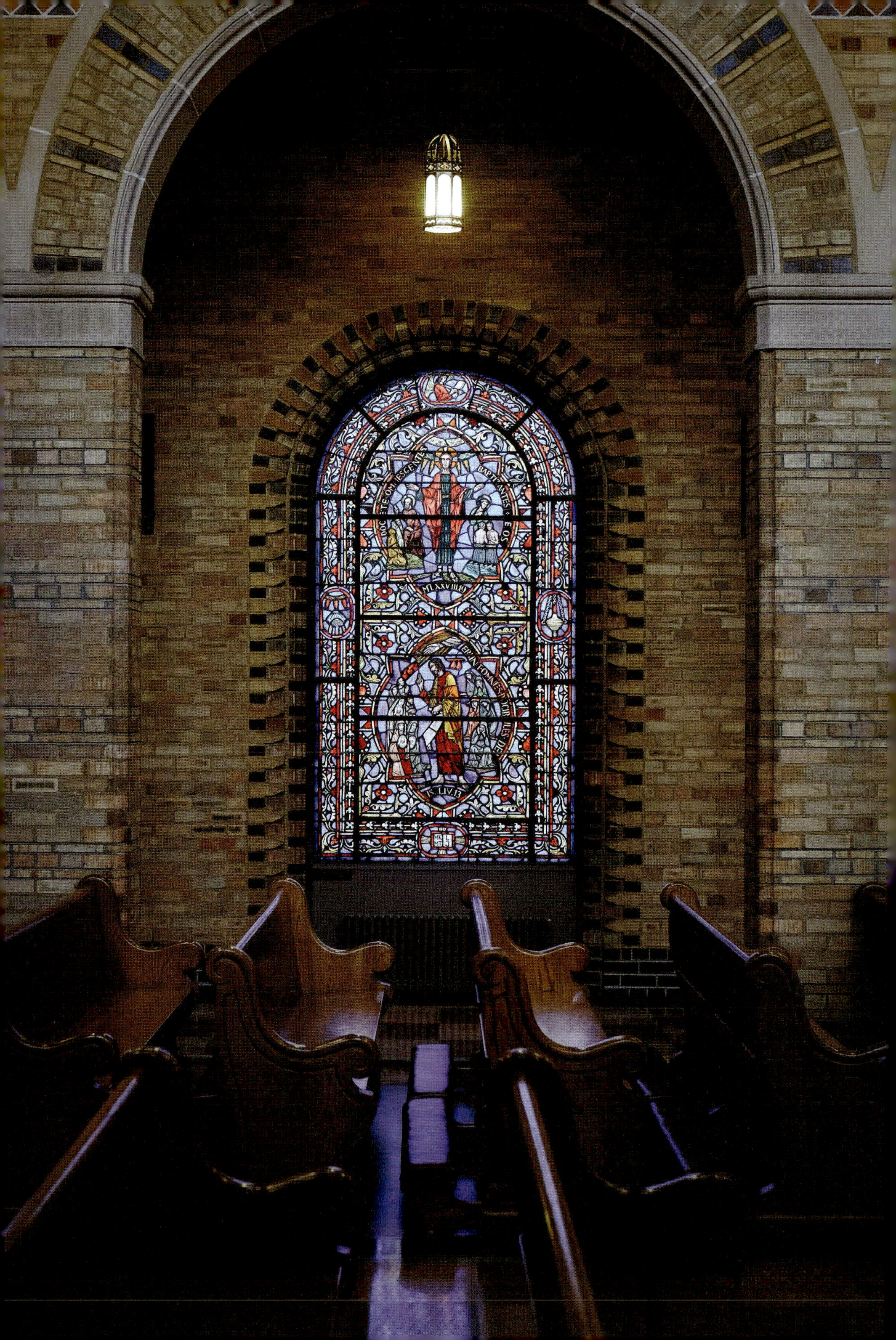

FAITH

A KINDERGARTEN TEACHER WAS OBSERVING HER classroom of children as they drew. She occasionally walked around to see each child's artwork. As she approached one little girl working diligently, she asked what she was drawing. The girl said, "I'm drawing God." The teacher paused and said with a smile, "But no one knows what God looks like." Without looking up from her drawing, the girl replied, "They will in a minute!"

Being in touch with reality means being in touch with all of reality, not only the reality that we perceive through our senses. Even on a natural level, we know some things on the testimony of others. I have never been to Alaska, for instance, but reliable sources tell me that Alaska exists. I trust them enough to believe in its existence.

Supernatural faith is like that, but with two differences. First, the object of faith is not about created things but God himself. Second, the authority by which we know supernatural truth is none other than God himself, who can neither deceive nor be deceived. It is therefore a gift of grace.

We can know the existence of God as an intellectual conclusion through the use of reason. If you are driving on a winter day and see a snowman by the side of the road, you will likely conclude that it was not a random drift of snow that formed itself into a snowman; a human being did it. So too can we conclude, if our mind is not too hindered by deliberate blindness and sin, that the intelligibility of the universe is the product of a rational being. This is not yet faith but simply a deduction of reason.

In order to assist our assent of faith, God provides other supports for belief, such as the miracles of Christ and the saints; Eucharistic, medical, and other miracles; prophecies; the witness of the martyrs; the holiness of the Church; personal spiritual experiences; and even the discoveries of science. These are all called "motives of credibility."

Motives of credibility are still not faith, but they can help us receive the gift of faith. More is needed. After all, even fallen angels know that God exists. "You believe that God is one; you do well," St. James writes. "Even the demons believe—and shudder" (Jas 2:19).

Faith is a grace that God bestows, ordinarily in the Sacrament of Baptism. When St. Peter confessed Jesus to be the Christ, the Son of the living God, the Lord answered him, "Blessed are you, Simon Bar-Jona! For flesh and blood has not revealed this to you, but my Father who is in heaven" (Matt 16:17).

We cannot see God with our senses, we cannot feel God with our emotions, and we cannot comprehend God with the unaided intellect; we can only grasp concepts about God. But the virtue of faith can touch

HOW DO WE GROW IN FAITH?

There are many ways that we and our children can grow in faith. Like a tiny seed that is nourished with water, light, and good soil, the faith planted in our hearts in baptism can be cultivated so that it grows strong and yields abundant fruit.

- First, the humility discussed in the previous chapter is an essential ingredient to a thriving faith. It gives us a docility of heart, a receptivity to listen, and an openness to grace. St. John Henry Newman wrote, "Difficulties in revelation mainly contribute to this end. They are stumbling-blocks to proud and unhumbled minds, and were intended to be such. Faith is unassuming, modest, thankful, obedient. It receives with reverence and love whatever God gives."*

- Second, we should ask for an increase of faith, like the father of the possessed boy who begged Jesus, "I believe; help my unbelief!" (Mark 9:24). When children—particularly teenagers—speak to you about their struggles with faith, begin by encouraging them to ask for a deeper faith. In fact, you can pray then and there for an increase of faith for you both!

- Third, since living faith is a relationship with God, we grow in the virtue by nurturing that relationship in prayer. Just as

---

* John Henry Newman, "The Christian Mysteries," Sermon 16 in *Plain and Parochial Sermons*, vol. 1 (London: Longmans, Green, 1907), 211.

God. Like the woman with the hemorrhage who touched Jesus and was healed (see Mark 5:25–34), when we exercise faith we touch God, and divine life—grace—is released. Faith is not, then, simply a rational deduction or an idea or an opinion. Faith is an encounter with a person. Anyone can know that God exists, but only someone with supernatural faith can live in personal union with him.

At this point we come up against an interesting question. Why does God ask for faith? Why not just reveal himself to us in more direct ways?

friends grow in friendship by spending time with each other, so too we grow in friendship with God by spending time with him. The more we get to know Jesus, the more we realize that he is not an abstraction but a real, living person who desires to be known and loved. No day should go by in a Christian home without parents leading their children in a devotion or other religious act.

- Fourth, faith grows through acts of faith and works of charity. Many who have a wavering faith have grown into men and women of unshakable conviction in the reality and goodness of God by explicitly renewing their faith many times, however dark things might seem, and by living an upright and generous life. All your efforts to form your children well, in other words, also contribute to their growth in faith.

- Fifth, like a lighted candle, our faith is not diminished but grows by sharing it with others. Encourage your children to be courageous witnesses of their faith in their actions and words. They will not only become more apostolic but their own faith will grow too.

OBSTACLES TO FAITH

Faith is a fragile virtue that can be weakened or even tragically lost. There are several pitfalls that we and our children can anticipate and turn into opportunities for growth.

The ways our culture discourages faith. We live at a time that oscillates between two poles. On the one hand, there is a hyper-rationalism that aggressively (and unscientifically) restricts knowledge to the data of the five senses. On the other hand, and paradoxically, there is a nihilistic rejection of meaning and even of objective reality. Both contaminate the healthy soil in which faith can grow. Helping our children be critical of our culture's blind spots, without rejecting the culture outright, will enable them to sustain their faith in today's environment.

The lie that faith restricts freedom. The fact is, we all give ourselves to something beyond ourselves. The only question is, to whom or what do we give ourselves? "Everyone is bound to have some belief," Joseph Ratzinger wrote, "since every man must adopt some kind of attitude to the basic questions of life. There is a realm which allows no other answer but that of entertaining belief, and no man can completely avoid this realm."* We all serve someone or something; it is in serving God, however, who knows all our needs and loves us without measure, that we attain true freedom.

Harmful reading. Faith is an intellectual virtue that grows or withers in intellectual ways. Reading, in particular, can either strengthen or weaken it. In this regard we are none of us quite as strong as we think. If we must read something that is potentially harmful—for school, for instance, or for an apostolic motive—it should be done with the advice and accompaniment of a spiritual guide. On the other hand, we reinforce our faith by taking in solid spiritual reading, good literature, and beauty. Faith can be strengthened especially with good apologetical books which are intended to clear away obstacles and overcome prejudices that can be detrimental to faith.

---

* Joseph Ratzinger, *Introduction to Christianity*, trans. J. R. Foster (San Francisco: Ignatius Press, 1990), 40–41.

The question presumes, first of all, that faith must be obscure. Part of our inheritance from Original Sin, though, is a darkened mind and rebellious passions (see Eph 4:18). We do not know exactly what Adam and Eve's relationship with God was like before sin, but clearly it was easy and familiar (see Gen 1–2). The difficulty we sometimes experience with faith, in other words, is not due to God being enigmatic but due to our own limitations as fallen human beings.

"Okay," one might say. "But God *knows* that we are fallen, that faith is therefore sometimes difficult. Why not reveal himself in more explicit ways?" There are three main reasons.

First, because faith gives us space for repentance. In several places the Gospels show Jesus "unable" to work miracles because the people lacked faith (see, for instance, Mark 6:1–6). This was not a lack of power on Jesus' part, since his divine power is unlimited, nor was it simply punishment for their unbelief. It was because miracles might have made their rejection of Jesus that much more culpable and spiritually disastrous for them. Faith, in other words, gives a certain distance from our sinful rejection of God which, if that rejection were made in the face of greater clarity, would deepen our rupture with him. Unlike the angels whose powerful intellects made their sin instantaneous and irrevocable, we have the merciful opportunity to repent and grow. Faith gives us the space to do so.

Second, faith is not something we acquire or achieve on our own. God gives us faith through the communion of the Church. "How are men to call upon him in whom they have not believed? And how are they to believe in him of whom they have never heard? And how are they to hear without a preacher? And how can men preach unless they are sent?" (Rom 10:14–15). Faith depends upon and fosters a community of believers. Faith flows from charity and leads to charity, which would not be the case were God to reveal himself directly to each of us in more immediate ways.

Finally, and most importantly, faith deepens our love for God. Take the instance of married love, which so beautifully echoes the love that God has for us. In a healthy marriage, the faith that spouses have in each other is a space where their love grows. In a struggling marriage, on the other hand, the constant need to prove their fidelity to each other is a source of irritation and distrust and saps the marriage of vitality. Similarly, our love for God grows when our faith is stretched and remains steadfast.

We cannot see God through our human senses, even in a precocious kindergartener's drawing. However, he can be known, and ever more deeply known, through the lens of faith. This priceless gift of grace enables us to grow in union with God until—please the Lord—he calls us home. When that blessed day arrives we will no longer need the sight conferred by faith because we will behold God face-to-face for all eternity.

> Have you ever shared with your family the story of your faith journey? Using age-appropriate language, share more deeply with your children a bit of your deeper conversion of heart or some dimension of your relationship with God. Encourage them to do the same.
>
> Ask your spouse what doubts or difficulties he or she is experiencing in the spiritual life. What help can you offer? A commitment to pray for your spouse? Are there devotional or apologetic resources that might be helpful?
>
> Who in your life has been a witness to the virtue of faith? How has that example impacted you?
>
> Look for natural opportunities to ask your children to share any questions about God they may have with you. Make sure these conversations are two-way and happen on a regular basis, depending on their age and particular stages of spiritual development.

ST. JOSEPHINE BAKHITA

Virgin
Born in Darfur
D. 1947
Feast day: February 8

Fight the good fight of the faith; take hold of the eternal life to which you were called when you made the good confession in the presence of many witnesses.

1 Timothy 6:12

Josephine Bakhita was born around 1869 in western Sudan to a respected family of the Daju tribe. She lived there for six happy years before Arab slave traders kidnapped her sister. Josephine herself was captured two years later. Since she forgot her own name in the trauma of her enslavement, her captor called her "Bakhita," which in Arabic translates to "Fortunate." Over the next several years, Bakhita was sold repeatedly to different owners, some of whom treated her with callous brutality. She was forced to convert to Islam, beaten, abused, bound with chains, and scarred across her chest and arms to identify her as a slave. Later in life, as she lay dying, these scenes of torture resurfaced and afflicted her grievously.

When Bakhita, as she was still known, was thirteen years old, she was sold to the Italian Vice Consul in Khartoum. He treated her well, and when he and his family fled in the midst of Sudan's mounting civil war, he brought Bakhita with them to Italy. He entrusted her to friends, Augusto Michieli and his wife Maria, who also treated her kindly. When they moved back to Sudan, the Michieli's placed Bakhita and their young daughter in the care of the Canossian Daughters of Charity in Venice. However, when they wanted Bakhita to move back to Sudan in 1889, she firmly refused. The good Sisters, with the help of the Patriarch of

Venice—a certain Giusseppe Sarto, the future Pope St. Pius X—brought the matter before a civil court, which ruled in Bakhita's favor. She was finally, legally, free.

The Sisters, through their kindness, virtuous life, and instruction, inspired faith in the heart of the young African woman. Bakhita was introduced to Jesus and began to take catechism instructions. In 1890, she was baptized, confirmed, and received first Holy Communion from the archbishop himself. Her baptismal name was Josephine Margaret Fortunata (the Latin translation of *Bakhita*), and she entered the Daughters of Charity novitiate three years later. In 1902, she was assigned to a convent in northern Italy, where she spent the rest of her life as doorkeeper, cook, and sacristan, endearing herself to the locals and their children with her kindness, infectious smile, and calm demeanor. She was always happy to share her story and made a point of saying that she had forgiven her many abusers.

Despite increasing pain that forced her to use a wheelchair, Josephine always remained upbeat and filled with faith. When asked how she was doing, she would reply, "As the Master desires." On February 8, 1947, surrounded by her Canossian sisters, she uttered exclamations of love for the Blessed Virgin as she was called home to her true Master's house.

> Heavenly Father, your beloved daughter Josephine Bakhita endured great physical and emotional suffering in her life, but with great mercy, she was able to forgive those who had tormented her. With the eyes of faith, she discerned your sovereign will to draw good even out of the profound evil inflicted by sinful men. And so she came to know her true Master, who became a slave so that we might be set free from the shackles of sin. Through her example and prayers, Father, strengthen our faith so that we may cling to you no matter what trials we experience in life. May we also come to our homeland in heaven, where we shall finally be truly free. We ask this through our Lord Jesus Christ, your Son, who lives and reigns with you and the Holy Spirit, God forever and ever. Amen.

PRUDENCE

Did you know that your job as parents was made harder by a man who lived seven hundred years ago? Well, it isn't *entirely* his fault, but it is *a lot* his fault. The man is William of Ockham, a prolific theologian who is known for his opposition to many of the scholastics who had preceded him, including St. Thomas Aquinas. He believed their closely reasoned claims about God were too bold, even arrogant, and limited God's omnipotence and freedom by suggesting that God was somehow constrained by the reality he created.

In an effort to protect divine sovereignty, Ockham taught that God's acts are completely independent, even of reason or logic. God did not create a world with inherent meaning, in other words, but gives the world meaning at each moment in a way that human beings cannot understand or predict. Ockham said, for instance, that God could have become incarnate as a stone, tree, donkey, or ox—or even as a donkey and a man at the same time. Things are right or wrong simply because God says so; Ockham argued that hatred for God, adultery, or robbery—any vice at all—would be meritorious if God commanded them.

What does this have to do with the formation of your children? All parents want to teach their children the difference between right and wrong. However, Ockham's ideas, by way of the Protestant Reformation, have seeped deeply into our collective Western consciousness. Ockham taught that it is God's will—that is, God's power—that determines moral truth. There is no basis in reality itself, Ockham said, to discern right from wrong.

That was a dangerous enough idea at a time when everyone believed in God. But what happens when, in the modern era, God himself is removed from the equation? Morality is still determined by a lawgiver, but that lawgiver is no longer God—it is the state, or society, or the spirit of the age, or anything else with the power to compel.

In practice this means that our approach to ethics and law, since William of Ockham, has more to do with compliance with "the rules" than it has

(continued on p. 138)

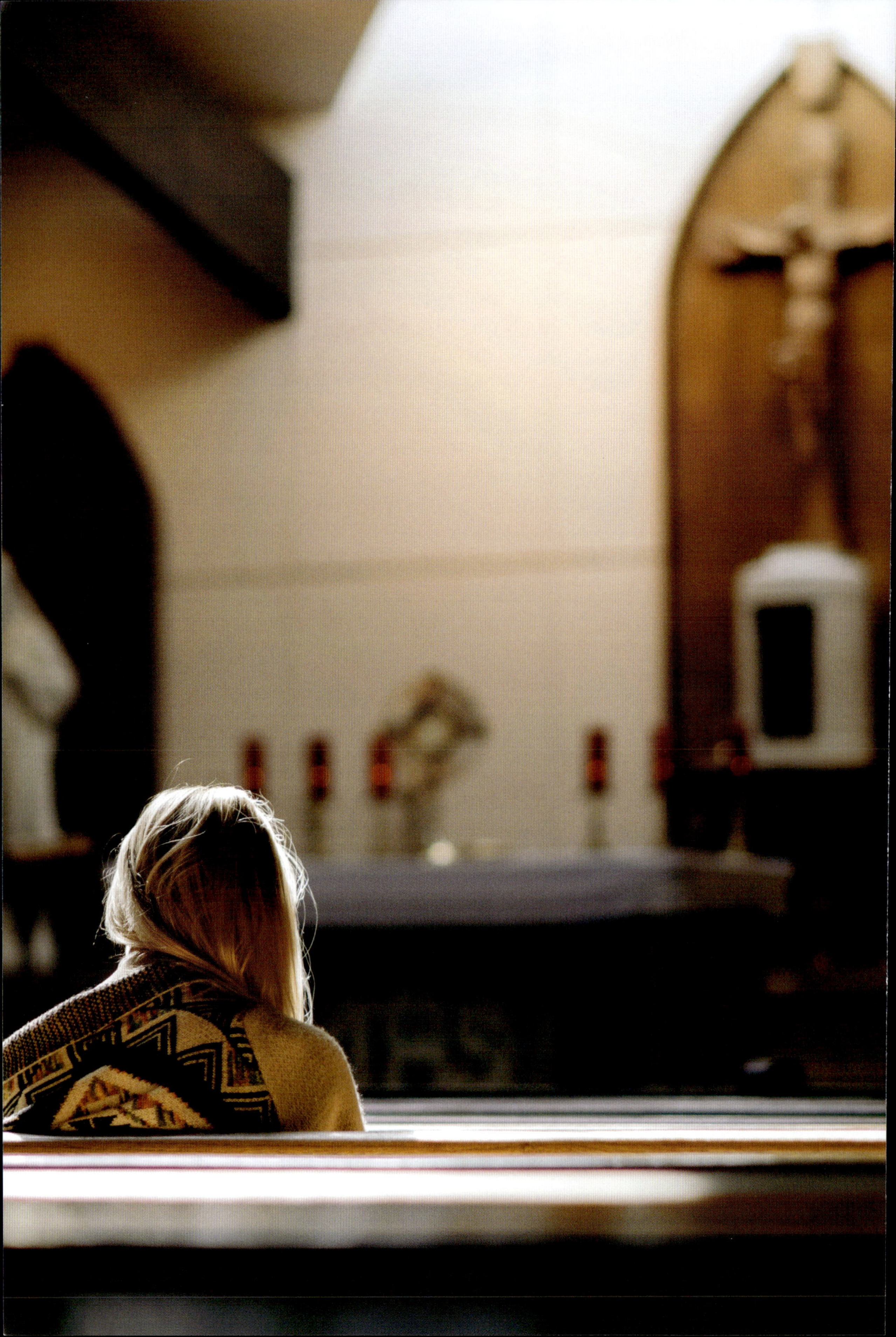

TOO MANY RULES?

Have you ever heard someone say that they could never become Catholic because there are too many rules that we have to follow?

From the outside, it might appear that the Church's (and the Gospel's) moral guidance is simply a set of prohibitions. These teachings, which are sometimes demanding, might even seem to reinforce the very voluntarism that is so harmful and contribute to an anxiety about following the "rules" to avoid divine punishment.

While the moral teaching of the Church *can* be taught as simply a list of prohibitions, and while some might understand the moral law in a defective way that contributes to anxiety and a fear of "getting it right," those approaches miss the mark.

The truth is exactly the opposite. It is not the command that comes first; it is the reality of how we are made, what will make us thrive, what will enable us to live more abundant lives, that precedes the commands. Good choices are not good because they are commanded; they are commanded because they are good—and make us good.

Nobody ever said that they wouldn't watch football, for instance, because it has too many regulations, or that learning the piano shouldn't be confined by so many rules, or that electricians shouldn't have to abide by so many safety requirements. These are all necessary conditions for greater goods. Human life is a great good indeed, and moral teachings are the "rules of life" that help us live it well. Prudence is the virtue that puts those moral teachings into practice.

Today, the "rules" to which many object are about sexual morality and family life. For someone living in a sexually permissive way, they may only see in Catholic teaching prohibitions of behavior they enjoy.

In her perennial wisdom, though, and having reflected deeply on the Gospel, guided by the Holy Spirit, the Church teaches those moral truths because they are how we live fuller and happier lives. Even a glance at the effects of the "freedoms" won in the sexual revolution—the catastrophic effects in the lives of children, women, men, families, and society at large—reinforces the point. The negative commandments, even those that seem most challenging, are all in the service of far more important positive goods.

to do with understanding their rational basis. This is called "voluntarism" since it puts all the weight of morality on the will (*voluntas* in Latin).

Good people want to know the rules and follow them; immoral people try to find ways to evade them.[1] When good people fail to follow the rules, they simply try harder to conform to them. This approach to morality, so common today, causes many people a great deal of tension, anxiety, scrupulosity, and fatigue.

Those steeped in voluntarism seek the security of knowing the right thing to do and they achieve that security by conforming to moral expectations as they understand them. Deep down, though, there is frequently a great deal of frustration, exhaustion, and, often enough, rebellion. That, in short, is a picture of our age and its anemic approach to moral authority. Voluntarism is pervasive, so pervasive that many have this outlook on morality without even knowing it.

Catholicism affirms that God has created an intelligible world. We can know things as they are, including right and wrong. Things are not good because they are commanded, but rather commanded because they are good. Forming children in a free and healthy relationship to moral authority means putting them in touch with the reality that underpins moral good and evil. That, in turn, means forming them in the virtue of prudence.

Prudence helps us make good choices in life. It engages both our intellect and our will. To take a simple example: We see a piece of chocolate, and the intellect judges it to be a good, something that should be eaten. The intellect sends that message to the will, which moves us to eat the chocolate.

We invariably choose something under the appearance of good. The portion of our intellect that makes that judgment is called the *practical intellect*. The *speculative intellect*, by contrast, gives us the power of understanding and knowing for its own sake.

Sometimes our practical intellect, swayed by our passions or emotions, obscures what is truly our good. When we know (through the speculative intellect) that something is wrong and yet we choose it anyway, it is because the practical intellect has judged it good for us here and now, despite us knowing better. That is called sin. Thus, if we choose to eat

---

[1] For my approach to this topic I am indebted to the discussion of prudence in Julio Diéguez, *He Knows Not How: Growing in Freedom*, trans. Dale Parker (Madrid: Letragrande, 2022).

HOW TO FORM PRUDENCE

- **BE PATIENT.** Formation in this virtue takes time. Much of the growth will happen as children grow into adolescence and beyond. Nevertheless, many of these suggestions can be instilled even in young children.

- **BUILD TRUST.** Learning prudence first means accepting moral principles from the outside. The more trustworthy your authority as a parent, the more you show your affection for your children, your understanding, your desire for their good, the more they will internalize the moral principles you teach.

- **BEGIN WITH THE GOAL.** Moral guidance means showing how good actions make us better people. It is not just a matter of telling them the correct conclusion. How will this act make me the kind of person I wish to become? Help children understand the reasons behind moral norms.

- **PAINT THE RIGHT PICTURE.** Talk about the moral life as positive, joyful, and fulfilling. Moral growth is useful since it helps us live fuller lives and prepares us to undertake new tasks and overcome struggles.

- **ALLOW YOUR CHILDREN TO MAKE MISTAKES.** Except when a misstep would be disastrous for them or others—which thankfully is rare—we should be comfortable giving children moral principles and letting them draw their own conclusions. Mistakes are an occasion for a discussion so that they can make better decisions in the future.

- **BE WITNESSES OF PRUDENCE.** You provide an example to your children when you are able to discuss your own moral decision-making with them. When you seek advice, listen to others, draw from your own life experience, and apply moral principles to concrete situations, they see prudence in action.

- **STORIES CAN HELP.** Lives of the saints, biographies, and even fictional stories and movies can all spark discussions about prudential judgments—when characters make good moral decisions and even when they don't. Good literature provides endless opportunities to talk about prudence.

- **NEVER OMIT GRACE.** It is only through grace that we can live the holy life to which we are called. But grace is inseparable from our freedom; it works through our freely chosen, prudential acts. Without formation in prudence, we will not be able to cooperate with the graces that God offers in order for us to live holy, joyful lives.

the chocolate even though we know it doesn't belong to us, or we made a Lenten resolution not to eat chocolate, or we know it would be harmful to our health, we are guilty of an immoral choice.

Forming our practical intellect to make better choices is the role of prudence. It is right reason in acting. Ancient philosophers called prudence the "charioteer of all the virtues" because no virtue—no virtue *at all*—can exist without prudence, since every virtue first requires that we know the good to be done.

This approach to morality is so different from voluntarism because it engages our intellect in every moral act; we know not just what is right, but *why* it is right. We see in moral behavior the opportunity to grow into better people, to live fuller lives, to be happy.

When we wish to do the right thing but lack the willpower to do so, then, the answer is not just to try harder. Neither is it to ignore what we know to be right. Rather the answer is twofold. First, we grow in prudence so that we can discern right and wrong. Second, we grow in the virtues that order our passions so that they help us make a good discernment rather than clouding our judgment. Prudence, in other words, is a clear and accurate understanding of moral reality and the ability to put that view of reality into action through the virtues. With prudence we can both choose and act well.

Formation in prudence begins at home, since the family provides the first set of moral principles that help children determine right from wrong. Over time, they learn to think in moral ways, to think prudentially.

From this it is also evident how harmful bad examples can be, whether from parents, siblings, friends, negative role models in movies or shows or video games, societal approval of immoral behavior, and so forth. Bad examples stunt our growth in prudence and therefore limit our capacity to make good choices.

As your children grow up, their moral formation matures by not simply securing their compliance but by helping them to think through situations in a moral way. When you put your children in touch with the reality created by God, a reality of good and evil that can be known and applied in everyday life, you are preserving them from one of the great intellectual limitations of our age: the prison of voluntarism and all the anxieties that accompany it. William of Ockham need not have the last word in your family.

Reread the opening of this chapter. Do you see any influence of voluntarism in your life? In the culture?

Rule following can have negative connotations for many. How would you describe the value of following authentic moral rules or laws?

Candidly discuss with your spouse whether your approach to establishing family rules is more about compliance or moral formation. Are you challenging your children to desire to choose the good or simply to avoid punishment?

Are there examples from literature or film that illustrate for your children positive examples of prudence? How can you help them draw connections from these examples for their own moral growth?

Forming Families, Forming Saints

ST. FRANCES XAVIER CABRINI

Virgin
Born in Italy
D. 1917
Feast day: November 13

*I have taught you the way of wisdom;
    I have led you in the paths of uprightness.
When you walk, your step will not be hampered;
    And if you run, you will not stumble.*

Proverbs 4: 11–12

Maria Francesca Cabrini (Frances) was born in Lombardi. She was the youngest of thirteen children, only four of whom survived childhood. Frances grew up in a devout home and was well formed in the faith. Due to her poor health, she was frustrated in her first attempts to enter a convent. At the age of twenty-four, however, she was invited to assist at an orphanage for girls, and three years later, she and some of those girls made a religious profession of vows at the hands of her bishop. She added Xavier to her religious name in honor of the missionary, St. Francis Xavier.

When that congregation had to disband due to calumnies spread by some of the women who worked at the orphanage, another bishop invited her to form a missionary convent, which became known as the Institute of the Missionary Sisters of the Sacred Heart of Jesus. Frances was named mother superior and remained so for the next thirty-seven years until her death. This Institute thrived, and within five years, there were seven convents around Italy. Pope Leo XIII approved the rule and constitution, and the order established houses in Rome. At that point, though Mother Cabrini's dream was to spread her Institute to China (following in the footsteps of St. Francis Xavier), the bishop instead encouraged her to found a convent in the United States to care for Italian immigrants. When she asked the pope for his guidance, he looked at her affectionately and said, "You will go not to the East, but to the West!"

Mother Cabrini and six sisters arrived in New York on March 31, 1889. Their convent, however, was not yet ready, so the archbishop of New York encouraged the women to return to Italy. Mother Cabrini said, however, that the pope had sent her and that she would remain. Finally they were able to move into their convent, and the sisters began to work with the poor Italians in Manhattan. They established free schools, founded orphanages and hospitals, and opened convents all over the United States and eventually throughout the world. In Mother Cabrini's lifetime, over one thousand young women joined her mission. Within ten years of her death, the Institute finally fulfilled Mother Cabrini's dream of establishing a convent in China. She became a naturalized citizen of the United States in 1909 and eight years later passed away at the age of sixty-seven. In 1946, she became the first US citizen to be canonized.

Mother Cabrini was an exceptionally talented woman. While remaining deeply prayerful and humble, she was also determined, industrious, highly organized, and zealous for souls. Her prudence was legendary as she always seemed to know what to do and how to do it. She was resourceful and wise in temporal administration, always finding people to donate money and time to her charitable works. In our busy lives, Mother Cabrini is an example of someone who never forgot the source of true success in working for God: remaining close to the Holy Spirit, whose inspirations guided her many decisions that reflect a profound natural and supernatural prudence.

> Heavenly Father, the prudence of St. Francis Xavier Cabrini brought compassion and relief to countless poor, ignorant, and suffering souls. As our family grows in this virtue, help us, through her intercession, always to follow the right path in the moral judgments that we face. May we have an ever deeper gratitude for the fullness of life to which, through virtue, you call us. We ask this through our Lord Jesus Christ, your Son, who lives and reigns with you and the Holy Spirit, God forever and ever. Amen.

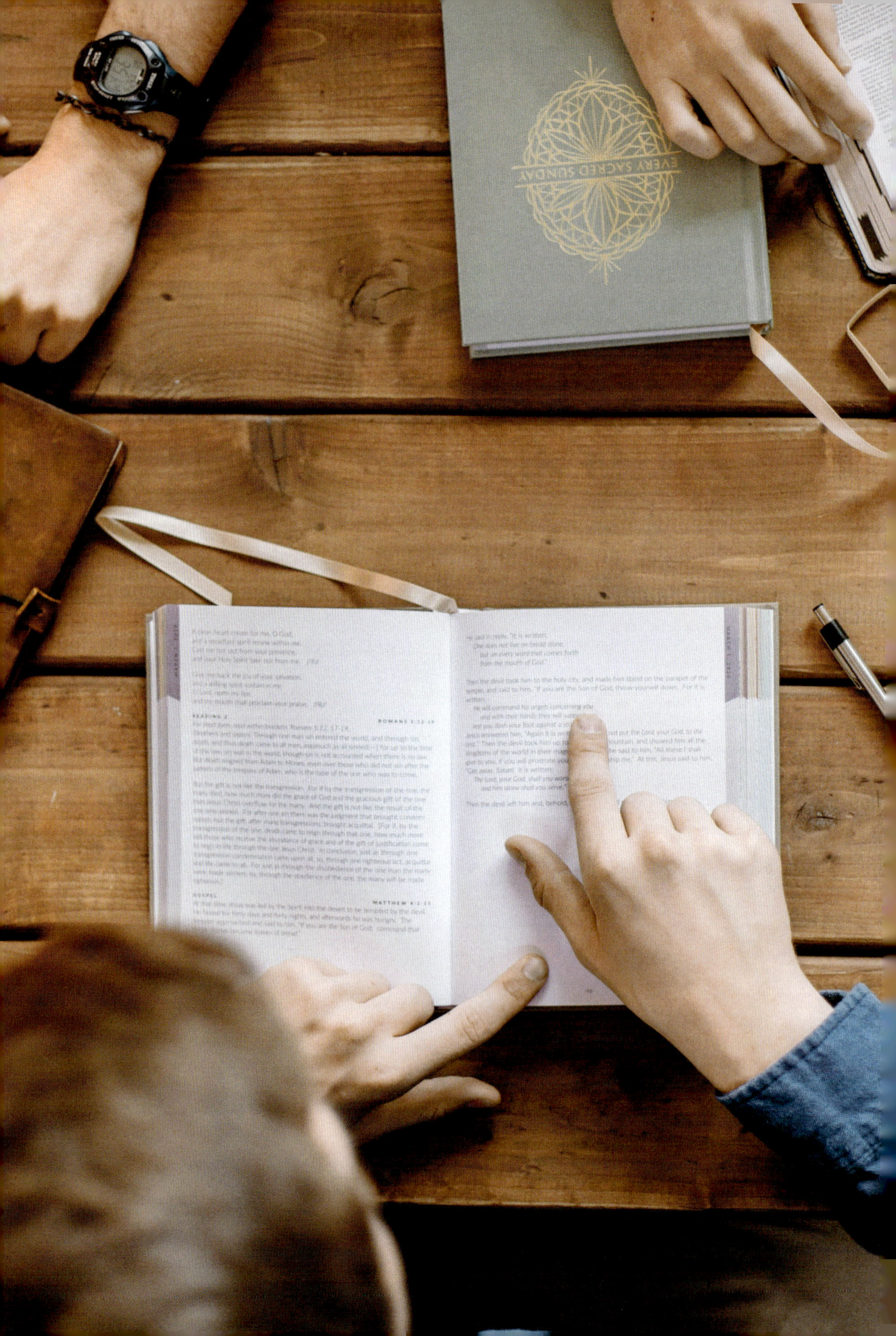
EVERY SACRED SUNDAY

SPIRITUAL READING

IN MY WORK WITH SEMINARIANS, I try to keep an eye on building habits that will enable them to continue growing well after they are ordained priests. I am convinced that three such habits are particularly important to cultivate so that formation can continue throughout life. First, fidelity to regular spiritual mentoring. Second, cultivating peer friendships that foster holiness. And third, good reading. All three are applicable to family formation, but this chapter will focus on the third practice: nurturing a love for good reading.

Children first experience the joy of reading when someone reads to them, perhaps at bedtime. Serious reading usually begins with school. Over time, we start to read literature and grow in cultural awareness. We continue to read for pleasure and to explore new interests. All of these are vitally important ways to get in touch with reality. Parents can do much to cultivate them in their children's lives with their example and advice.

An especially valuable kind of reading promotes the soul's relationship with God. The primary focus of this chapter is to consider ways that reading can continue to nourish our knowledge of the faith and our interior life, a practice collectively called spiritual reading.

It would be difficult to overestimate the importance of this kind of reading. C. S. Lewis ascribes the beginning of his Christian conversion to reading G. K. Chesterton and George MacDonald, a Scottish author and Congregational minister. In *Surprised by Joy* Lewis wrote, "In reading Chesterton, as in reading MacDonald, I did not know what I was letting myself in for. A young man who wishes to remain a sound Atheist cannot be too careful of his reading."[1]

There are many reasons to acquire the habit of spiritual reading. Most reading is done to gain information. This happens in spiritual reading too, but it's primary purpose is to gain wisdom. Through good reading we grow in appreciation for the richness of our Catholic faith. It widens our horizons, opens our minds, illuminates the world from a perspective of faith, and feeds our prayer with insights and inspirations. St. Josemaría

---

[1] C. S. Lewis, *Surprised by Joy: The Shape of My Early* Life (London: Harcourt Books, 1955), 191.

Escrivá wrote that spiritual reading "builds up a store of fuel.... It looks like a lifeless heap, but I often find that my memory, of its own accord, will draw from it material which fills my prayer with life and inflames my thanksgiving after Communion."[2]

Most importantly, good reading helps us grow in holiness. St. Josemaría advises: "Don't neglect your spiritual reading.... Reading has made many saints."[3] Reading can inspire, convict, and console.

St. Augustine famously attributes his conversion to reading the Epistles of St. Paul after he heard a child's voice calling out, *"Tolle lege, tolle lege"*— "Take up and read, take up and read."

St. Ignatius of Loyola was converted by reading the lives of the saints while recovering from a battle wound.

As an atheist, Edith Stein was staying with friends outside Freiburg when she poked through their bookshelf looking for something interesting to read. Spotting St. Teresa of Avila's autobiography, she pulled it from the shelf and sat down for a few minutes' diversion. The next morning, having read all night, she laid the book on the table and declared, "That is the truth." She was baptized a few weeks later.

There are many reasons, then, to build a habit of spiritual reading. Let's consider what, when, and how to read. When you try to build these habits yourself, you will naturally pass them on to your children as well.

What to Read

- It is always good to start with the classics. These are titles that have stood the test of time. Countless books have been written by saints and these, too, should be given priority. St. Philip Neri advised his directees to read authors whose names begin with S!

- One approach to a reading plan is to cycle through different types of books. Several book suggestions, in various categories, are given in the sidebars both for you and your children. Though fiction books are not usually ideal for spiritual reading, you might occasionally use a work of fiction that is particularly suitable to spiritual growth.

---

[2] Josemaría Escrivá, *The Way* (New York: Scepter Publishers, 1954), no. 117.
[3] Escrivá, *The Way*, no. 116.

READING SUGGESTIONS FOR PARENTS

Prayer

Difficulties in Mental Prayer
　by Eugene Boylan

Prayer Primer
　by Thomas Dubay

Listening at Prayer
　by Benedict Groeschel

The Fulfillment of All Desire
　by Ralph Martin

Thirsting for Prayer
　by Jacques Philippe

Discipleship

Frequent Confession
　by Benedict Baur

I Believe in Love
　by Père Jean du Coeur
　de Jésus D'Elbée

This Tremendous Lover
　by Eugene Boylan

The Seven Storey Mountain
　by Thomas Merton

Introduction to the Devout Life
　by St. Francis de Sales

Doctrine

A Father Who Keeps His Promises
　by Scott Hahn

The Creed in Slow Motion
　by Ronald Knox

Making Sense Out of Suffering
　by Peter Kreeft

The Screwtape Letters
　by C. S. Lewis

Theology and Sanity
　by Frank Sheed

Our Lady

Mary: Mirror of the Church
　by Raniero Cantalamessa

The Reed of God
　by Caryll Houselander

True Devotion to the Blessed Virgin
　by St. Louis de Montfort

The World's First Love
　by Fulton Sheen

Mary of Nazareth
　by Federico Suarez

Saints (and nearly so)

Confessions
　by St. Augustine

St. Francis of Assisi
　by G. K. Chesterton

With God in Russia
　by Walter Ciszek

Story of a Soul
　by St. Thérèse of Lisieux

Edmund Campion
　by Evelyn Waugh

- There is nothing wrong with rereading certain books, even multiple times. I always enjoy finding books that move me deeply, yet differently, at various points in my life.
- It is good to know what book you will be reading next so that you do not lose the habit by breaking the chain.
- If you find yourself dreading spiritual reading, perhaps it is time to change books. Often a book that leaves me cold at one point is exactly what I will need later. Exchange it for one that will rekindle your enjoyment of reading.
- Since the greatest book of all is the Bible, consider starting your period of spiritual reading with a chapter of the New Testament before diving into your regular book.
- Finally, when in doubt, it is advisable to consult with your parish priest, a spiritual director, a well-read Catholic friend, or another trusted source for good reading.

When to Read

- The main thing is consistency. Read every day. It is an easy habit to neglect if we do not make it a daily priority.
- Earlier in the day is generally better than later, and try to avoid doing it late at night or right before bed (or in bed).
- If you miss your normal time of reading, don't let the "perfect become the enemy of the good." Just do some reading when you can and how you can. If you're traveling and forget your book, read something online. If you use an e-reader, keep a few spiritual books on it for such occasions.
- Reading does not need to be for a long stretch. Fifteen minutes a day will cover a lot of ground. If you read ten pages a day, that is a two-hundred-page book every three weeks. That's seventeen books in a year!

How to Read

- Begin by placing yourself in God's presence and asking for his assistance, and that of your guardian angel, before reading.

- Some reading is merely for information, which can be done more quickly. Some reading, like lectio divina, is slow and prayerful. Spiritual reading strikes a middle ground. Read attentively and give yourself permission to pause and reflect.

- Many find it helpful to take a few notes on book margins or on a separate piece of paper. This will help with retention and may provide you with something to reflect on later in the day or in your time of prayer.

- I suggest reading one book at a time, from beginning to end, rather than having several books going at the same time. There are, as always, exceptions. Some books lend themselves to being picked up and put down more easily, such as diaries of saints and books of homilies.

On the fiftieth anniversary of his priestly ordination, Pope St. Pius X wrote to the priests of the world on priestly sanctity and included some advice on spiritual reading. "Everyone knows the great influence that is exerted by the voice of a friend," he wrote, "who gives candid advice, assists by his counsel, corrects, encourages and leads one away from error." Then he continued:

> We should, then, count pious books among our true friends. They solemnly remind us of our duties and of the prescriptions of legitimate discipline; they arouse the heavenly voices that were stifled in our souls; they rid our resolutions of listlessness; they disturb our deceitful complacency; they show the true nature of less worthy affections to which we have sought to close our eyes; they bring to light the many dangers which beset the path of the imprudent. They render all these services with such kindly discretion that they prove themselves to be not only our friends, but the very best of friends. They are always at hand, constantly beside us to assist us in the needs of our souls; their voice is never harsh,

their advice is never self-seeking, their words are never timid or deceitful.[4]

His advice is applicable to everyone, not only priests. May these good and holy friends never leave our side!

> How is reading valued in your home? Are other forms of entertainment prioritized? What can you to do support good reading hygiene for yourself and your children?
>
> Reflect on books that were instrumental in your spiritual and moral development. Have you shared these books with your spouse or children?
>
> Even in religious life, reading out loud is a common practice. Does your family have a habit of reading out loud for the benefit of all? If not, consider what type of material would be suitable for your family at this time. Perhaps a little poetry or Scripture could be read aloud after dinner. Or one of the many books listed in this chapter. Find something that will engage all members of the family.
>
> Is there a spiritual classic you have always wanted to read but have never started? Could now be the time to try?

---

[4] Pope Pius X, Exhortation to the Catholic Clergy on Priestly Sanctity *Haerent Animo* (August 4, 1908), § 3.3.

READING SUGGESTIONS FOR CHILDREN

From board books to chapter books, there are excellent lives of the saints that are enriching to the spiritual life for all ages. The following lists suggest other opportunities for solid spiritual reading for your children.

Young Children

The emphasis here is on learning the story of the Gospel, recognizing God's presence, and cultivating a relationship with God and an openness to prayer that goes beyond rote recitation.

The Weight of a Mass: A Tale of Faith
   by Josephine Nobisso

Angel in the Waters
   by Regina Doman

Tomie dePaola's Book of Bible Stories
   by Tomie dePaola

The Beautiful Story of the Bible
   by Maite Roche

The Gospel for Little Ones
   by Maïte Roche

God Is Calling: Seeing His Signs in Your Life
   by Br. François Fontanié

Catholic Tales For Boys and Girls,
   vols. I and II
   by Caryll Houselander

Jesus, Were You Little?
   by Sally Metzger

The Monk Who Grew Prayer
   by Claire Brandenburg

Marian Consecration for Families with Young Children
   by Colleen Pressprich

Middle Schoolers

For this age group, literature depicting the life of virtue is a good option. Lives of the saints are particularly helpful here. The *Vision Books* series from Ignatius Press is excellent, as is the series listed below by Judith Boullic.

A Life of Our Lord for Children
   by Marigold Hunt

The Chronicles of Narnia
   by C. S. Lewis

The Door in the Wall
   by Marguerite de Angeli

The Interior Castle: A Boy's Journey into the Riches of Prayer
   by Judith Bouilloc

The Bronze Bow
   by Elizabeth George Speare

Outlaws of Ravenhurst
   by Sr. M. Imelda Wallace

The Little Way: A Journey to the Summit of Love
   by Judith Bouilloc

Heavenly Hosts: Eucharistic Miracles for Kids
   by Kathryn Griffin Swegart

*The Garden of Wonders:
A Journey into the Works of God*
   by Judith Bouilloc

*Beatitales: 80 Fables about
the Beatitudes for Children*
   by Jared Dees

Teens

Personal witness is so important at this age that autobiographies make for some of the most powerful spiritual reading. There are also simple spiritual classics that are appropriate for this age as well.

*Trustful Surrender to Divine Providence:
The Secret of Peace and Happiness*
   by Jean Baptiste Saint-Jure and
   St. Claude de la Colombiere

The Hiding Place
   by Corrie Ten Boom

Mere Christianity
   by C. S. Lewis

The Imitation of Christ
   by Thomas à Kempis

Story of a Soul
   by St. Thérèse of Lisieux

The Long Loneliness
   by Dorothy Day

The Way
   by St. Josemaría Escrivá

Treasure in Clay
   by Fulton J. Sheen

*Happy Are You Poor: The Simple Life and
Spiritual Freedom*
   by Thomas Dubay

*My Dear Young Friends: Pope John Paul II
Speaks to Teens on Life, Love, and Courage*
   by Pope St. John Paul II

Family Film Recommendations

At times, a family movie night can be an enriching experience for children and parents alike. Here are four picks that can prompt further discussion and reflection. Be sure to check CommonSenseMedia.org for age appropriateness and thematic elements.

The Sound of Music (20th Century Studios, 1965, G, 2hr 52min) Set in 1940s Austria and told through the lens of vocation discernment, this classic musical offers tremendous insight into self-gift.

The Straight Story (Disney, 1999, G, 1hr 52min) Based on the true story of a man on an unconventional journey to reconcile with his brother, this film highlights the dignity of ordinary people.

The Miracle Maker (Lionsgate, 1999, G, 1hr 30min) A claymation film about the life of Christ that does not water down the Gospel message. A great choice during Lent or Holy Week.

A Hidden Life (20th Century Studios, 2019, PG-13, 2hr 53min) Powerfully juxtaposing the simple beauty of family life and the urgent obligation to do what's right, this depiction of the life of Bl. Franz Jägerstätter gives older teens an unforgettable witness of grace and courage.

ST. TERESA BENEDICTA OF THE CROSS (Edith Stein)

Virgin and Martyr
Born in Breslau, Germany (present-day Poland)
D. 1942
Feast day: August 9

Guard what has been entrusted to you. Avoid the godless chatter and contradictions of what is falsely called knowledge, for by professing it some have missed the mark as regards the faith.

1 Timothy 6:20

Edith Stein (St. Teresa Benedicta of the Cross) was born into a prominent Jewish family, the youngest of eleven children, eight of whom survived infancy. Her father died when she was two years old, but her mother was able to support the family and give her children an excellent education. Though her parents were devout Jews, Edith became an atheist at fourteen years old. She studied at a local university before attending the University of Göttingen, where she pursued her doctorate in philosophy under the renowned professor of phenomenology, Edmund Husserl.

When World War I broke out in 1914, Edith volunteered with the Red Cross, where her experience of suffering found its way into her doctoral thesis, which explored empathy from a phenomenological perspective. She received her doctorate at the age of twenty-five and followed her mentor, Professor Husserl, to the University of Freiburg.

During a 1921 summer visit with her friend Hedwig Conrad-Martius, a pioneer in German philosophy and a recent convert to Catholicism, Edith picked up an autobiography of St. Teresa of Avila. Having read all night, Edith put the book down and declared, "That is the truth!" Within weeks, she was baptized. From 1923 to 1931, Edith taught history, philosophy, and German to girls at the Dominican convent of St. Magdalene in Speyer. She became a lecturer at the Catholic Institute for Scientific Pedagogy in Münster but was soon forced to resign because of anti-Semitic legislation passed by the Nazi government.

A year later, Edith was received into the Discalced Carmelite Monastery of Our Lady of Peace in Cologne. She took the religious name Sr. Teresa Benedicta of the Cross in honor of St. Teresa of Avila and St. John of the Cross. After Hitler came to power, Sr. Teresa Benedicta's Jewish background became a source of increasing danger to her and her Sisters, so the Carmelite superiors secretly transferred her and her sister Rosa to their monastery in Echt, Netherlands. When the Nazis invaded the Netherlands in 1940, however, Sr. Teresa Benedicta was once more at risk. In 1942, the Dutch bishops issued a statement read at all Masses that condemned Naziism and their persecution of the Jews. The Nazis retaliated by arresting all Catholic converts from Judaism, including Sr. Teresa Benedicta and her sister. They were taken to Auschwitz, where they perished in the gas chambers on August 9, 1942. Sr. Teresa Benedicta was fifty-one years old.

St. Teresa Benedicta of the Cross is a model of intellectual honesty. She pursued the truth wherever it led her, even if it meant leaving behind family, friends, and career. Her powerful intellect contributed much to the study of philosophy (her writings fill seventeen volumes) but her most important work was to discover the truth of the Gospel and share it with others.

> Heavenly Father, your daughter St. Teresa Benedicta of the Cross sought the truth throughout her life. By your grace and the gift of reading, she discovered that truth in your divine Son, who is "the way, the truth, and the life." Through St. Teresa Benedicta's prayers and example of intellectual honesty, may we, too, seek you in the exercise of our reason and so come to embrace more fully the truths of our faith. We ask this through our Lord Jesus Christ, your Son, who lives and reigns with you and the Holy Spirit, God forever and ever. Amen.

BEAUTY

PAUL CLAUDEL WAS EIGHTEEN YEARS old and walking through the streets of Paris on a cold and rainy afternoon. It was Christmas Day, 1886. Claudel was, like many in France at the time, a skeptic and an atheist. The young man decided to escape the rain and ducked into the Cathedral of Notre Dame where Vespers were being sung. Decades later he remembered where he stood, "near the second pillar at the entrance to the chancel, to the right, on the side of the sacristy."

> Then occurred the event which dominates my entire life. In an instant, my heart was touched and I believed. I believed with such a strength of adherence, with such an uplifting of my entire being, with such powerful conviction, with such a certainty leaving no room for any kind of doubt, that since then all the books, all the arguments, all the incidents and accidents of a busy life have been unable to shake my faith, nor indeed to affect it in any way.[1]

Claudel went on to become a diplomat and one of France's most famous poets and dramatists. He never swerved from his Catholic faith, born in an experience of pure beauty.

Together with truth and goodness, beauty is one of the three transcendentals, which are timeless properties of all beings. They reflect the original goodness of the world, the divine origin of creation. To recognize beauty is to make an act of gratitude to God. It can awaken in us and our children a longing for the beauty of God.

Beauty is a first evangelist, so to speak, because it can be less remote than the claims of truth and less daunting than the moral demands of goodness.

The attraction of beauty, however, must not be divorced from the other two transcendentals. Unmoored from them, beauty can easily

---

[1] Quoted in Louis Chaigne, *Paul Claudel: The Man and the Mystic* (Westport, CT: Greenwood Press, 1978), 48. Interestingly, that very same day, one hundred and twenty-five miles away in the small town of Lisieux, Thérèse Martin attended midnight Mass in the local cathedral. On that same Christmas Day, she later wrote, "I received the grace of leaving my childhood, in a word, the grace of my complete conversion." Thérèse of Lisieux, *Story of a Soul: The Autobiography of St. Thérèse of Lisieux*, trans. John Clarke, OCD (Washington, DC: ICS Publications, 1972), 98.

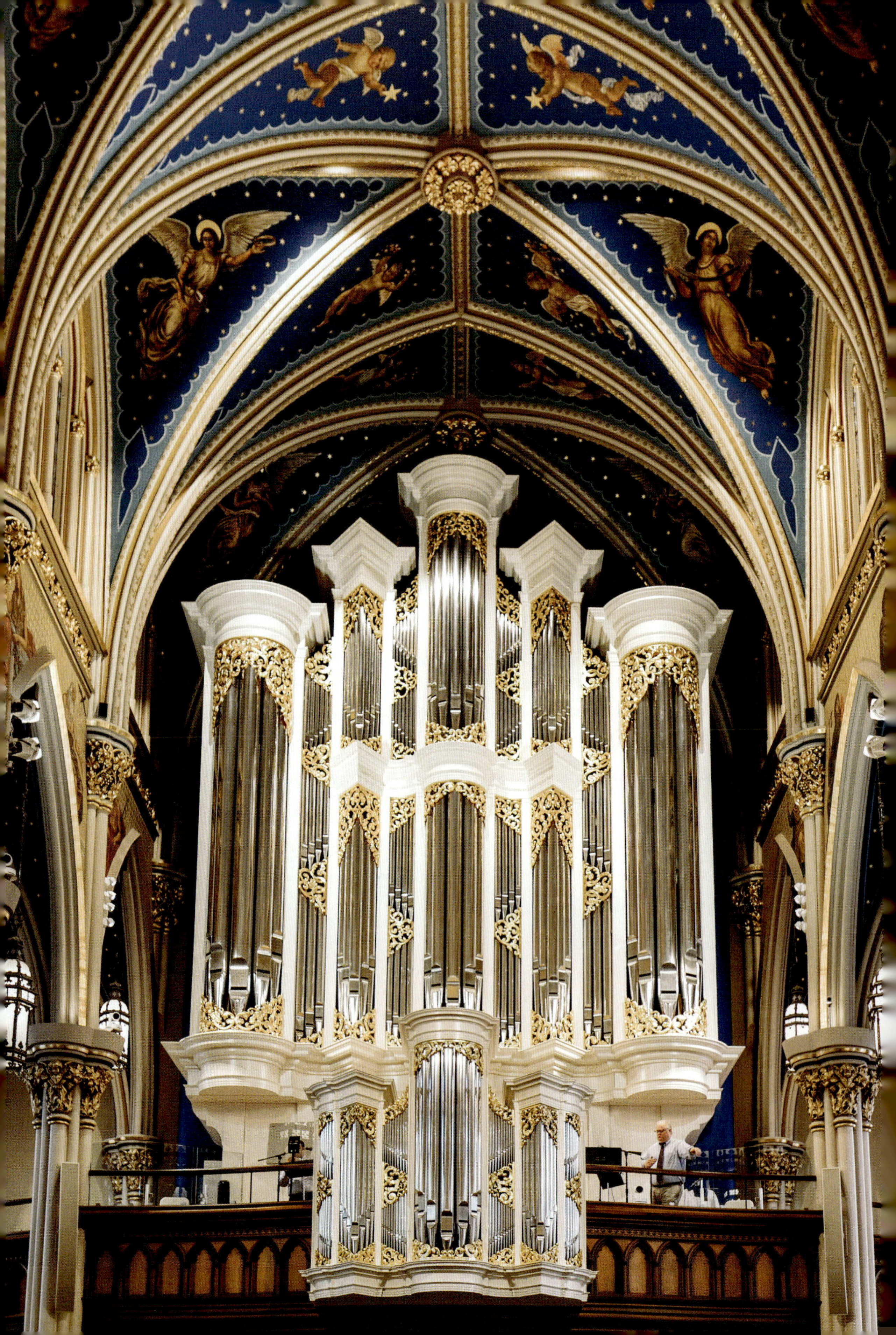

become a competitor to God, an idol, directing our attention not to the source of beauty but to itself as a substitute god. This is true even of sacred art. Plenty of atheists visit Chartres Cathedral and admire its beauty, untroubled in their atheism.

As Dostoevsky wrote in *The Brothers Karamazov*, "The awful thing is that beauty is mysterious as well as terrible. God and the devil are fighting there and the battlefield is the heart of man."[2] That battle for the true purpose of beauty rages all around us.

Despite greater access to beauty than ever before, what should be a golden age of beauty is not. We can easily travel to enjoy places of stunning natural splendor. We can go to art museums and see the fruits of man's creative genius. With one click we can hear the greatest music ever composed.

And yet, we who should be celebrating beauty more than any other generation are instead subjected to an endless barrage of the bland and the conventional, and too often the celebration of the ugly. It is further proof that truth, goodness, and beauty stand or fall together. In a time of doctrinal and moral confusion like ours, we cannot wonder that beauty follows in their wake.

The urgency to recover authentic beauty, then, has never been greater. It is capable of drawing us, like Paul Claudel, towards a profound experience of faith, though it can also lure souls away from God. Beauty makes it easier to receive the truth and to aim for the good, while its counterfeit can confuse and undermine them.

Given this urgency, how can true beauty be incorporated into your family life in such a way that it contributes to the Christian formation of your children?

The physical environment of the home is one place to start. Beauty does not mean luxury. Neither does it mean expensive, though at times it will be wise to spend a bit more to have something truly beautiful and lasting.

Beauty in the home can be fostered in small ways—for instance, in selecting pleasing colors and in choosing furniture that is solid, well-made, and attractive.

---

[2] Fyodor Dostoevsky, *The Brothers Karamazov*, trans. Constance Garnett (New York: Lowell Press, 1912), 131.

BEAUTY IN THE LITURGY

We Catholics have access to the most beautiful experience on earth: the sacred liturgy. Liturgy is, and must be, beautiful because it is our direct and daily contact with the all-holy, all-good, and all-beautiful One.

For centuries the Church was the greatest patron of the arts because she appreciated the importance of beauty in the lives of her children and because she wished to surround the source of all beauty with beautiful sights, sounds, and smells. In recent decades, this traditional appreciation for beauty has tapered off somewhat, though more recently there has been a growing resurgence in many parts of the Catholic world.

Hopefully your parish has liturgies that are adorned with splendid music, tasteful statues, and articulate homilies in an exquisite church building—liturgies that would captivate a young skeptic like Paul Claudel were he to rush into your parish church to escape the rain.

If that is not the case, perhaps there are ways that you and your family can encourage and assist your pastor in improving that external beauty which does so much for our internal dispositions and our reverential attitude.

However, even if that is not possible, know that there is a beauty beyond those externals, the beauty of the "fairest of the children of men" (Psalm 45:2) who comes to meet you and your family and to usher you into the source of all that is true, good, and beautiful.

St. Augustine wrote in the *Confessions*, "Late have I loved Thee, O Beauty so ancient and so new; late have I loved Thee!"* Late—but it is never *too* late to love him better, the One to whom all earthly beauty points, the One whose beauty we and our children will, please God, one day behold together for all eternity.

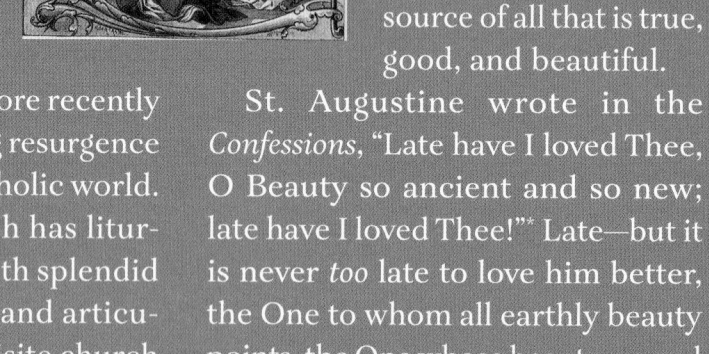

---

* Joseph Ratzinger, *Introduction to Christianity*, trans. J. R. Foster (San Francisco: Ignatius Press, 1990), 40–41.

Beautiful artwork for the wall, especially today, does not cost much more than the aluminum-framed posters that dominate many homes. Perhaps some of those posters, especially in the statelier parts of the home, like a living or dining room, might be replaced by a couple of nicely framed oil painting reproductions.

Keeping a clean house and tending to the yard also contribute to a clean, bright, beautiful home.

Family communication is another place to instill beauty. In our conversations with each other, our hospitality to guests, our good manners, even the way that we disagree with each other—these can be either ugly or beautiful. It is a matter of setting and keeping expectations for courtesy that gives rise to beauty in family interactions.

Exposing children to timeless art, literature, and music cultivates in them an instinct for the truly beautiful. As children grow up, take them to places where beauty is appreciated, such as museums, concert halls, and the theater.

In these matters less is often more. Learning in depth about two or three paintings and seeing only those at a nearby museum, or even online, will do more to pique their interest than dragging them through endless exhibits. Studying and listening to a single Mozart piano sonata at home might be a better approach than sitting through two hours of live classical music. As the children grow up, of course, the hope is that their capacity to experience beauty will also grow and they will appreciate more and longer exposure to beautiful art.

Finally, nature itself is a marvelous (and usually free) way to experience beauty. Most of us live in a world dominated by asphalt, plastic, and digital screens. Getting in touch with the three-dimensional world of creation, rather than the two-dimensional world of the screen, is particularly vital today.

Exposure to natural beauty can instill a sense of wonder that ultimately leads us back to God. "The proud are so full of themselves," Thomas Dubay wrote, "that there is little room to marvel at anything else. Saints are typically awestruck at an insect, a flower, a star because they are burning with love and rooted in a perceiving honesty."[3] Taking a walk through the

---

[3] Thomas Dubay, *The Evidential Power of Beauty: Science and Theology Meet* (San Francisco: Ignatius Press, 1999), 77.

woods, with all our senses open, can sometimes do more for our spiritual lives than an hour of mental prayer.

Just as your family is the place where your children will first experience truth and goodness, so will they first experience beauty in your family. There are countless ways to include beauty in your life. Even if they don't always compare to sung Vespers in the Cathedral of Notre Dame, these small touches may one day be fondly recalled by your children as brief glimpses of God.

> What are some ways that you can expose your children to more authentic beauty?
>
> Do you have a favorite piece of classical or sacred music? If so, play it for your family this week. Invite them to share whether the music moved them. Do they have a favorite piece that they can share with the rest of the family?
>
> Walk through your home and consider: What elements of beauty are present? Are there areas that could benefit from a simple piece of art or plant life?
>
> Challenge yourself to instill beauty in your family communication this week. After a week or so of concentrated effort, reflect on any impact you see your efforts having on the rest of the family.

A Personal Reflection from Parents
— Daniel and Kari Flynn —

The domestic church is most beautiful when the home is spreading seeds of virtue among all who pass through it. Exterior beauty and order can create an atmosphere that welcomes God and virtue more easily.

When we were newly married, we agreed that creating a beautiful home was high on the priority list. Being on a teacher's salary, our budget was meager, so we chose wisely and intentionally what we purchased.

We picked out few knick-knacks but bought classic furniture and decor that would stand the test of time. Dried floral arrangements created welcoming centerpieces, warm paint colors and religious artwork were carefully chosen, and boxes for organizing were installed.

Though the simple, beautiful decor was created in the beginning, as our family grew to now fourteen children after twenty-two years of marriage, the demands of the housework grew as well and was hard to keep up. We have learned that beauty in the home does not mean perfection at all times.

Perfection can come from a disordered desire for control and actually create more angst in the family rather than peace. Seeing piles of Legos on the floor or a sink filled with dirty dishes needed to be approached more with gratitude for the opportunity to serve the souls which the Lord has so generously given to us as gifts. We have learned over the years that a daily twenty-minute cleanup after dinner, with all hands on deck, can help maintain order, while not always perfection.

Sundays are usually spent as family days after morning Mass, hiking a nearby trail, visiting a museum, attending a local festival, or handing out burgers to the homeless, experiencing God in beautiful ways beyond the walls of our home and known only to each child.

Admittedly, as our children grew older, getting out the door for these excursions was often filled with strife and complaints. Limited screen time, little access to video games, and encouragement to read edifying literature was not always welcomed by our teens.

However, our adult children have since encouraged us to forge ahead in these endeavors because these were some of the most memorable and powerful experiences of their childhood as they look back. Often it takes more work and it can be hard to seek something better to love.

By expanding our children's exposure to beauty both inside and outside of the home, we are expanding the capacity for God in their souls.

BL. JOHN OF FIESOLE (Fra Angelico)

Religious
Born in Italy
D. 1455
Feast day: February 18

Whatever is true, whatever is honorable, whatever is just, whatever is pure, whatever is lovely, whatever is gracious, if there is any excellence, if there is anything worthy of praise, think about these things.

PHILIPPIANS 4:8

JOHN OF FIESOLE (FRA ANGELICO) was born near Florence around the year 1400. He began painting as a young boy and studied under the tutelage of a local painting master. Though Florence was the cultural center of Europe at the time, young Guido, as he was known, resisted the allure of fame and fortune and asked for admission to a Dominican convent at the age of twenty. He took the name Br. Giovanni (John) and spent most of his life in prayerful work within Dominican convents. He was humble and modest and was called *Angelico* ("Angelic One") because his paintings depicted calm, religious scenes and because of his deep prayerfulness and piety. Though he did serve as prior of the convent in Fiesole (hence his official name), his preference was to remain in the background. When Pope Eugenius asked him to serve as archbishop of Florence, for instance, Fra Angelico respectfully declined, preferring the quiet and simple life of a friar.

As a painter, he spent much of his career on projects within the monastery of San Marco, where he and other friars moved in 1436. Among these is his famous and incomparable fresco of the Annunciation. For four years, from 1445 to 1449, he also painted frescoes in several chapels of the Vatican Palace. The most famous are in the Niccoline Chapel and depict scenes from the lives of St. Steven and St. Lawrence. They are considered by some to be the very pinnacle of the era's "Christian humanism."

In the tradition of icon painters from the Eastern Church, Fra Angelico believed that his painting was a form of prayer. It is said that he wept continuously while painting scenes of the Crucifixion. His art is simple and pure, with figures carefully arranged and usually unadorned. Michelangelo once said of Fra Angelico, "One has to believe that this good monk has visited paradise and been allowed to choose his models there." The simple beauty of his paintings lifts the well-disposed viewer to the contemplation of God. True to his Dominican vocation, he was a preacher of the Gospel, proclaiming the Good News with his words and with his life but also through the beautiful paintings, which were the overflow of his prayer, labor, and study.

St. John Paul II named Fra Angelico the patron of artists because his life and art remind us so powerfully of the importance of beauty in our faith. Fra Angelico allowed beauty to draw his own soul ever closer to the Lord, and through the centuries, the Lord has drawn countless souls to himself through Fra Angelico's beautiful paintings. Though his artistic talent was prodigious, it was his own holiness of life that imbued these paintings with an otherworldly peace that continues to inspire us today.

> Heavenly Father, you granted your servant Fra Angelico talents that allowed him to unveil your beauty to the world. Help us, through his intercession, to discover ways that we, too, can be agents of beauty in the world today. May we always receive the sources of beauty that you place in our lives as opportunities to draw closer to you, the Source of all beauty. We ask this through our Lord Jesus Christ, your Son, who lives and reigns with you and the Holy Spirit, God forever and ever. Amen.

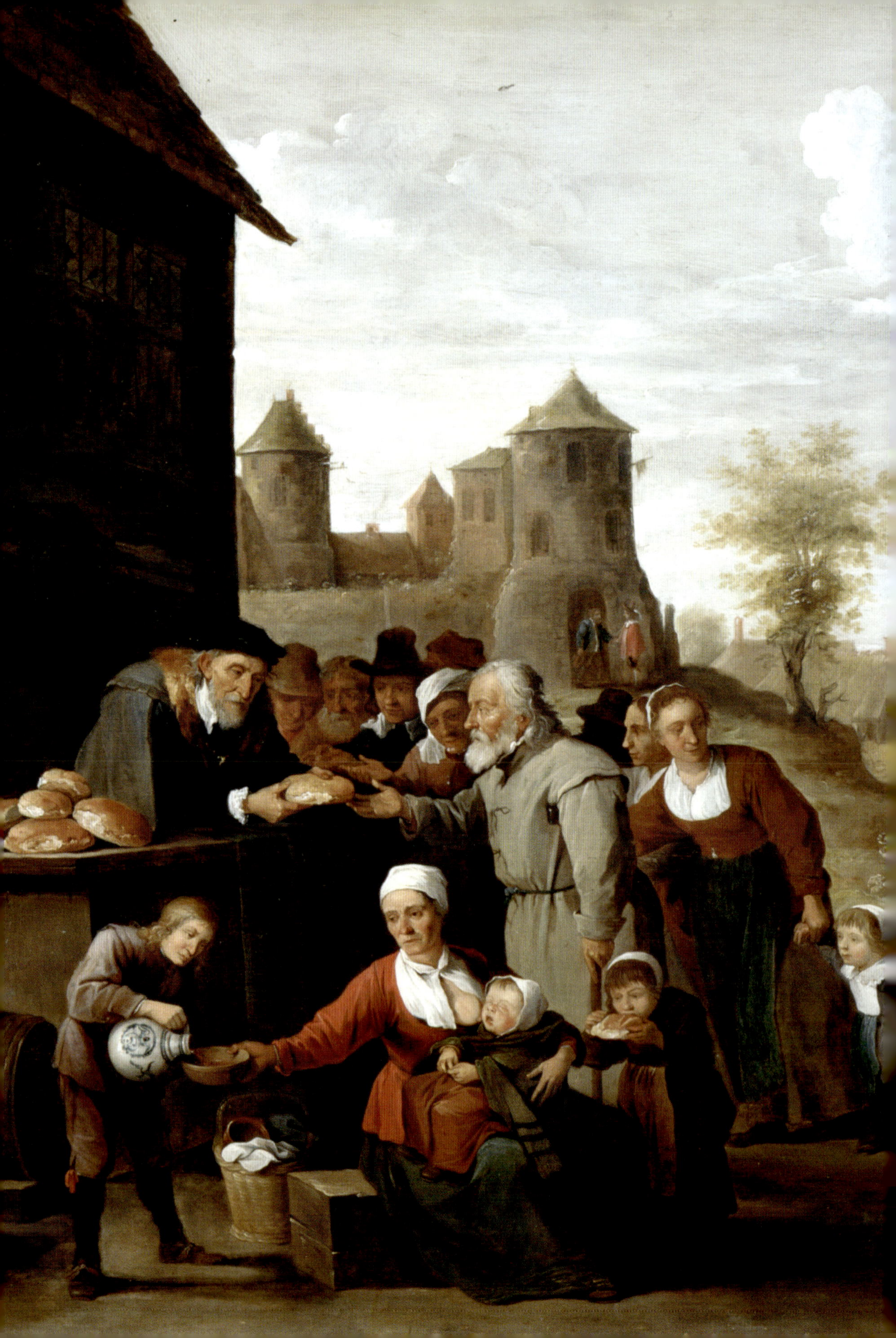

PILLAR IV

Apostolic Formation

"The family, like the Church, ought to be a place where the Gospel is transmitted and from which the Gospel radiates. In a family which is conscious of this mission, all the members evangelize and are evangelized. The parents not only communicate the Gospel to their children, but from their children they can themselves receive the same Gospel as deeply lived by them. And such a family becomes the evangelizer of many other families, and of the neighborhood of which it forms part."

POPE ST. PAUL VI
Apostolic Exhortation *Evangelii Nuntiandi*

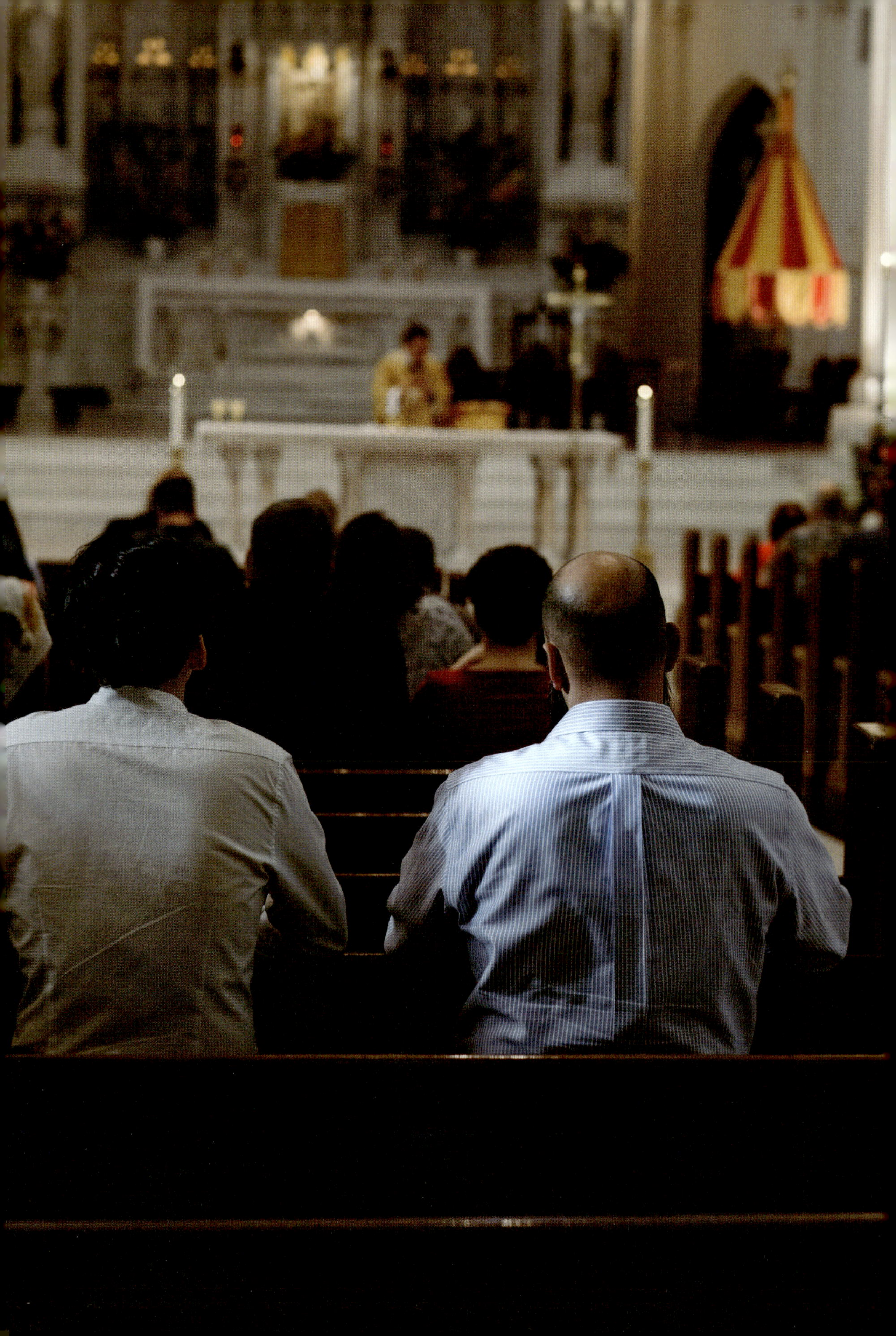

INTRODUCTION TO APOSTOLIC FORMATION

A FRIEND OF MINE WAS ONCE at a restaurant when the building across the street suddenly caught fire. Firetrucks arrived, hoses were laid out, and several firefighters went into the building to rescue anyone trapped inside. My friend and his dinner companions rushed outside to help but were politely yet firmly asked to leave and "let the professionals handle it." They had no choice but to return to the restaurant, where they reluctantly and quickly finished dinner as people across the street were possibly fighting for their lives.

Historically, when it came to the apostolic commission of the Church—"Go therefore and make disciples of all nations" (Matt 28:19)—too often laypeople were politely asked to let the professionals handle it.

Even several decades after the Second Vatican Council decisively reaffirmed the right and duty of the lay faithful to engage in the apostolic mission of the Church, there is still too much disengagement of laypeople from this essential element of the Church's life. Laypeople themselves often have too modest a view of their apostolic role.

A new generation of Catholics, intentionally and confidently apostolic—raised by families like yours—is needed to unleash more of the Church's apostolic potential that has laid dormant for too long.

The Church is quite clear on the matter. In addition to the clergy, the Second Vatican Council declared, "the laity likewise share in the priestly, prophetic, and royal office of Christ and therefore have their own share in the mission of the whole people of God in the Church and in the world."[1] That is not simply a commission from the Church:

> The laity derive the right and duty to the apostolate from their union with Christ the head; incorporated into Christ's Mystical Body through Baptism and strengthened by the power of the Holy

---

[1] Second Vatican Council, Decree on the Apostolate of the Laity *Apostolicam Actuositatem* (November 18, 1965), § 2.

Spirit through Confirmation, they are assigned to the apostolate by the Lord Himself.[2]

While laypeople are sometimes called upon to assist in more formal evangelization efforts, their normal field of apostolate is their everyday lives, families, and work. "Since the laity, in accordance with their state of life, live in the midst of the world and its concerns, they are called by God to exercise their apostolate in the world like leaven, with the ardor of the spirit of Christ."[3]

Through his Church, Jesus asks every Catholic to be a part of his saving mission, in all "those things which make up the temporal order, namely, the good things of life and the prosperity of the family, culture, economic matters, the arts and professions, the laws of the political community, international relations, and other matters of this kind."[4]

This fourth pillar of formation might be the most daunting to parents. After all, human, spiritual, and intellectual formation are more or less contained within the walls of the home, parish, and school. Apostolic formation, of its very nature, means going out and encountering others, even strangers, with all the unpredictability that goes along with it.

In addition, many Catholic parents were raised in families that did not emphasize this element of Christian life and might feel somewhat adrift as they think about forming it in their children.

The following chapters endeavor to provide some practical advice that can strengthen the confidence of parents forging the next generation of Christian apostles. The most basic requirement, and the subject of the first chapter, is that children develop the interpersonal skills needed to interact well with others, a crucial element of formation even apart from its apostolic value. The second chapter will consider the underlying attitude of all apostolate, which is the love of souls and taking seriously our duty to help them to grow in holiness and attain eternal life. The third chapter will consider ways to address the disputed issues of our day through the study of apologetics. The fourth chapter delves into the indispensable role of parents in helping their children discover and respond to their divine vocation. Finally, we will explore the apostolic value of hope. The

---

[2] Second Vatican Council, *Apostolicam Actuositatem*, § 3.
[3] Second Vatican Council, *Apostolicam Actuositatem*, § 2.
[4] Second Vatican Council, *Apostolicam Actuositatem*, § 7.

most effective apostolate today is often the steady witness of hope that Christians provide to a world caught in the grip of despair.

Formation for the apostolate, however, goes beyond skills and attitudes. All the areas of formation contribute to our children's apostolic fruitfulness. The human, spiritual, and intellectual pillars culminate in this fourth and final pillar.

All the hard work you do, in other words, in forming your children will bear fruit in their apostolate. Your beautiful work as good parents will contribute to the salvation of many souls, well beyond the confines of your family.

The Christian life is never turned inwards. Our religion is ordered not only to ourselves but to others, to their union with God. We Catholics have received, in the gift of faith, the greatest gift imaginable. It is our duty, in fact our joy, to introduce others to Jesus and to his Church.

Your efforts to form your children into future apostles will give them the tools they need to share their faith and to rejoice in bringing others into a saving relationship with the Lord. It is in this fourth pillar that the many sacrifices you make as parents will most deeply redound to your joy one day when you stand before the Lord to give an account of your life.

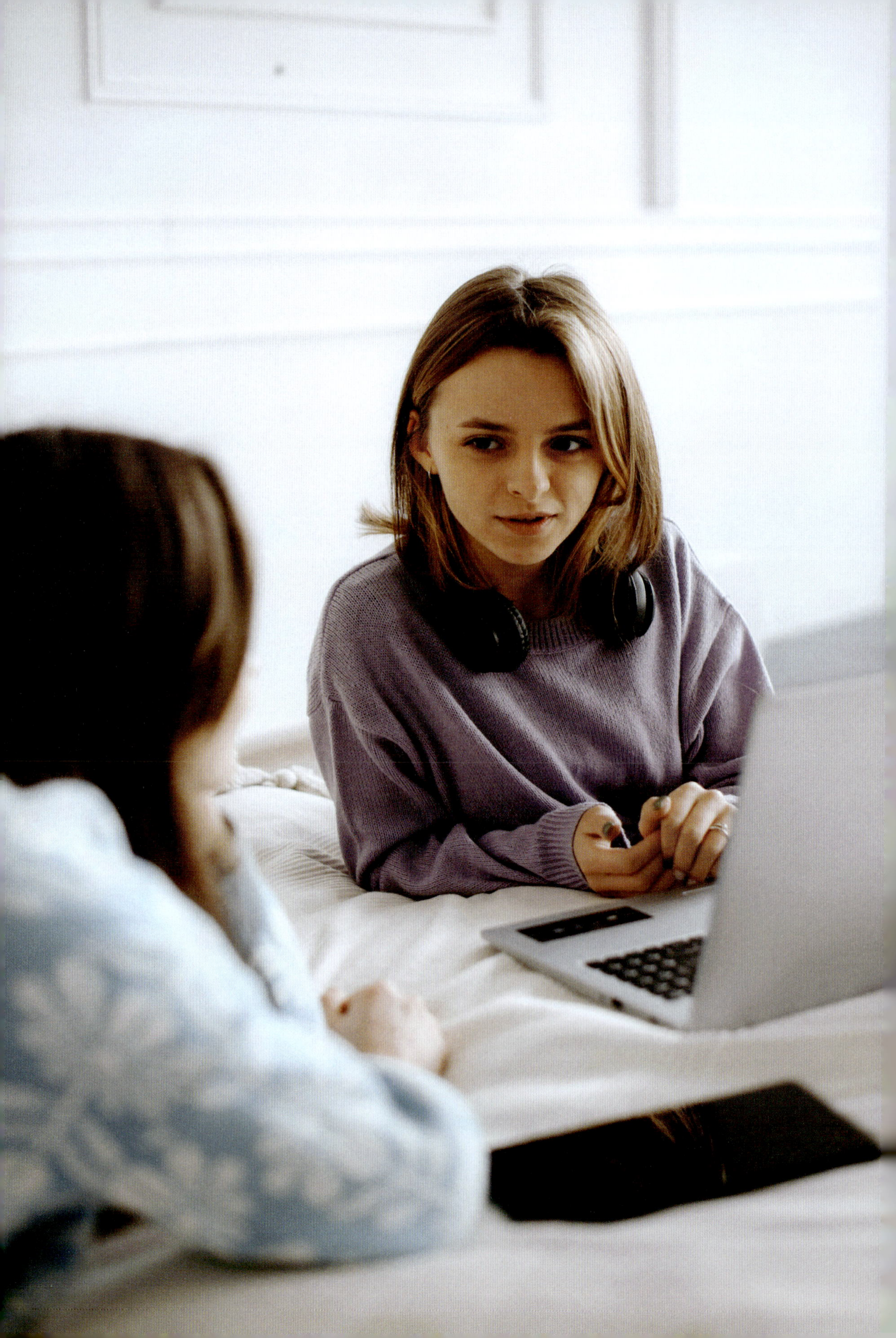

INTERPERSONAL SKILLS

THERE IS A LEGEND OF an old, suffering knight who guarded the Holy Grail. He tells a group of travelers that he will entrust the sacred chalice to the one who asks the right question. One asks, "How can I know the truth?" Wrong question. Another asks, "How do I get to heaven?" That, too, is the wrong question. The third traveler asks, "What are you suffering?" That one received the Grail. He was the only one who was thinking of someone besides himself.

In the age of smartphones and social media—despite their pretensions to enhance our opportunities to communicate—interpersonal skills are suffering. We are made for communion with God and others, however, so proficiency in human interactions is essential for a flourishing life.

These skills are also an indispensable ingredient for anyone who wishes to be an effective apostle. Courtesy warms hearts, opens minds, heals divisions, and overcomes misunderstandings. Engaging well with others clears a path for the Gospel. This chapter offers some suggestions to develop these skills in your family.

Focus on Others

Mother Teresa famously said that "thoughtfulness is the beginning of great sanctity."[1] In our prosperous time, when we are all a little more spoiled and demanding, how can we grow in thoughtfulness?

We can start by simply being interested in others. There is something worth learning about everything and everyone; we just have to find it. Boredom is typically a sign of being stuck in our own lives and our ego.

Another sign of thoughtfulness is respect. When parents show consideration for the dignity of others, whether their own peers, authority figures, or those who serve us, children will do the same. Polite and mannerly children absorb those habits in the family.

---

[1] Teresa of Calcutta, quoted in Malcolm Muggeridge, *Something Beautiful for God: Mother Teresa of Calcutta* (New York: Collins, 1971), 69.

ST. JOHN HENRY NEWMAN'S DEFINITION OF A GENTLEMAN

It is almost a definition of a gentleman to say he is one who never inflicts pain. This description is both refined and, as far as it goes, accurate. He is mainly occupied in merely removing the obstacles which hinder the free and unembarrassed action of those about him; and he concurs with their movements rather than takes the initiative himself.

His benefits may be considered as parallel to what are called comforts or conveniences in arrangements of a personal nature: like an easy chair or a good fire, which do their part in dispelling cold and fatigue, though nature provides both means of rest and animal heat without them. The true gentleman in like manner carefully avoids whatever may cause a jar or a jolt in the minds of those with whom he is cast;—all clashing of opinion, or collision of feeling, all restraint, or suspicion, or gloom, or resentment; his great concern being to make every one at their ease and at home.

He has his eyes on all his company; he is tender towards the bashful, gentle towards the distant, and merciful towards the absurd; he can recollect to whom he is speaking; he guards against unseasonable allusions, or topics which may irritate; he is seldom prominent in conversation, and never wearisome.

He makes light of favours while he does them, and seems to be receiving when he is conferring. He never speaks of himself except when compelled, never defends himself by a mere retort, he has no ears for slander or gossip, is scrupulous in imputing motives to those who interfere with him, and interprets every thing for the best. He is never mean or little in his disputes, never takes unfair advantage, never mistakes personalities or sharp sayings for arguments, or insinuates evil which he dare not say out. From a long-sighted prudence, he observes the maxim of the ancient sage, that we should ever conduct ourselves towards our enemy as if he were one day to be our friend.[*]

---

[*] John Henry Newman, *The Idea of a University* (London: Longmans, Green, 1907), 208–9.

At the seminary we have a "speaking tradition" (which I learned from my father's experience at Washington and Lee University in the 1960s) that is simple: you should acknowledge, by word or gesture, people who you pass in the hallways or on campus. It is a small but important mark of respect that is easy for every child to do.

Simple kindness is also a sign of thoughtfulness. The other day, someone at the seminary dropped a plate of food at dinnertime. I wasn't pleased with the food scattered all over the floor, but I was really pleased by the response. Nobody laughed, clapped, or joked at the expense of the young man who dropped the plate. Several seminarians jumped up, helped him clean up the mess, and made a place at their table for him. They brushed it off with a smile and continued the conversation. The seminary, I realized, is a great place to drop your plate of food.

Children who learn respect and kindness at home will wear their own authority lightly—for instance, by looking after the lonely, reaching out to the outcast, and protecting the underdog among their school-fellows or companions. Any occasion, in fact, which gets children thinking about others, and how their actions affect others, is valuable. Noticing and encouraging such behavior will go a long way towards forming courteous and thoughtful children.

Conversation

Conversation is a particularly important arena for developing interpersonal skills, and it starts with becoming good listeners. There was a prominent surgeon who asked his resident students what the doctor's most important instrument is. The students suggested several medical devices, but he said no; it was a chair, so that he could sit down and listen to his patients!

Here are some pointers for good listening to model and instill in your children:

- If you are in a conversation, put away the phone and *please* don't look at your watch.
- Give verbal and non-verbal feedback (eye contact, head nods, leaning forward).

- Respect the ebb and flow of conversation and resist the temptation to interrupt.
- Try to avoid formulating your response while listening.
- As the conversation progresses, topics might arise that could be brought up if the discussion starts to stall. Practice storing those away and returning to them when the conversation lags.
- Listen empathetically, with an open mind, and avoid being defensive. Listening attentively does not mean agreement.
- Ask yourself if you can summarize what the other person is saying.

In addition to good listening:

- Learn the art of asking open-ended questions. There is nothing wrong with small talk, but many people are eager for more substantial discussions.
- Model cheerfulness. Even when serious matters are discussed, there is a way of doing it that doesn't indulge in anger or cynicism. As Christians our conversations should be seasoned with faith and a supernatural outlook.
- Know what is appropriate subject matter for the occasion.
- Never resort to crass, vulgar, suggestive, or offensive humor. Avoid being too personal or edgy. Self-deprecating humor, in moderation, is often the best.
- Learn how to engage a table with several people without pigeonholing one or two.
- Learn how to discuss difficult issues respectfully. Arguing can be done without quarreling, so to speak. As an aside, be intentional about forgiving and asking for forgiveness in the family. There is no better way to form children in the art of conflict resolution.
- Learn how to end a conversation smoothly.

Naturalness

An atmosphere of naturalness in the family also fosters interpersonal skills. Naturalness means that we do not seek the spotlight and do not intentionally draw attention to ourselves, especially in our dress, speech, and grooming. When parents are modest in their demeanor and avoid affectation and showiness, they prepare children to be pleasant and enjoyable companions.

Naturalness includes formation in etiquette: teaching children to say please and thank you, to eat and drink properly, to greet and introduce people, to attend to guests, and to give a firm handshake while smiling and looking someone in the eye. Good manners are not a way to demonstrate our superior formation; they are a way of putting others at ease and showing respect.

Outside the Family

Finally, families can form children in interpersonal skills by showing them how to interact with people outside the family, including strangers. Consider volunteering for events (at the parish, for example) where children will need to interact with people of all ages.

Visit the less fortunate and lonely, perhaps at a nursing home, even (or especially) if such visits are not entirely comfortable. Such interactions will expand horizons, deepen concern for others, and show your children how to engage with a variety of individuals.

Whether they show it or not, children watch closely when you talk to strangers in a store, for instance, or on a train or airplane. Take a risk and show them how it's done. They will also see how you engage with difficult or eccentric people with tact and understanding.

Interpersonal skills will give your children a big leg up in their personal lives and in their future careers. Even more importantly, these simple courtesies will make your children effective apostles. I once heard a prayer asking God to "make bad people good, and good people nice." There is no reason why we and our children cannot be both good and nice: faithful and courageous apostles whose engaging, pleasant, confident presentation of the Gospel will be all that more credible and appealing.

> Be mindful of whether you model interest in others for your children. Where and how do you set an example for them?
>
> Is there an expectation that good manners will be used in and outside of your family? How can you better support your children to be polite and show respect to others?
>
> Pay attention to how your children engage in conversation. Discuss with your spouse the positive habits they display and whether some gentle course-correction is in order.
>
> What interpersonal skills do you value the most? Do you see a connection between those skills and the pursuit of holiness?

THE DINNER TABLE

SOME YEARS AGO the National Center on Addiction and Substance Abuse at Columbia University issued a study reporting that teens who regularly eat dinner with their family are *four times* less likely to use drugs. The reason is not the food; it is the conversation, the interaction, the sharing, the relationships.

The dinner table is perhaps the single most important place where parents can cultivate the interpersonal skills that make those relationships so rewarding. Here are some ideas for taking advantage of family meals:

- Consistency is key: eating dinner together should be the norm, even when job commitments prevent one parent from being present. If nothing else, find a few times during the week when the whole family can have a meal together. I know some families whose father returns home for dinner on weeknights so that he can be there with his wife and children—even if he has to return to work in the evening. Not possible for everyone, but perhaps for some!

- Children should be involved in preparing for dinner (setting the table for instance) and cleaning up afterwards.
- The television is never on at dinnertime and smartphones and other devices are left in another room.
- Children stay at the table until they are excused, normally at the end of the meal.
- Everyone says something during the meal. Here are some ways to do this:
  - Each person can share the best part of his or her day.
  - Each person can be asked to bring a topic for discussion to the table.
  - Children can be asked to memorize something short (a poem, a snippet from literature, a quote) and recite it at dinner. Discussion about it can follow.
  - Alternatively, one of the parents can read something, perhaps from the Catechism or a life of a saint, for discussion.
- If adult guests are present, it is appropriate to speak somewhat about the children and to the children, but that should not constitute the bulk of the conversation. Children have enough sources of self-absorption already. In addition, adult guests provide an opportunity for children to learn how mature adults interact. If the conversation goes long, the children can be excused after an appropriate length of time.

FORMING FAMILIES, FORMING SAINTS

BL. PIER GIORGIO FRASSATI

Layman
Born in Italy
D. 1925
Feast day: July 4

Let love be genuine; hate what is evil, hold fast to what is good; love one another with brotherly affection; outdo one another in showing honor. Never flag in zeal, be aglow with the Spirit, serve the Lord. Rejoice in your hope, be patient in tribulation, be constant in prayer. Contribute to the needs of the saints, practice hospitality.

Romans 12:9–13

Pier Giorgio Frassati was born into a wealthy family in Turin, Italy, in 1901. His mother was a painter, and his father owned an influential newspaper. Though his mother was not deeply religious and his father was an agnostic, Pier Giorgio showed signs of piety early in life, even obtaining permission to receive daily Communion when he was attending a Jesuit school. Throughout his life, he had a heart for the poor, often giving his small allowance to people who were needy. At the age of seventeen, he joined the St. Vincent de Paul Society and spent much of his spare time serving the sick and the poor, caring for orphans, and assisting the wounded servicemen returning from World War I.

His deep devotion to the Blessed Virgin Mary and to the Holy Eucharist—frequently spending long hours in nighttime adoration—nourished a deep commitment to the Catholic faith. Pier Giorgio was even forced to physically defend his faith at times, first against anti-clerical Communists and later against fascists. He never hid his views, however, even after fascists broke into his family's home one night to attack him and his father. He was a formidable opponent. On the night of that particular attack, Pier Giorgio beat them off and chased them down the street.

Pier Giorgio was a natural leader and had exceptional interpersonal skills. He was vibrant, engaging, and athletic. He had many good friends and shared his faith with them with naturalness and sincerity. He enjoyed the theater, opera, and museums. He could quote whole passages from Dante. Pier Giorgio was also an avid outdoorsman and loved hiking, riding horses, skiing, and mountain climbing. He would often organize climbing expeditions and use them as opportunities to bring friends to Mass, read Scripture, and pray the Rosary. He loved to laugh and was renowned among his friends for his good-natured practical jokes. Pier Giorgio's sister, Luciana, said of her brother, "He represented the finest in Christian youth: pure, happy, enthusiastic about everything that is good and beautiful."

After what would be his final mountain climb, he wrote a note on a photograph: "*Verso L'Alto,*" which means, "To the heights!" This phrase has come to encapsulate his whole approach to life.

Just before he could graduate from university in 1925, Pier Giorgio contracted polio, probably from the sick whom he tended in the poverty-stricken neighborhoods of Turin. Even at the end, as he lay dying, he scribbled a message to a friend, asking him to take certain medicines to a poor man whom he had been visiting. During Pier Giorgio's funeral procession, his family was shocked to see thousands—mostly poor—line the streets of the city to bid farewell to this remarkable young man whose attractive humanity brought so many souls closer to his beloved Lord.

> Heavenly Father, your son Pier Giorgio Frassati developed the human gifts you bestowed on him so that he could be all things to all people and draw many souls to you. Help us, through his example and intercession, to grow in our capacity to engage others through our conversations, friendships, and attentiveness to their needs. May our family be a source of radiant joy for others so that they may draw near to the banquet of eternal life. We ask this through our Lord Jesus Christ, your Son, who lives and reigns with you and the Holy Spirit, God forever and ever. Amen.

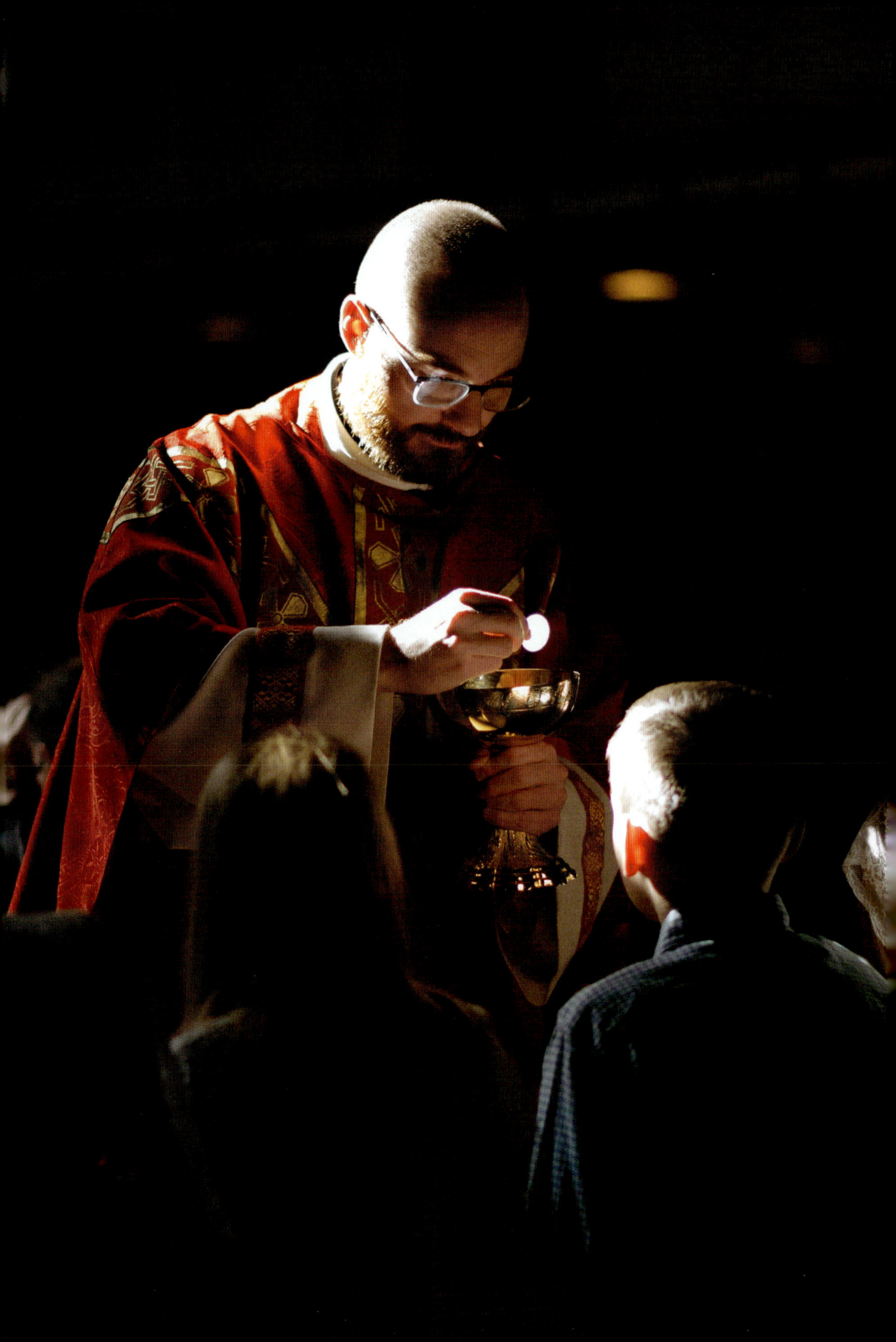

LOVE FOR SOULS

THE GOAL OF A DOCTOR is to restore good health to those who are ill. Christian apostles are like doctors of souls, striving to restore supernatural health to those who suffer from spiritual illnesses. Unlike doctors, though, who can only stave off bodily death temporarily, apostles aspire, through God's grace, to prepare immortal souls for eternal life.

Salvation of souls only makes sense if we believe that souls need saving. Our Lord spoke about the dangers of hell far more than he spoke about the joys of heaven—not because he considered heaven unimportant, but because he loved us too much to remain silent about the danger of damnation.

We also must love souls too much to stay silent. The magician Penn Jillette, an avowed atheist, made this point in a memorable way:

> If you believe that there's a heaven and a hell, and people could be going to hell or not getting eternal life, and you think that it's not really worth telling them this because it would make it socially awkward . . . how much do you have to hate somebody to believe everlasting life is possible and not tell them that? I mean, if I believed, beyond the shadow of a doubt, that a truck was coming at you, and you didn't believe that truck was bearing down on you, there is a certain point where I tackle you. And this is *more* important than that.[1]

Jesus used the image of salt to describe the work of apostles who carry on his redemptive work. "You are the salt of the earth; but if salt has lost its taste, how shall its saltness be restored?" (Matt 5:13). Salt has three effects: it protects from corruption, it instills thirst, and it enhances taste.

First, salt protects from corruption. It is in giving good doctrine that apostles can preserve souls from the corrosion of worldly philosophies. This does not mean that we badger or bludgeon anyone into the faith. Neither is it a false charity where we cowardly shy away from tough teachings or apologize for our faith. Rather it is the charitable teaching of Jesus, always strong and clear, and never spiteful or disparaging.

---

[1] Beinzee, "A Gift of a Bible," YouTube video, July 8, 2010, 5:11, https://www.youtube.com/watch?v=6md638smQd8&t=145s.

Sharing the Gospel means being confident in its goodness, confident that the teachings of the Church, even the difficult ones, always contribute to life in its fullness. It means the conviction to speak with authority, not like the scribes and pharisees, not like popular wisdom or the mass media. At times, giving good doctrine will be difficult. Like Jesus, we will sometimes be rejected. That does not always mean that we've failed.

The apostle patiently waits, always looking for opportunities to speak about the Good News of Jesus. I am reminded of a story about Lord Collingwood, Lord Nelson's second-in-command at the famous Battle of

WHERE TO EXERCISE APOSTOLATE

- **WITHIN YOUR FAMILY.** It should be normal to discuss apostolic efforts among family members. Parents should not hesitate to talk (kindly) about their own friends who do not know the Lord or who are estranged from the Church. Children can do the same. When a child expresses concern that a friend at school is not going to church, for instance, you might encourage an invitation to your own church one Sunday.

- **AMONG FAMILIES.** Your witness as Christian parents will have a profound effect on other families. In your upright way of life, in your fidelity to each other and commitment to the indissolubility and sacredness of marriage, you are uniquely suited to be Catholic witnesses. When possible, gather like-minded families together to discuss the struggles and opportunities of parenting today and to give the children opportunities to meet and play. Small groups of families that meet for discussion, mutual support, and recreation can be enormously fruitful.

- **IN THE PARISH.** Helping engaged couples prepare for marriage, teaching catechesis, supporting married couples and families in crisis, and bringing fallen away or non-Catholics to prayer or classes of adult religious formation are all ways to assist the parish's apostolic efforts.

- **WITH THE DISADVANTAGED.** The Second Vatican Council taught:

Trafalgar.[2] He never left his home in Northumberland without a handful of acorns in his pocket. As he walked along the hills with his dog, Bunce, he would stop every now and again, lean down, and press an acorn into the soil when he saw a fine spot for an oak tree. He knew that eighteenth-century England was protected by the "wooden walls" of the Royal Navy, and her survival depended on having enough oak trees to keep those wooden walls strong. He never missed an opportunity to plant

---

[2] See Dudley Pope, *Life in Nelson's Navy* (Looe, Cornwall: House of Stratus, 1981), 30.

---

parents have the task of training their children from childhood on to recognize God's love for all men. By example especially they should teach them little by little to be solicitous for the material and spiritual needs of their neighbor. The whole family in its common life, then, should be a sort of apprenticeship for the apostolate.*

Simply speaking kindly to homeless people and bringing them some food can leave a powerful impression on young hearts. Taking your children to visit the elderly who have no one else to visit, volunteering at a parish clothing drive, or helping at a soup kitchen or other outreach are all great ways to instill an apostolic instinct in your children.

- **IN SOCIETY.** All honorable work contributes to the good of society and can be an instrument of the apostolate. When we infuse a Christian spirit in our workplace, for example, we can quietly draw souls to the Lord. On a broader level, Catholics promote the common good by fulfilling their civic duties, by remaining involved in public affairs through voting, political and economic discussions, and even by holding political office or other positions (such as sitting on school boards) that can have a deep impact on the wider culture.

---

* Second Vatican Council, Decree on the Apostolate of the Laity *Apostolicam Actuositatem* (November 18, 1965), § 30.

another oak tree, and some of those trees still flourish centuries later, in the era of the nuclear submarine.

We Christians can be no less committed to finding opportunities to plant new seeds. We take advantage of favorable moments to evangelize in our families, among our friends, and at work when we inject a note of faith into our conversations. We plant seeds when we gently encourage a friend to go to Confession after a long time away, lend a sympathetic ear to someone going through a difficult time, volunteer to bring food and other necessities to the less fortunate, pray outside an abortion clinic and endure the hurtful remarks, or simply smile and make friendly conversation with the person at the grocery store register.

Each of these seeds can grow and become, like a mustard seed, a great tree which "puts forth large branches, so that the birds of the air can make nests in its shade" (Mark 4:32). Like Lord Collingwood, you will be planting trees everywhere you go.

Second, salt instills a thirst for God. It is only through prayer and sacrifice that we can foster that thirst in the hearts of others. This includes our own prayer but also bringing souls to prayer.

A woman once brought a non-Catholic friend to Eucharistic adoration at her parish church. During Benediction, the non-Catholic woman felt an intense power radiating from the monstrance that hit her, almost physically, during the blessing. She turned to her Catholic friend and whispered, "What *is* that?" The Catholic woman, without taking her eyes off Jesus, said, "It's complicated. I'll tell you later." In bringing her to adoration she was doing what good apostles do; she was instilling a thirst for God in the heart of her friend.

Third, salt enhances taste. So many today endure a drab, flavorless existence. It is union with God that restores the relish and joy of life. We Catholics have the secret to happiness and peace, both in this life and in the next, and it is our privilege to share that secret with others by making him visible in our lives.

People become Christian only by meeting other Christians. St. John Paul II said that "the men and women of our own day—often perhaps unconsciously—ask believers not only to 'speak' of Christ, but in a certain sense to 'show' him to them."[3] Being an apostle in every age, but especially

---

[3] Pope John Paul II, Apostolic Letter at the Close of the Great Jubilee of the Year 2000 *Novo Millennio Ineunte* (January 6, 2001), § 16.

in ours, is really a call to holiness so that the Lord can be perceived in the witness of our lives.

Cultivating a love for souls means being convinced that redemption is real, that salvation is necessary, and that there are eternal repercussions in the way we live our lives. It will not always be easy. There will come a time, perhaps many times, when your children ask why your family is Christian, why they have to be different, why "we can't just be like everybody else."

The answer is that we are *not* like everybody else and we do not intend to become like everybody else. This is a healthy and humble exceptionalism that children absorb early on. You and your family have a mission that makes you different.

As "doctors" in the order of grace, you are called to be apostles of God's love, to bring healing and life through the means of sanctification, and to lead many souls to the eternal joys of the heavenly banquet.

Have you ever been called to share the message of salvation with others? Find an age appropriate way to share your experiences with your family. Ask your children what they would do in similar situations.

What seeds are you and your spouse planting to help evangelize those you know? Are there certain family members or friends with whom you feel the Holy Spirit is prompting you to share your faith in a more intentional way?

Do you truly believe that the Catholic Church has the secret to happiness and peace? Why?

Spend time in prayer this week asking for a deeper love of souls—first of all, those of your spouse and children.

LOVE FOR THE CHURCH

Our apostolate as Catholics is never detached from the Body of Christ. Love for souls is inseparable from our love for the Church. For many this has become more difficult in recent years with revelations of sexual abuse by the clergy, doctrinal confusion permitted (or even promoted) by members of the hierarchy, overbearing or indifferent pastors, and religious mediocrity among many of our fellow Catholics.

The Church, however, is not a merely human institution. Neither is she another denomination or simply one voice among many. She is the Bride of Christ, founded by the Lord Jesus to continue his ministry of redemption through space and time. She is the guardian of the deposit of faith, steward of the sacraments as arteries of grace, and mother of all the faithful.

Despite all the human failings of her members, including her shepherds, she remains resplendent, unshakable through the tempests of every age. "It is a very untidy outfit you're hooking up with," Walker Percy wrote to Mary Lee Settle, a fellow novelist, when she became Catholic. "But it's the one thing that will be around till the end."*

---

* Walker Percy, *Signposts in a Strange Land*, ed. Patrick Samway (London: Picador, 2000), xiii.

How can we love the Church more?

- By praying for the Church every day and offering a daily sacrifice for her with the desire to see her grow and thrive.

- By being faithful to her teachings, even those which are most counter-cultural. Just as parents should reinforce each other's authority with their children, so should parents reinforce the Church's authority by discussing and promoting even her difficult teachings.

- By loving her shepherds, particularly those who care for us, such as our pastor, our bishop, and the Holy Father. We respect and obey them in all matters under their responsibility, even if sometimes we disagree with their prudential decisions. We also pray earnestly for them, sacrifice for them, and help our children respect and appreciate the gift of their authority. We should give our shepherds the benefit of the doubt whenever possible. They have a difficult and even perilous task for which they will answer to God one day. They should at least be able to count on our prayers!

- By promoting unity in the Church. The Evil One (*diabolos* means "separator") is constantly sowing seeds of disunity. Wise Catholics will be on the lookout for a diabolical spirit of disunity in their hearts, in their families, in their conversations, and in the websites and news sources they read. The goal is not a false unity that papers over disagreements, but a genuine unity that is the fruit of charity and supernatural faith.

- The best way to love the Church is by growing in holiness and fostering the holiness of your children. Speaking in France, St. John Paul II once remarked, "Just when night engulfs us, we must think about the dawn coming, we must believe that every morning the Church is revived through her saints."[†] Saints are an endless source of renewal for the Church. Your growth in holiness is the greatest gift you can offer her.

[†] Pope John Paul II, "Homily for the Eucharistic Celebration on the Occasion of the 15th Centenary of the Baptism of King Clovis at the Airport of Reims," September 22, 1996, quoted in Jason Evert, *Saint John Paul the Great: His Five Loves* (Lakewood, CO: Totus Tuus, 2014), 204–5.

FORMING FAMILIES, FORMING SAINTS

ST. TERESA OF CALCUTTA

Virgin
Born in Macedonia
D. 1997
Feast day: September 5

"Abide in me, and I in you. As the branch cannot bear fruit by itself, unless it abides in the vine, neither can you, unless you abide in me. I am the vine, you are the branches. He who abides in me, and I in him, he it is that bears much fruit, for apart from me you can do nothing."

JOHN 15:4–5

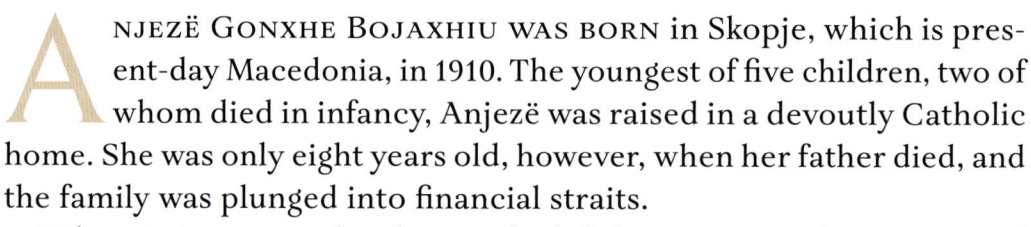

ANJEZË GONXHE BOJAXHIU WAS BORN in Skopje, which is present-day Macedonia, in 1910. The youngest of five children, two of whom died in infancy, Anjezë was raised in a devoutly Catholic home. She was only eight years old, however, when her father died, and the family was plunged into financial straits.

When Anjezë turned eighteen, she left home to join the Institute of the Blessed Virgin Mary in Ireland, also known as the Loreto Nuns. She particularly wished to serve the poor in India, so she was assigned to their house in Darjeeling. In 1931, she made her first profession of vows, taking the religious name of Teresa after St. Thérèse of Lisieux. Mother Teresa, as she became known, spent almost twenty years teaching at a Catholic girls' school in Calcutta. When she was thirty-six, she was traveling by train to the motherhouse in Darjeeling for her annual retreat when she heard a distinct call from Jesus to "give up all and to follow Him into the slums—to serve Him in the poorest of the poor." Mother Teresa said, "I knew it was His will and that I had to follow Him. There was no doubt that it was going to be His work."

After two years of discernment and testing by her spiritual director and the archbishop, Mother Teresa founded the Missionaries of Charity on August 17, 1948. Living in the poorest villages of Calcutta, dressed in a white sari and sandals—the common attire of an Indian woman—she visited families, washed the sores of children, cared for the elderly lying sick on the side of the road, and nursed those dying of hunger and tuberculosis. She opened a school for poor children. Over time she received the help of many who donated food, clothing, and supplies.

Within months, the foundation started to attract other women, beginning with some of her former students. By the 1990s, the Missionaries of Charity had set up houses on every continent, including nearly every Communist country. By the time of Mother Teresa's death in 1997, the Missionaries of Charity numbered about four thousand sisters across 610 foundations in 123 countries. Though she became an international figure and exercised enormous influence on the world stage, Mother Teresa remained deeply humble and devoted to her "call within a call" to quench the thirst of Jesus by serving the poorest of the poor.

Though at first, Mother Teresa received many interior locutions guiding her and calling her to trust in God, she soon experienced a painful inner darkness, a complete loss of feeling God's presence, which lasted the rest of her life. Her love for souls, her exercise of charity, became pure and absent all selfishness. Jesus asked her to slake his infinite thirst for souls and to find himself in the "distressing disguise of the poor" without benefit to herself, even without interior consolation. This she did with supernatural generosity and courage until the day of her death on September 5, 1997.

> Loving Father, you called St. Teresa of Calcutta to be a radiant witness of your love for souls. May her love for every person inspire us to see you in those around us, including those afflicted with the deepest material and spiritual poverty. May our hearts grow to embrace all the souls we encounter and to earnestly desire their well-being on earth and their salvation for all eternity. Through our Lord Jesus Christ, your Son, who lives and reigns with you and the Holy Spirit, God forever and ever. Amen.

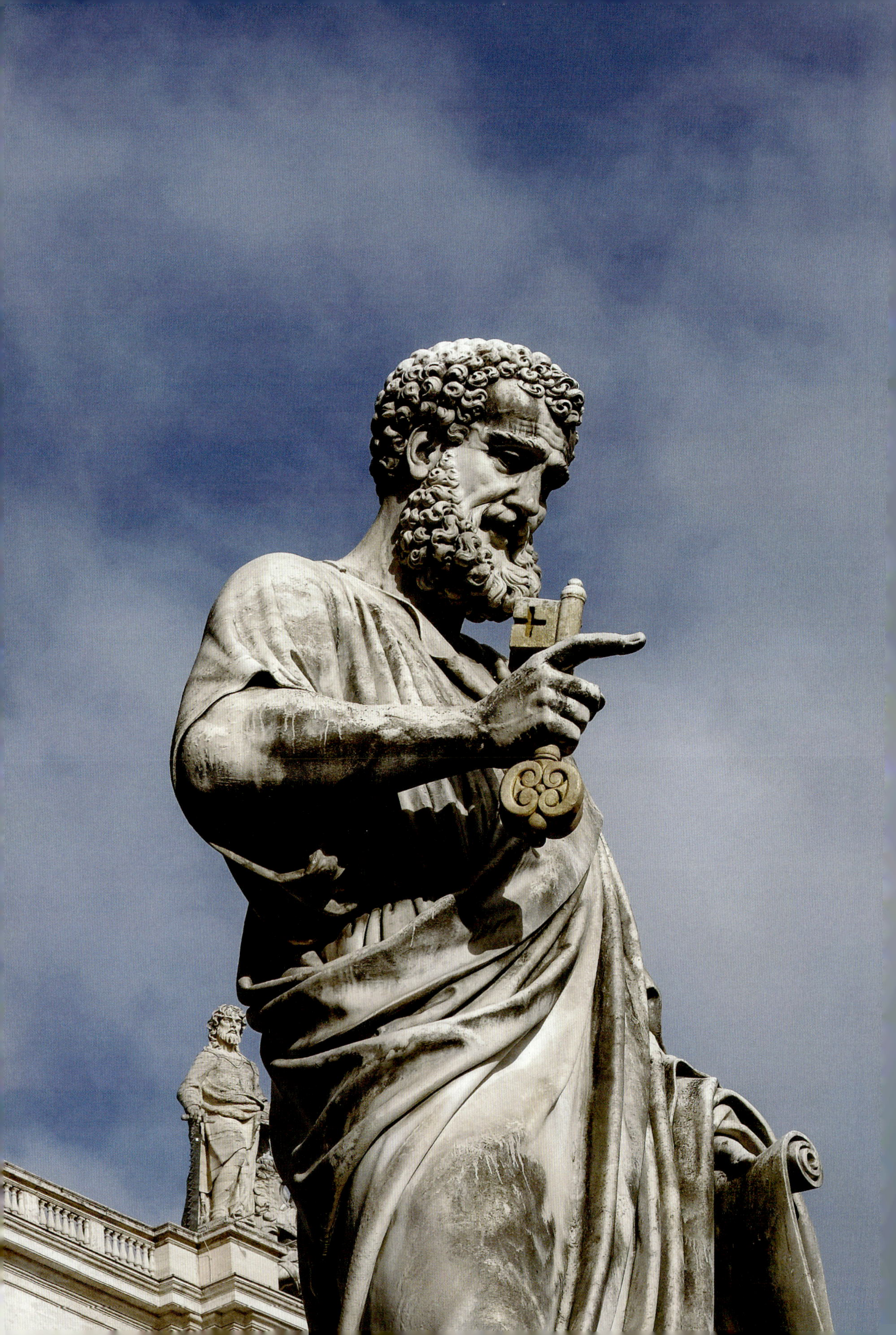

APOLOGETICS

G. K. Chesterton's Father Brown novels are about a quiet priest who stumbles into crime scenes and solves them with shrewd insights into human nature. In the first novel, *The Blue Cross*, the villain, Flambeau, is a thief masquerading as a priest. He succeeds in fooling the authorities and almost deceives Father Brown until he makes a fatal mistake.

During a conversation Flambeau says, "These modern infidels appeal to their reason, but who can look at those millions of worlds and not feel that there may well be wonderful universes above us where reason is utterly unreasonable?" At that point Father Brown sees through the charade and turns Flambeau in to the police.

As Flambeau is being arrested, he asks how Father Brown saw through his disguise. "You attacked reason," said Father Brown. "It's bad theology."[1]

As Catholics we are confident that God, who is truth itself, can never contradict himself. There can be no real conflict between our beliefs and the legitimate conclusions of reason. The Church's teachings never contradict the truth revealed in the Scriptures, the truths discovered by philosophy, or the truths uncovered by science.

When there is a perceived contradiction, we can be quite sure that we have misunderstood Catholic teaching, or that we have reached erroneous conclusions from Scripture, philosophy, or science.

The first pope exhorted the early Christians to "always be prepared to make a defense [Greek: *apología*] to anyone who calls you to account for the hope that is in you, yet do it with gentleness and reverence" (1 Pet 3:15).

As that verse suggests, "apologetics" comes from the Greek word meaning "defense," usually a legal defense or a reasoned defense of one's position. By engaging the apparent contradictions between faith and reason, apologetics seeks to defend the faith by showing its cogency and reasonability. Catholics have nothing to fear from the truth, whatever its source.

---

[1] G. K. Chesterton, *The Blue Cross*, in *The Father Brown Omnibus* (New York: Dodd, Mead, 1951), 16.

TEN TOPICS TO JUMP-START YOUR STUDY OF APOLOGETICS

1. How can we know that God exists?
2. Was the Resurrection a literal, historical event?
3. Why do Catholics pray to the saints?
4. How can a good and all-powerful God allow suffering?
5. Can we be saved only through the Catholic Church?
6. Why must I confess my sins to a priest?
7. Why can't women be ordained priests?
8. Why is transgenderism not compatible with Catholic teaching?
9. Why is using pornography a serious sin?
10. Why does the Church teach that same-sex attractions are disordered?

Reasoned thought about Catholic doctrine does not remove all difficulties. Many teachings, after all, we know only from revelation and cannot be apprehended through reason alone. Pascal wrote that "the last proceeding of reason is to recognize that there is an infinity of things which are beyond it. It is but feeble if it does not see so far as to know this."[2]

In the case of truths that we know only through revelation, apologetics can demonstrate that the teaching is never against reason, or irrational, even when it is beyond or above reason. We can show that embracing the faith will never require anyone to do violence to his or her intellect. On the contrary, a candid acknowledgement of perceived difficulties and opposing arguments shows a confidence in the truth of Catholic teaching and a willingness to engage any and all well-disposed interlocutors.

There are at least three good reasons for your family to study apologetics.

First, because we believe that the Catholic faith is true and everyone has a right to hear the truth. In baptism every Catholic receives a personal, apostolic commission from the Lord to help others embrace that truth. The more convinced we are by the truth, beauty, and goodness of the Gospel—the full Gospel proclaimed by the Catholic Church—the more earnestly we desire others to receive it. The study of apologetics can help us to articulate the faith in ways that others, whether non-Catholics or fallen-away Catholics, are more likely to grasp it, appreciate its truth and splendor, and ultimately embrace it.

Second, we study apologetics because there are many prejudices and misunderstandings about the Catholic faith which impede others from accepting it. As Venerable Fulton Sheen once wrote,

> There are not over a hundred people in the United States who hate the Catholic Church. There are millions, however, who hate what they wrongly believe to be the Catholic Church. . . . As a matter of fact, if we Catholics believed all of the untruths and lies which were said against the Church, we probably would hate the Church a thousand times more than they do.[3]

One person, for instance, believes that the Church discriminates unjustly against women by forbidding their priestly ordination. Another

---

[2] Blaise Pascal, *Pensées*, trans. W. F. Trotter (New York: E. P. Dutton, 1958), no. 267.
[3] Fulton J. Sheen, preface to *Radio Replies*, by Leslie Rumble and Charles Mortimer Carty, 3 vols. (Radio Replies Press Society, 1938; repr. Tan Books, 1979, 2012), ix. Citation refers to the 2012 TAN edition.

TEN SCRIPTURE VERSES TO MEMORIZE

On the Primacy of Peter
"You are Peter, and on this rock I will build my Church, and the gates of Hades shall not prevail against it. I will give you the keys of the kingdom of heaven, and whatever you bind on earth shall be bound in heaven, and whatever you loose on earth shall be loosed in heaven."—Matthew 16:18–19

On Celibacy
"For there are eunuchs who have been so from birth, and there are eunuchs who have been made eunuchs by men, and there are eunuchs who have made themselves eunuchs for the sake of the kingdom of heaven. He who is able to receive this, let him receive it."—Matthew 19:12

On Marian Devotion
"Elizabeth was filled with the Holy Spirit and she exclaimed with a loud cry, 'Blessed are you among women, and blessed is the fruit of your womb! And why is this granted me, that the mother of my Lord should come to me?'"—Luke 1:41–43

On the Real Presence of Jesus in the Eucharist
"He who eats my flesh and drinks my blood has eternal life, and I will raise him up at the last day. For my flesh is food indeed, and my blood is drink indeed."—John 6:54–55

On Confession
"He breathed on them, and said to them, 'Receive the Holy Spirit. If you forgive the sins of any, they are forgiven; if you retain the sins of any, they are retained.'"—John 20:22–23

On Calling Priests "Father"
"For though you have countless guides in Christ, you do not have many fathers. For I became your father in Christ Jesus through the gospel."—1 Corinthians 4:15

On Receiving Holy Communion Worthily
"Anyone who eats and drinks without discerning the body eats and drinks judgment upon himself."—1 Corinthians 11:29

On Apostolic Tradition, Not Only Scripture
"So then, brethren, stand firm and hold to the traditions which you were taught by us, either by word of mouth or by letter."—2 Thessalonians 2:15

On the Church as Pillar and Bulwark of the Truth
"If I am delayed, you may know how one ought to behave in the household of God, which is the Church of the living God, the pillar and bulwark of the truth."—1 Timothy 3:15

On the Need for Good Works
"Faith by itself, if it has no works, is dead."—James 2:17

that the Church requires the elderly and sick to be kept alive for as long as possible, with every medical procedure available, regardless of pain or expense. Another that each word that a pope utters or writes is to be accepted as infallible by Catholics. These are simply mistakes, but very common ones—and difficult to dislodge. Apologetics can help overcome these stubborn preconceptions which pose false obstacles to conversion.

Third, apologetics increases the Catholic's own confidence and love for the faith. Reasoned argumentation can help us appreciate the beauty of our religion, the scriptural and rational roots of its doctrine, and the proportion and balance and interplay among its various teachings. Perhaps even more importantly, apologetics can help us understand and respect the arguments made against our faith, giving us a wider vision and more generous approach to those who disagree with us.

Our intellectual opponents are not personal enemies. The vast majority are not malicious or slow-witted. At the same time, their arguments against Catholic doctrine are not unanswerable. It is true that often in a conversation we do not know to respond. Sometimes, our best answer will be "I don't know but I'll find out!" It is apologetics that gives us the confidence that we *will* find out. We can be certain that someone, somewhere, has thoughtfully considered the objection already and addressed it calmly and thoroughly.

Apologetics is an intellectual instrument that, like any instrument, can be used or misused. The goal is not to vanquish an opponent in a debate. If we wield apologetics like a club, we will probably find ourselves welcoming very few friends into full communion with the Catholic Church. And we may well find ourselves falling deeper and deeper into the sinkhole of spiritual pride.

St. Peter said that we should "be prepared to make a defense to anyone who calls you to account for the hope that is in you"—and then he added "*yet do it with gentleness and reverence*" (1 Pet 3:15, emphasis added). Our explanations of the faith must be delivered calmly, rationally, and charitably. That is how we show reverence both for the doctrines themselves and for the sacred ground which is the human soul.

Zeal for the faith is admirable and must be fostered, today more than ever, but how tragic it would be if the outburst of our own zeal became the very obstacle for another soul in its encounter with the Lord.

Teaching apologetics to your children is not difficult, and it can be both fun and edifying for you as well. Since they are not intended to be comprehensive studies of the faith but rather address specific questions, most apologetics manuals are conveniently divided into short and discrete chapters than can easily be discussed in one sitting. As your children grow up, the questions considered can be more complex and suitable to their age.

With seminarians I find it helpful to start by trying to raise some objections to Catholic teaching, and then addressing the objections one by one.[4] You may also find it helpful to teach, in short lessons, the Catholic approach and then let additional questions arise naturally. It can also be beneficial to memorize some Scripture verses together that have particular relevance for apologetics (such as the examples given in the second sidebar of this chapter).

Our Blessed Lord called himself "the way, the truth, and the life" (John 14:6). This is not simply a listing of three characteristics but rather an

---

[4] This is the approach I take in *Cross Examined: Catholic Responses to the World's Questions* (Steubenville, OH: Emmaus Road Publishing, 2021). Some of the questions addressed in that book can be found in the first sidebar of this chapter.

itinerary in itself. The "way" of discipleship reaches eternal "life" because each touches the "truth" of the Gospel.

Studying apologetics can contribute to a deeper love for the faith we hold dear, a firmer desire for others to embrace it, and a greater boldness to speak about our beloved Jesus and his life-giving doctrine—so that more and more souls may walk on the way of truth towards the joy of eternal life.

> What apologetics resources have you made available to your family?
>
> Consider what apologetics topics are particularly relevant to your family. Are all members of the family equipped to address those topics?
>
> Discuss with your spouse how to naturally implement some apologetics training into your family life. Start slowly and help your children build both knowledge and confidence.
>
> Pray about whether you perceive those who disagree with Church teaching as personal enemies. Do you need a change in perspective in order to more peacefully engage with those who disagree with your beliefs?

ST. MIGUEL PRO

Religious and Martyr
Born in Mexico
D. 1927
Feast day: November 23

The Lord's servant must not be quarrelsome but kindly to everyone, an apt teacher, forbearing, correcting his opponents with gentleness. God may perhaps grant that they will repent and come to know the truth.

2 Timothy 2:24–25

José Ramón Miguel Agustín Pro Juárez (Miguel Pro) was born in 1891 to a prosperous, devout family in Guadalupe, Mexico. Though the country had experience waves of anti-Catholic sentiment since its independence from Spain, by the time Miguel was born, the government had a more tolerant approach. It allowed the Church to operate independently and freely despite its anti-Catholic constitution that had been in place since 1857.

When he was twenty years old, Miguel entered the Jesuit novitiate in El Llano. That same year, a new government was established that steadily intensified persecution of Catholics. The tide of sentiment was turning against the Church again. Miguel's novitiate was closed by government authorities and, together with the other scholastics, Miguel fled to the United States, then to Spain, and finally to Belgium, where he continued his studies for the priesthood. He was ordained in 1925, the very year that President Plutarco Calles, a notorious anti-Catholic, was elected president of Mexico. Despite poor health, Miguel begged to return to his homeland to serve as a priest. His superiors granted his request.

By the time he returned to Mexico in 1926, the government had outlawed all forms of public worship, confiscated Church property, forbidden religious education, and expelled priests from the country.

St. Miguel Pro

This led to a peasant revolt called the Cristero Wars, which lasted until 1929. Their battle cry in the teeth of oppression was *¡Viva Cristo Rey! ¡Viva la Virgen de Guadalupe!* "Long live Christ the King! Long live the Virgin of Guadalupe!" Miguel began his priestly service in disguise. He celebrated Mass, heard confessions, administered the sacraments, and catechized children in the faith—all in secret.

In order to celebrate the sacraments and teach the faith, Miguel adopted many interesting stratagems. For instance, he would arrive at a Catholic home in the middle of the night disguised as a beggar. He showed up at a jail in the garb of a police officer in order to bring Communion to condemned Catholics. He went to fashionable neighborhoods dressed as a well-to-do businessman to beg for the poor. His naturally joyful (and mischievous) temperament helped him through many scrapes and enabled him to continue to serve souls, preach the Gospel, and teach the faith.

Eventually Miguel was arrested on trumped-up charges of treason. Without any evidence, President Calles ordered his execution. As Miguel walked from his cell, he knelt before his executioners, clutching a rosary in one hand and a crucifix in the other. "May God have mercy on you," he said, "May God bless you! Lord, You know that I am innocent! With all my heart I forgive my enemies!" He then rose, faced the firing squad, extended his arms as if on a cross, and prayed in a loud voice, "Viva Cristo Rey!"

Calles specified that Miguel's execution should be photographed and printed in the papers as a way of deterring the Cristeros. However, this plan failed miserably, as forty thousand Mexicans lined the streets for Miguel's funeral.

> Heavenly Father, the love for souls that filled the heart of St. Miguel Pro fostered in him a desire to teach the faith and bring the sacraments of salvation to your people, whatever the cost to himself. May his evangelical zeal and joyful attitude, even in the midst of persecution, inspire us to defend the faith with reason and calm, and so help many souls on their path toward salvation. Through our Lord Jesus Christ, your Son, who lives and reigns with you and the Holy Spirit, God forever and ever. Amen.

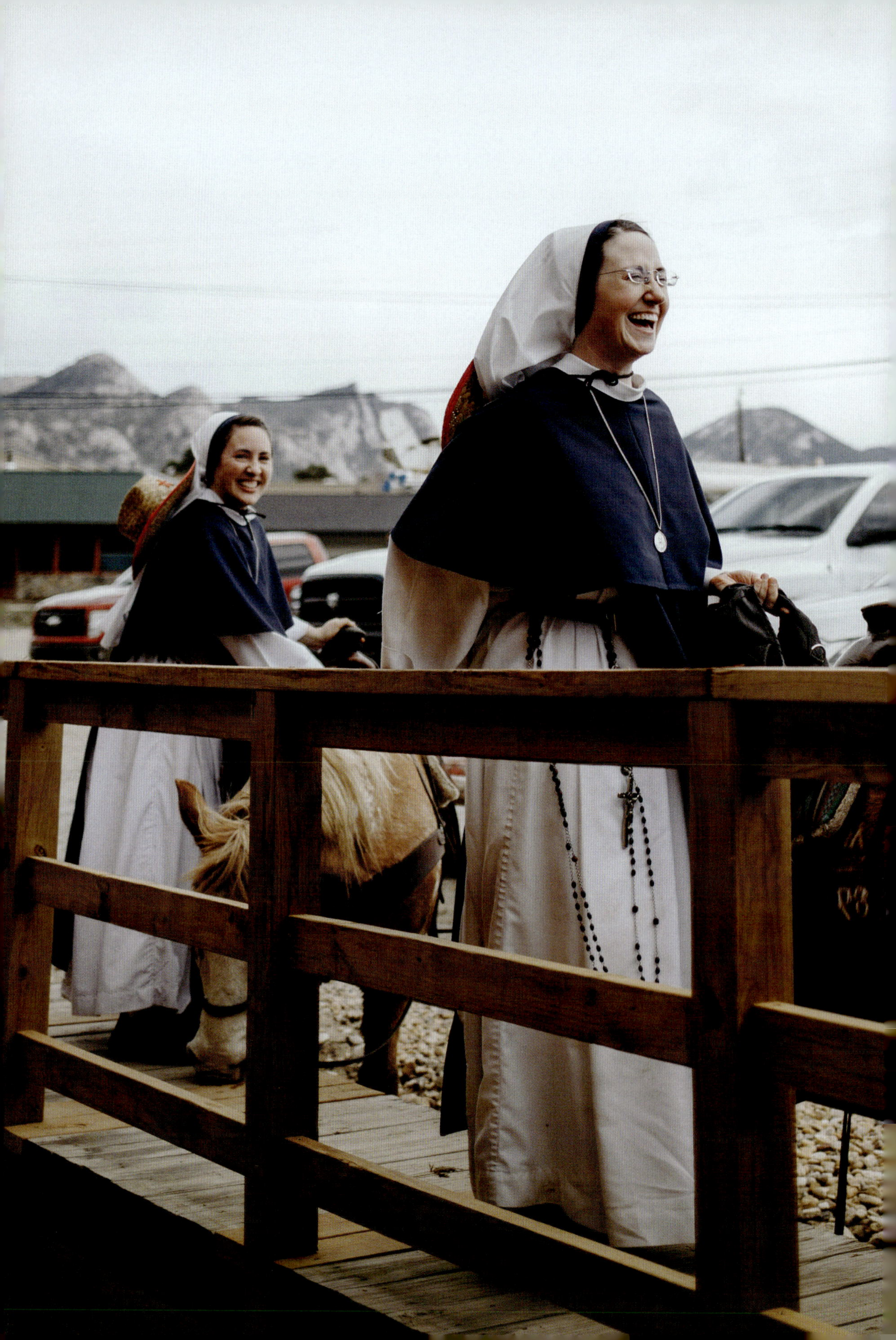

VOCATIONS

Every semester our seminarians have an experience of street evangelization. They go out in pairs to speak to passersby, asking people if they have any prayer intentions and seeing where the conversation goes. As you can imagine, the responses range from gratitude to flat rejection. It requires a bit of courage and some thick skin!

A few years ago we did our street evangelization at a nearby parish. Half of the seminarians prayed in Eucharistic adoration while the others were out meeting people. It was in the evening and the church remained dimly lit, their faces radiated by the altar candles as they prayed. After an hour, the first group returned to the church and those who had been praying went out in pairs to speak to strangers about the Lord.

It was a beautiful moment, seeing those courageous young men, filled with potential, giving their lives to Christ, walking into the night like soldiers on a campaign of peace. Leaving the lighted church behind, with nothing but the light of Christ in their hearts, they went in search of souls.

In that grace-filled evening, as at every graduation from the seminary, as at every priestly ordination, I have a glimpse of what it must be like for parents to see their sons and daughters set out on their own.

As they take up their role in the Church and in the world, our hearts are full of joy, pride, hope . . . and a little apprehension. How will they be treated? What success or failure will they have? Will they be happy in life?

Those are understandable questions in the mind of every parent. As Christians, what matters most is that our sons and daughters discern and follow their vocation. Their calling from God is their path to sanctify themselves and others and the surest path to true joy. Their vocation is the reason for their existence. Fr. William Faber put it this way:

> There has never been precisely the same vocation since the world began. . . . No matter what our position in life may be, no matter how ordinary our duties may seem, no matter how commonplace the aspect of our circumstances, we each of us

have this grand secret vocation. We are, in a certain inaccurate and loving sense, necessary to God. He wants us in order to carry out his plans, and nobody else will quite do instead of us.[1]

How can we help our children discover their purpose in life? How can we build a culture of vocations in our home?

The Second Vatican Council taught that the family is the "domestic church." It is the universal Church in miniature and the seedbed of vocations. When you pray for your children, make sacrifices for them, give

---

[1] Frederick William Faber, *Spiritual Conferences* (London: Thomas Richardson and Son, 1859), 405–6.

VOCATION TO SINGLE LIFE?

In recent years some have argued that in addition to marriage, priesthood, and religious life there is also a vocation to the single life. Such a calling, it is thought, would give those who have not—or cannot—embrace one of the other vocations a better sense of belonging in the Church. So is there a special calling from God to remain single?

It depends on what one means. If a calling to the single life is meant a vocation in the proper sense—that is, a state in life confirmed by either a sacrament or the profession of vows—then the answer is no. Vocations in the strict sense have an established form of life and are mediated and ordered by the Church.

Declaring oneself single by vocation, in fact, can cause someone to become closed to the possibility of marriage (or another calling) later on in life. One should not permanently commit to the single state because it is unnecessarily restrictive. God may have other plans later!

What is called the vocation to the single life is really the baptismal vocation when it is not further specified by another calling. There is no need to discern or profess it because it is the baptismal vocation itself. Those who do not marry or become priests or religious *already* have a vocation from God through their baptism: it is the vocation to holiness. This is the most important calling that any of us have, in

them an example of faith, teach them the Catechism, form them in virtue, and bring them to the sacraments, you are living out the domestic church and preparing the ground for future vocations.

Human formation is particularly important. Every vocation is a way to give oneself, and that capacity to sacrifice is what separates childhood from adulthood. The perpetual adolescence sadly common today, in which grown men and women are mired in self-indulgence and reluctant in self-sacrifice—the true cause of our vocations crisis—is not inevitable. Your efforts to form your children into men and women of maturity and generosity will yield fruit in many ways, not least in an openness to their vocation.

fact, surpassing even the importance of marriage, priesthood, and religious life.

There is a long and illustrious history of people who never marry, are never ordained, and never take vows and yet whose lives are sterling examples of holiness.

Many saints, canonized and uncanonized, have lived a single life with joy and fidelity and deep sanctity. Anyone who remains single because he or she has not found a spouse or cannot marry for whatever reason, then, or whose life circumstances or family situations suggest remaining single, should never feel excluded from the life of the Church. Such men and women *do* have a vocation. It is the baptismal vocation, the most important calling that any of us have: the vocation to become saints.

A Personal Reflection from Parents
— Eric and Grace Morrison —

God has abundantly blessed our marriage with seven children. Of our adult children, two sons are ordained priests, another son is in priestly formation, one daughter is in a holy marriage, and another daughter is a novice in a religious community. As their parents, we watch with a sense of joy and contentment because of their docility to God's call for their lives and their response of generosity and courage.

This openness to vocations was fostered by raising our children in the beauty of the Catholic Church. We chose to homeschool, which gave them knowledge of the faith and allowed frequent participation in the sacraments, and they grew up with other families striving to live the Church's teachings.

Praying the Rosary for the intentions of future vocations and visits to the adoration chapel were part of our regular routine. Silent time before the Blessed Sacrament was essential to help them grow in love and intimacy with the Lord and primed them to hear his call.

In their teens, a time when they consider their future, we encouraged them to seek out friends who would challenge them to grow in holiness; we called this "positive peer pressure."

We intentionally provided interaction with holy priests and religious—for meals, retreats, and homeschool camping trips—so that they could see the happiness in the lives of priests and religious.

In our home the Church's saints were our heroes. We enjoyed reading about their lives, watching saint movies, and celebrating their feast days, which emboldened our family with a sense of excitement to live courageously for the Lord.

Our children's response to the Lord's call has been a source of joy, but it has also required sacrifice. As parents, although imperfectly, we needed to accept daily dying to ourselves in order to raise our children in a nurturing, God-centered environment. Witnessing this, our children grew in charity for the family and for others.

Now as our adult children have entered the priesthood, holy matrimony, and discernment for religious life, we step back with surrender and trust, which at times can be heavy on our hearts considering the weight of their vocations. We understand that all holy vocations will require sacrifice, perhaps heroic sacrifice, but we also find great consolation in knowing that their vocation will be their path to joy and happiness here and for all eternity.

Here are some more specific ways to foster a culture of vocations within your family:

- Pray with your children for vocations in general and for their own vocations.
- Offer small sacrifices as a family for vocations to holy matrimony, priesthood, and religious life.
- Speak to your children regularly about the excitement of discovering what God has in store for them. Keep these conversations serious, peaceful, and supernatural in tone.
- Encourage your children to trust in the Father's love. He wants nothing but the very best for them.
- Two key periods in a young person's life are "11 and 11"—at eleven years old and eleventh grade. Those are times especially to focus on their vocational discernment.
- Young people are looking for lives to imitate. They will naturally have more contact with married people, so giving them opportunities to meet priests and religious (perhaps at vocations events or even in your home over a meal) is a great way to expand their capacity to discern those vocations.
- Strive for a holy indifference in your own hearts, wanting nothing but what God wants, being open to religious and priestly vocations without pressuring children one way or another. The goal is to create an environment where children are truly free and open for whatever God has in store for them, with your vocal and heartfelt encouragement to pursue whatever it is.

Since marriage is both a natural and a supernatural vocation, and the great majority of people are called to holy matrimony, it makes sense to form your children for that vocation. But when you prepare your boys to become fathers and your girls to become mothers, you are in fact preparing them for any vocation. It so happens that the virtues of a great Mom or Dad (and wife or husband) are precisely the same virtues that make a great religious or priest!

There may be in your family one or more vocations of complete dedication to God. When the first stirrings of these vocations emerge, be encouraging without being pushy in either direction. Let your child know that he or she will not disappoint or fail you whatever decision is reached. Help him or her see how beautiful and rewarding such a life would be.

The capacity to discern those vocations, however, ultimately extends beyond the family. Spiritual direction with a wise priest or religious will help your son or daughter take the next steps, which might be entering a formation program such as a seminary or beginning an aspirancy period at a religious community.

Even then, discernment is far from complete; the first task of these formation environments is to help the young candidates discern, and for the Church to discern, if it is the right fit.

Generosity in fostering vocations among your children is a great gift to the Church and is always rewarded by God. Whatever God has in store for your children, accept it with joy—his plan is always better than ours—and give him thanks for drawing forth and nurturing those fine fruits of your marital fidelity. By cultivating holy vocations to marriage, priesthood, and religious life, you are making the greatest contribution imaginable to the future of the human family and to the salvation of souls.

List the virtues and habits you see developing in each of your children. How will those positive traits aid them later in their primary vocation—whatever it may be?

What exposure have your children had to the various states of life? Ask them what their thoughts are about celibate vocations. Do they see those vocations as limiting or as potentially fulfilling?

Have you ever shared with your children the story of your own vocation discernment? Consider if they are ready to discuss your experience and whether they are at an age where they might benefit from hearing the vocation stories of others—priests and religious included.

Decide with your spouse how together you can pray or fast regularly for the future vocations of your children.

STS. LOUIS AND ZÉLIE MARTIN

Layman and Laywoman
Born in France
D. 1877 (Zélie) and 1894 (Louis)
Feast day: July 12

For as in one body we have many members, and all the members do not have the same function, so we, though many, are one body in Christ, and individually members one of another. Having gifts that differ according to the grace given to us, let us use them: if prophecy, in proportion to our faith; if service, in our serving; he who teaches, in his teaching; he who exhorts, in his exhortation; he who contributes, in liberality; he who gives aid, with zeal; he who does acts of mercy, with cheerfulness.

ROMANS 12:4–8

Louis and Zélie Martin are the second couple in the history of the Church to be canonized. Louis Martin was born in Bordeaux in 1823, and Marie Azelia (Zélie) Guerin was born in Alençon in 1831. They had both discerned religious life but eventually determined that they were called to marriage.

After marrying on July 13, 1858, the couple lived for almost a year without marital intimacy but changed their minds when a confessor encouraged them to reconsider. Then they decided to have as many children as God desired for them. The Martins had a warm and loving home. They cared for their children, the poor, and the sick. During the Franco-Prussian war, they were forced to billet nine German soldiers, but they received this humiliation with peace and treated the soldiers with charity.

One of their children, Léonie, had a difficult temperament as a child, screaming sometimes for hours until she received what she wanted. She was even expelled from school because she was so unmanageable. It was

Forming Families, Forming Saints

only through heroic patience and tact that the parents (especially Zélie) were able to win over the heart of the girl. Léonie eventually discovered her own calling to be a Visitation nun. She lived to an old age and was known especially for her humility and gentleness of spirit.

Louis and Zélie had to confront many of the challenges that families face today. They worked hard in small businesses (Louis was a watchmaker and Zélie an expert lace maker) while raising a large family. They had to care for a fractious child in the midst of her tantrums. They took responsibility for their elderly parents. They struggled to find time to pray and take part in parish activities. They grieved the loss of four of their nine children. And they had to endure painful diseases, including Zélie's breast cancer, which led to her premature death, and Louis' humiliating experience of mental illness and forced confinement in a psychiatric hospital.

After Zélie's death, Louis' daughters left home, one by one, to enter religious life. Despite his loneliness, he said, "It is a great, great honor for me that the Good Lord desires to take all of my children. If I had anything better, I would not hesitate to offer it to him."

It is sometimes said that Louis and Zélie were canonized because of St. Thérèse. In a sense, the case is exactly the opposite: Thérèse became a saint largely because of her parents. The Martins created a home that fostered holiness and nurtured vocations. The parents became saints because they corresponded to the grace that God gave them, through their sacramental marriage, to follow him heroically and to help their children do the same. As St. Thérèse herself wrote, "God gave me a father and a mother who were more worthy of heaven than of earth."

> Loving Father, you called Louis and Zélie Martin to follow you closely in the state of matrimony. Through the example of their individual lives and the pattern of their family life, and through their intercession from heaven, may our family also be a Christian oasis of love, peace, and joy. Help us to foster an atmosphere in which our children can freely discern and respond courageously to the vocation that you have chosen for them. We ask this through our Lord Jesus Christ, your Son, who lives and reigns with you and the Holy Spirit, God forever and ever. Amen.

HOPE

People who become trapped in the dark—after a mining accident, for example, or getting lost in a cave—recall hungering for light, as a person lost in the desert craves water. It is an apt image for our darkening age of despair.

Widespread anxiety, loneliness, rage, bitter divisiveness, low birthrates, rising suicide rates, and a craving to escape real existence through sex, drugs, video games, virtual reality, and other outlets all point to the hopelessness of the age.

"Today we often see in the faces of young people a remarkable bitterness," Cardinal Joseph Ratzinger wrote years ago,

> a resignation that is far removed from the enthusiasm of youthful ventures into the unknown. The deepest root of this sorrow is the lack of any great hope and the unattainability of any great love: everything one can hope for is known, and all love becomes the disappointment of finiteness in a world whose monstrous surrogates are only a pitiful disguise for profound despair.[1]

We Christians have the privilege of bearing the hope that people so desperately need today. Like offering water to a man in the desert, sharing our hope fulfills a demand of justice. It also happens to be one of the most irresistible sources of apostolic effectiveness in the modern age.

Every other year we take seminarians on pilgrimage to Poland in order to walk in the footsteps of St. John Paul II. Built into the itinerary is an almost visceral experience of the contrast between despair and hope. We first spend a few pleasant days visiting Krakow and other locations important in Karol Wojtyła's life. Then we take a detour to visit a site of almost inexpressible evil: Auschwitz concentration camp.

Auschwitz is a place where innocent people were cruelly sent to work or to die—a decision made by a Nazi officer, trivially, with a lazy flick of his wrist. It is a place where children were subjected to savage

---

[1] Joseph Ratzinger, *The Yes of Jesus Christ: Exercises in Faith, Hope and Love* (New York: Crossroad, 1991), 69.

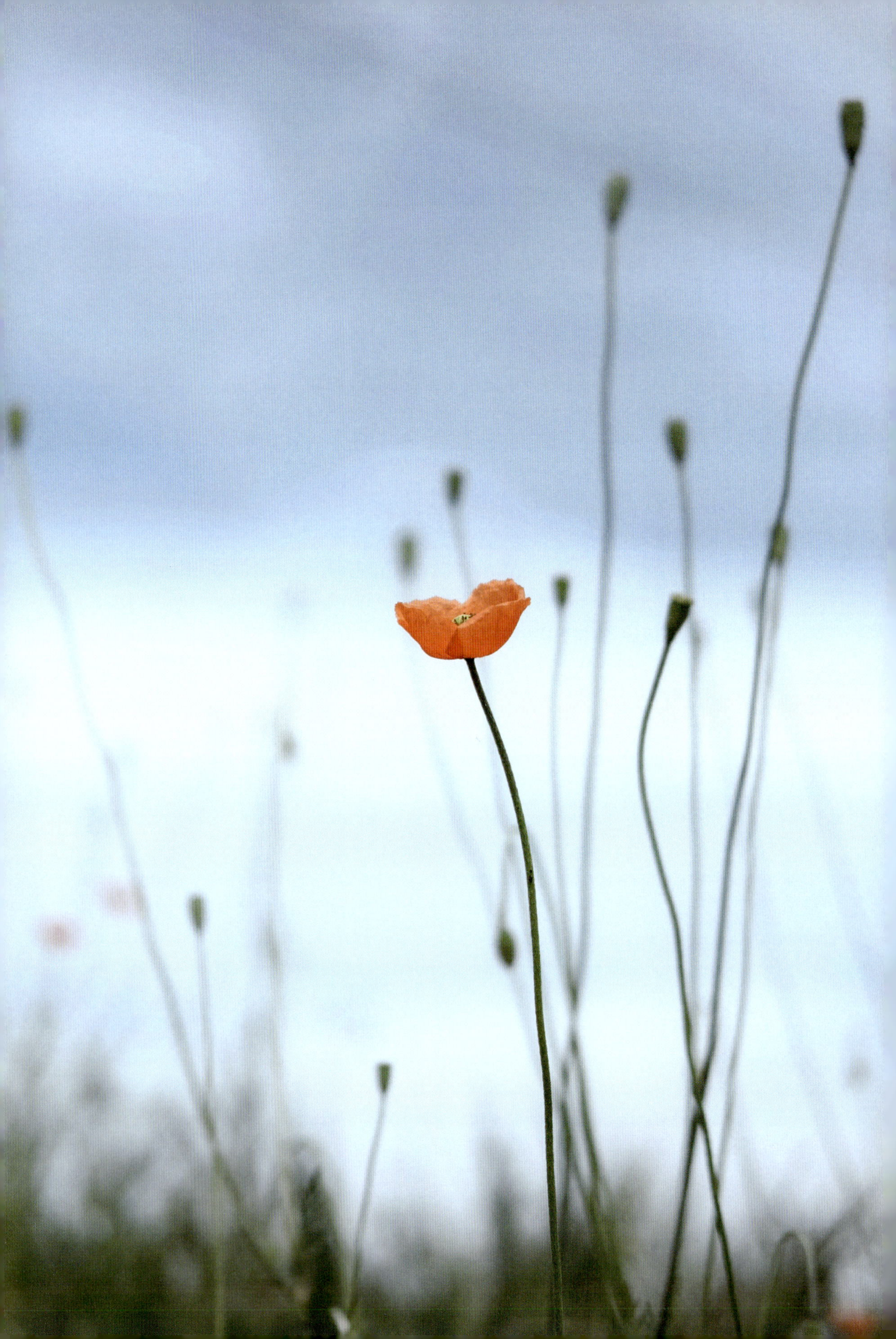

medical experimentation, where people were herded like animals into gas chambers, subjected to chemical poisoning and suffocation, where prisoners were hanged or shot, dehumanized, mocked and beaten. A place of barbed wire, watchtowers, electric fences, and harsh, cold winds. A place designed to foster despair, a master stroke of the Father of Despair. In the decades following the war, "after Auschwitz" became a rallying cry for those who refused any longer to believe in a good God—or any God at all.

We take the seminarians to Auschwitz for three reasons. First, to pray for the souls of those who perished there. Second, because the atrocities unleashed by violent ideologies like Naziism and Communism must not be forgotten by future generations. Such ideologies are no mere relic of the past and priests can do much to form a culture resistant to their lure and their lies. The third reason is vitally important too: because of where we go next.

With the heaviness of Auschwitz on our hearts, we get into the bus and drive to Jasna Gora, the monastery that houses the image of Our Lady of Częstochowa, the Queen of Poland, the "Black Madonna" revered around the world. It is a place of peace, warmth, natural beauty, and quiet prayer. The contrast between the two places could not be more stark.

Auschwitz is an icon of evil, a window into a world of death, suffering, and despair. It is a testament to the depths of man's capacity for cruelty to man. It is also a reminder that we are unable to heal ourselves, to redeem ourselves, to save ourselves.

Our Lady of Częstochowa, in contrast, is an icon of goodness, a window into a world of life, healing, and hope. Our Lady's icon is a reminder that evil can be overcome only by God, that Jesus her Son has achieved victory over sin and death, and that we can face evil—really face evil—only through the lens of the Resurrection.

The best way to ensure that your children grow up to become witnesses of hope is by being men and women of hope yourselves.

Like all virtues, children first learn hope at home, and primarily by example. Being hopeful does not mean a buoyant optimism, a naturally cheerful disposition, or simply repeating to ourselves that everything is going to be okay.

Hope is a virtue bestowed in baptism, the power to trust that Christ will never let us down. Sometimes that means hoping against all odds.

"Hope means hoping when things are hopeless, or it is no virtue at all."[2] It is the audacious confidence that flows from our Catholic faith—the conviction that God has it all in hand, that he knows what he is doing, no matter how dark things seem to get. It is the fruit of a supernatural outlook that sees all things in the light of faith.

You might think that hope would be the one virtue that doesn't need to be taught to young people: after all, they have their life ahead of them and seemingly endless possibilities. The reality is quite the reverse. Chesterton wrote that many think "hope goes with youth, and lends to youth its wings of a butterfly; but I fancy that hope is the last gift given to man, and the only gift not given to youth." He writes that "the power of hoping through everything,

---

[2] G. K. Chesterton, *Heretics*, in *The Collected Works of G. K. Chesterton*, vol. 1 (San Francisco: Ignatius Press, 1989), 125.

NURTURING HOPE

Nurturing authentic hope in your children is the best way to preserve them from the despair of the age and forge them into witnesses of hope. Here are some practical ways to foster this virtue in the hearts of your children:

- **Talk to them about the difference between optimism and hope.** Hope is more than giddy feelings or earnestly wishing that everything will turn out all right. It is the solid conviction that God has a plan and that nothing is outside of it. Help children to see their own difficulties, however small, from a supernatural point of view. Hope is a virtue, an achievement—and it is not always easy. It is a seed planted in baptism that must be nourished.

- **Help your children become souls of prayer.** Cardinal Ratzinger said that "those who pray hope in a goodness and in a power that transcend their own capabilities. Prayer is hope in execution."[*] The more you

---

[*] Joseph Ratzinger, *The Yes of Jesus Christ: Exercises in Faith, Hope and Love* (New York: Crossroad, 1991), 69

the knowledge that the soul survives its adventures, that great inspiration comes to the middle-aged; God has kept that good wine until now."[3]

Having lived and seen more, you are perfectly placed to help your children grow in hope, particularly when they weather the inevitable difficulties of life.

We cling most strongly to God—that is, we grow most in hope—during times of trial, when we renew our conviction that God is greater than any evil and suffering.

There is a moment in *The Lord of the Rings* when Sam and Frodo are in the midst of the darkness of Mordor. All seems hopeless. At that moment, the wind suddenly shifts and the dark clouds part for a few minutes.

---

[3] G. K. Chesterton, *Chesterton on Dickens*, in Collected Works, 15:58.

---

form habits of prayer, the more you form the virtue of hope.

- **ENCOURAGE CHILDREN TO LOOK FORWARD TO HEAVEN AS THE TRUE AND LASTING SOURCE OF OUR HOPE.** (See next sidebar)

- **BE SINCERE ABOUT TEMPTATIONS AGAINST HOPE.** An open atmosphere in the home that gives children (particularly teenagers) permission to speak about occasional feelings of hopelessness will give you an opportunity to frame the struggles in a more supernatural light. Help them see temptations against hope as temptations that can be resisted with the help of grace.

- **THE SAINTS ALL LIVED THE VIRTUE OF HOPE TO A HEROIC DEGREE.** Reading the biographies of saints is a way to instill hope at every stage of your children's lives.

- **LOOK TO OUR BLESSED MOTHER.** Mary is called the Mother of Hope because she was filled with hope even in the bleakest moment of her life, her moment of greatest pain: when she stood at the foot of the Cross. Devotion to Mary will draw the hearts of your children ever more deeply into the hidden treasures of hope, even—perhaps especially—when life is most difficult.

DESIRE FOR HEAVEN

WE TEND TO THINK OF this world as more real than the next. Precisely the opposite is the case.

Like a movie that opens with a black and white photo and transitions into a vibrant and colorful moving scene, our transition through death will not be into a shadowy underworld but into the bracing vitality of true life.

Authentic hope grows when we become convinced of that truth. Hope in heaven is an affirmation that, if we remain faithful, all will ultimately be well.

However radiant we imagine heaven to be, our imagination will always fall short of the reality. We do not have clear enough eyesight, or keen enough minds, or strong enough faith. St. Paul insists that "eye has not seen, ear has not heard, nor has it so much as dawned on man, what God has prepared for those who love him" (1 Cor 2:9). The reality will be greater and more beautiful than we can possibly imagine.

The first Christians had that conviction, born of hope, and it drove their lives. They yearned with every fiber of their being for the Lord's return, when their bodies would be glorified and all creation would be transformed into the dwelling place of saints. They were pilgrims on a journey home, citizens of the world to come, and were homesick. They longed to be in heaven in the presence of their beloved Lord and in the company of angels and saints.

We, too, can nourish in our hearts, and in the hearts of our children, a burning hope for heaven, a heaven which will surpass every expectation, every desire, and every dream that we have.

Without in any way shirking our earthly responsibilities or diminishing our love for the world that Jesus came to save, we can nevertheless make our own the passionate hopes of those first Christians. With longing in our hearts, we can acclaim with them the words that they cried so often, the words that conclude the Sacred Scriptures: *"Marana tha!"* Come, Lord Jesus! Come!

> There, peeping among the cloud-wrack above a dark tor high up in the mountains, Sam saw a white star twinkle for a while. The beauty of it smote his heart, as he looked up out of the forsaken land, and hope returned to him. For like a shaft, clear and cold, the thought pierced him that in the end the Shadow was only a small and passing thing: there was light and high beauty forever beyond its reach.[4]

Christians have a window into a world of hope that is as refreshing to modern man as a drink of cold water is to a man lost in the desert. Against the reality of sin and suffering, against the despair so prevalent today, our faith is a beacon of hope to those who live in darkness.

Like Our Lady of Częstochowa, we hope in the goodness of God, in the redemptive value of suffering, and in the final victory over evil. Through hope we and our children can bring many souls into the light, into an oasis of peace, where they can encounter the divine Son, the very source and the end of all our hope.

What do you see as the biggest threat to the flourishing of hope in your family? Do certain members of the family struggle with despair? What needs to be done to better assist them through their difficulties?

In times when hope has been hard for you to grasp, what helped draw you back to this great theological virtue?

It is not difficult to see the lack of hope in our world today. What strategies do you and your spouse employ to rise above the darkness of the culture?

Spend some time this week meditating on the virtue of hope. In your relationship with Christ, how firm is your foundation of hope?

---

[4] J. R. R. Tolkien, *The Return of the King: Being the Third Part of the Lord of the Rings* (Boston: Houghton Mifflin, 1955), 199.

ST. MARK JI TIANXIANG

Martyr
Born in China
D. 1900
Feast day: July 7

*They who wait for the LORD
shall renew their strength,
   they shall mount up
with wings like eagles,
they shall run and not be weary,
   they shall walk and not faint.*

ISAIAH 40:31

ST. MARK JI TIANXIANG was born in 1834 in southeastern China. He was raised in a Christian family and trained as a physician. In his mid-thirties, suffering from a stomach ailment, Mark Ji treated himself with opium. This was a common course of treatment at the time but highly addictive since opium is essentially a pure form of heroin. The future saint was soon in the clutches of a powerful addiction.

He prayed to be delivered of his habit and went regularly to confession. Eventually his confessor told Mark Ji he would not give absolution since Mark Ji did not seem serious about fighting his urges. Our understanding of addictions has grown since the mid-nineteenth century, and a confessor would likely not give such advice today. Nevertheless, Mark Ji remained a practicing Catholic and continued to attend Mass, even though he could not receive Communion. He never stopped trusting in God's mercy though he never completely overcame his addiction. He struggled with it for almost thirty years until his death.

Between 1899 and 1901, the Boxer Rebellion erupted between Chinese nationalists and those they considered enemies of China: foreigners and Christians. More than thirty thousand Chinese Christians were massacred during those two years. In 1900, the Boxers arrested Mark Ji together with dozens of other Christians, including many members of his family. He was given the opportunity to apostatize, but he stoutly refused. As Mark Ji and the others were led to their execution, he asked to go last so that he could comfort the others as they were killed. He sang the Litany of the Blessed Virgin Mary as he awaited his own death.

This Chinese layman who died over a century ago has become an inspiration and a source of hope to many today who also suffer with addictions. Mark Ji prayed for release from his addiction, but a miraculous release never came. He fought to overcome his cravings but often failed to do so. He was ashamed and felt powerless, an apparent failure in the sight of God and man. Still, he never lost hope, never lost trust, and never turned away from the Lord. He stayed in the fight to the very end.

The resolute courage he showed in his martyrdom was, perhaps, the fruit of many daily struggles with his drug addiction, some of which he won and some of which he lost. In an age when so many have fallen into the grip of despair, St. Mark Ji is a remarkable example of hope that God never gives up on us, and as long as we do not give up on him, no matter what happens, he will see us through.

> Loving Father, thank you for the gift of St. Mark Ji's witness of perseverance in the midst of his struggles with drug addiction. Through his intercession, safeguard all the members of our family from the clutches of addiction and help us to overcome whatever bad habits separate us from you. Keep us faithful to you and preserve us in your grace up to the moment when you call us home and we are freed of all attachments and snares that separate us from your love. We ask this through our Lord Jesus Christ, your Son, who lives and reigns with you and the Holy Spirit, God forever and ever. Amen.

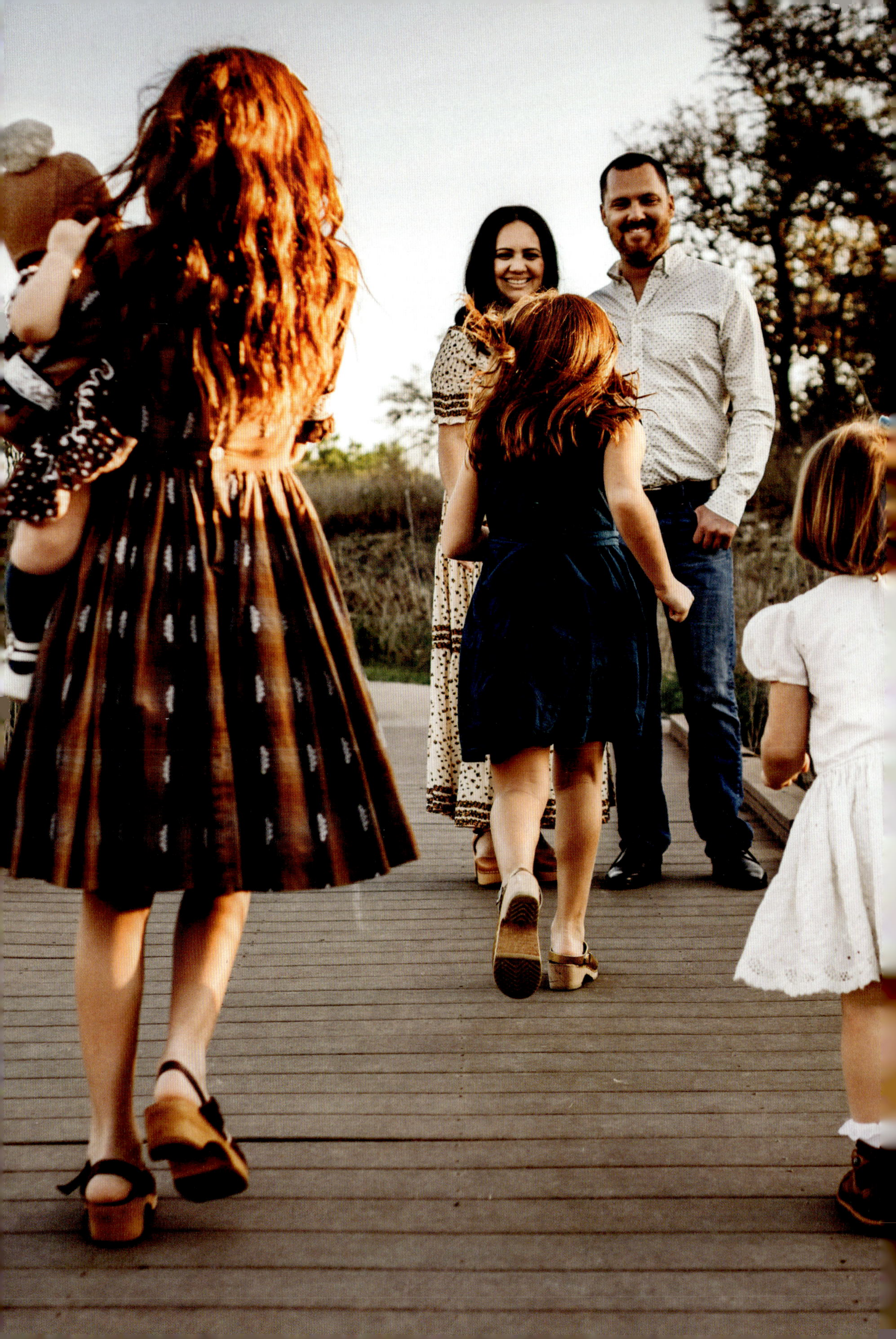

CONCLUSION

You are not the only parents intentionally fostering a specific way of life and a definite purpose in the hearts of children.

The children of the secular elite are even now being carefully formed to assume a role of leadership in an increasingly non-Christian, perhaps anti-Christian, future.

Progressive ideals are being scrupulously instilled from a young age; selective schools keep the scions of Silicon Valley from the addictive devices, entertainment, and media that their elders have invented; and an almost evangelical zeal is fostered to spread the "good news" of radical progress, intellectual skepticism, self-creation, and freedom from moral restraint.

Unless something dramatic changes, this will be our leadership class for decades to come.

In striving to form future saints, well-formed Catholic families will perhaps be the most significant voice of dissent in this bleak, brave new world. The work you do in preparing your children, the next generation of Catholics, to thrive in life is therefore a prodigiously important work.

The sacrifices you make, often heroic sacrifices, day in and day out, to raise mature and virtuous children are important not only for their own happiness and freedom; they are also vitally important for the future of the Church and indeed of our civilization.

The poet Ovid once mused, "Let others praise ancient times; I am glad I was born in these." We live precisely at the time willed by God. It is our age. These are our difficulties, our challenges, and our hopes. If we cannot find a way to thrive, nobody will.

Catholic families have the grace of office, so to speak, to show a better way to live in a world that has in many respects gone astray. However humble or exalted their calling in life, your children will be living witnesses of a different, and better, way of life.

Therefore, Catholic spouses have an irreplaceable role to play in the age to come. As your children grow up, invite them into that responsibility. Help your children become comfortable with being different. Like you

Conclusion

they are being entrusted with carrying the message of truth, love, and peace into a world increasingly desperate, angry, divided, and despairing. Allow your children to take a holy pride in being ambassadors of our Blessed Lord and of his Gospel to the world he came to save.

As the history of salvation shows, such humble exceptionalism is no contradiction in terms. The history of Israel and of the Church demonstrates, time and time again, that God uses chosen instruments, single prophets, small tribes, individual saints, and specific families to act as leaven in seasons of renewal. They were each called to be decisive, and yet humble, agents of reform.

We cannot therefore indulge the temptation to retreat from the great movements of the age or simply hunker down until the storm passes. Our children cannot be sheltered indefinitely from the dangers that surround them. We are the holy resistance movement prepared by the Lord, from all eternity, precisely for our time.

It will not always be easy and it will involve sacrifices. There will also be victories, both small and great, that advance the cause of the true, the beautiful, and the good in our lives, our families, and the wider culture. May we always be ready for those sacrifices and worthy of those victories.

I have profound admiration for every Catholic couple striving to raise children today. The suggestions I make in these pages, I hope, together with my heartfelt prayers, will be an encouragement and a support as you form the next generation of saints.

Above all, I pray that the Lord, his holy Mother, and his faithful angels guide your footsteps as you walk with your children along the path of salvation.

One day, please God, we will all be united as members of the great family of saints in our blessed homeland where peace never fails, love never fades, and joy never ends.

ACKNOWLEDGEMENTS

IT'S NOT OFTEN THAT ONE gets to collaborate with a hero of one's youth, but publishing with Emmaus Road has enabled me to do just that. Dr. Scott Hahn is one of the great evangelizers of our age and is responsible for a good part of my own conversion in college and that of countless others. It is a singular honor for me to work with him in the enormously fruitful work of Emmaus Road Publishing and the St. Paul Center of which it is a part.

The exceptional team at Emmaus Road has once again helped to guide me through a book from conception to completion. I thank Melissa Girard for her excellent editing in the midst of so many other professional and family responsibilities, as well as Kate Ternus and Katie Takats, who did the proofreading and final editing. I am equally grateful to Emily Muse Morelli, who designed the book so beautifully.

Richard and Leah Moss, Michael and Maureen Ferguson, Daniel and Kari Flynn, and Eric and Grace Morrison wrote inspiring sidebars for this book. To each of them I am deeply grateful. I also wish to thank Charles and Susan Griffin, Scott and Tonya Mullins, and Michael and Julia Chandler for slogging through earlier drafts of the manuscript.

I am grateful for Melissa Girard's help with many aspects of this project. In addition to her masterful editing, she provided the insightful list of reading suggestions for children (a subject well out of my league) in the "Spiritual Reading" chapter and helped me brainstorm (together with Bishop William Byrne and Msgr. Robert Panke) and prepare the "saints" section at the end of each chapter.

Lastly, a word of gratitude and acknowledgement to the seminarians and priests in whose formation I have had the privilege to play a part. Much as mothers and fathers must sometimes ask clemency from their children for their parental trials and errors, so too I am grateful for your forbearance as I learned my role in forming future priests. And yet, just as parents are rightfully proud when their children eventually become more peers than children, so too I take tremendous satisfaction in the many seminarians whom I now proudly call my brother priests. You have made any and all sacrifices more than worthwhile!